Studies in the History of Cape Town

Studies in the History of Cape Town

Volume Seven

edited by

Elizabeth van Heyningen

Cape Town History Project
Department of History
in association with
the Centre for African Studies,
University of Cape Town

1994

UCT Press (Pty) Ltd
University of Cape Town
Private Bag
Rondebosch
7700
South Africa

Published by UCT Press in association with the Centre for African Studies

Studies in the History of Cape Town
Editorial Board
Dr Vivian Bickford-Smith
Professor Rodney Davenport
Dr John Iliffe
Professor Paul Maylam
Professor Bill Nasson
Professor Stanley Trapido
Dr Elizabeth van Heyningen

Note on Terminology: Throughout this volume 'black', 'coloured', and 'white' are frequently used as ethnic labels. Logically they ought to be capitalised, like 'African' or 'Malay'. Conventional usage does not make this distinction, however, and for this reason we have not retained it.

All rights are reserved. No part of this publication may be reproduced, stored in a retrieval system, or transmitted in any form or by any means, electronic, mechanical, photocopying, recording or otherwise, without prior permission of the publisher.

Cover photograph: Cape Town scene, c.1840s
Typesetting and cover design: Karren Visser
Printed and bound by Creda Press

Copyright: Individual Authors
University of Cape Town
First published: 1994
ISBN: 0-7992-1511-2

Contents

Introduction — vi

1
Wayne Dooling — 9
The Castle in the history of Cape Town in the VOC period

2
Nigel Worden — 32
Slave apprenticeship in Cape Town, 1834–1838

3
Harriet Deacon — 45
Leprosy and racism at Robben Island

4
Vivian Bickford-Smith — 84
Protest, organisation and ethnicity among Cape Town workers, 1891–1902

5
Mohammed Adhikari — 109
"A drink-sodden race of bestial degenerates": Perceptions of race and class in the *Educational Journal*, 1915 – 1940

6
Muchaparara Musemwa — 133
The struggle for survival: The municipalisation of business enterprise in Langa Township and the African response 1927–1948

7
Naomi Barnett — 162
The planned destruction of District Six in 1940

8
Uma Shashikant Mesthrie — 184
"No place in the world to go to" – Control by permit: The first phase of the Group Areas Act in Cape Town in the 1950s

Introduction

The sixth volume of *Studies in the History of Cape Town* was published in 1988. Since that date the Council for Research Development (CRD) has made a three-year grant for research into Cape Town history. A workshop, held in November 1991, from which these papers were drawn, was partly the product of this funding.

As with previous workshops no attempt was made to limit the range of topics of the papers submitted. The full list reflects work in progress rather than polished final pieces. A proportion are by Honours students engaged in their first attempts at original research. While they often demonstrate exciting new avenues and open up questions especially about the history of black people in Cape Town, their preliminary nature has precluded them from inclusion in this volume.

The first part of this issue of *Studies* Volume 7 is devoted to the period before 1900. Although there has been substantial research in recent years on the late nineteenth century, our knowledge of Dutch Cape Town, the effect of the incorporation of the city into the British empire, and the social and economic transitions which accompanied the abolition of slavery, remain limited. Under the aegis of Dr Nigel Worden a start has been made on a re-examination of these issues. Most notable has been the publication of Andrew Bank's MA thesis.

In chapter 1, Wayne Dooling's paper, based on work for a research project on the Castle, funded by the CRD, throws new light on the relationship between the Castle and the town. Traditionally the Castle has been seen as the seat of the ruling élite. Dooling has shown that the common soldiers played a complex role within and apart from the town, forming a significant element of the mobile emerging proletariat.

Nigel Worden himself has broadened the scope of slave studies in Cape Town with his article published here of the apprenticeship period, part of a broader study of slave apprenticeship in general, which delineates further the distinctions between urban and rural slavery. Like Dooling, he introduces the themes of marginality and protest which link all the chapters in this volume.

The symbol of marginalisation in Cape Town history since the inception of the settlement has always been Robben Island. In chapter 3, Harriet Deacon's paper which is part of a larger doctoral project, explores the complex responses to leprosy, the archetypal pariah disease, and the role it played in emergent racial thought in the nineteenth century.

Vivian Bickford-Smith's paper is an expansion of his doctoral thesis. In chapter 4, picking up on the motifs of race and protest, he explores the role of ethnicity in shaping worker consciousness in the critical period of early South African industrialisation.

In the second part, confined to the twentieth century, all these elements of marginalisation, racism, segregation and protest lead up to the creation of the early apartheid state. Together they contribute to our greater understanding of the nuances of this process and the effects which it had on the outcasts of Cape Town society.

In chapter 5, Mohamed Adhikari deals with the difficult subject of identity for coloured teachers, whose class affinities would otherwise have led them to seek assimilation into middle-class white society. Rejected, their contradictory responses reflected both their aspirations and their need for self-esteem. Theirs was, in fact, another form of marginalisation.

In the same period Africans were overtly excluded from any possibility of absorption into Cape Town society. Traditionally Cape Town has been regarded as a liberal municipality. Mucha Musemwa has shown that the municipal council's treatment of its African residents was as autocratic and arbitrary as it was in cities like Durban. As far as the Langa citizens were concerned, legislated segregation, implemented at municipal level, was firmly in place well before 1948. Nevertheless, like the subjects of Adhikari's paper, they struggled to create a viable world within the confines of the restrictions placed upon them.

In chapter 7, Naomi Barnett's paper contributes to more recent studies on planning in the pre-apartheid city, which suggest that urban planners, especially, played a significant role in shaping future segregation in the South African cities. Beguiled by planning theories on the management of urban slums, the demise of District Six was on the drawing boards well before the Group Areas Act was passed. The local response, even in 1940, suggests that its inhabitants were able to orchestrate a more organised resistance than those of less cohesive communities.

The last chapter in this volume, Uma Mesthrie's paper, comes out of a larger project on the operation of that Act. This is a pioneering study in the administration of the early apartheid state. Dr Mesthrie demonstrates convincingly how ad hoc the formative stages of the "Grand Plan" of apartheid really was. Tragically, it was precisely the makeshift quality of the "permit" system which made it difficult for many communities to recognise the threat of dissolution in the way in which District Six did.

The Cape Town History Project has been fortunate enough to obtain renewed funding from the CSD. It is hoped that this will enable us to focus on specific aspects of Cape Town history. Work is to be continued on Dutch Cape Town, on the role of women in Cape Town society and on the twentieth century. Despite the research already undertaken on political consciousness, on squatting and on township history, the modern period remains under-researched in all South African cities. We still know very little about the social and economic impact of the two World Wars, for instance, on the lives of different citizens.

Because South Africans have so many histories, the Cape Town History Project has never believed that it is possible to write a definitive history of Cape Town. A history which is accessible to the general public has always been one of our objectives, however, and we hope to begin work on this within the next year. The editions of Studies which have been produced over the last ten years have now made this a practical possibility. While such a volume may be a marker in Cape Town historiography, we expect that the city will continue to be a focus of progressive and expanding research.

1

The Castle: Its place in the history of Cape Town in the VOC Period

Wayne Dooling

Introduction

This chapter is an attempt to place the history of the Cape Town Castle within a broader and recent historiography of the early Cape. Existing studies of the Castle have an almost exclusive focus on the architecture of the building.[1] Older histories of colonial Cape Town normally also include sections on the Castle.[2] These works, for the most part, are either not referenced or are too brief in their sections on the Castle, and are thus of limited value to the historian. More recent work on the Castle has been undertaken by the University of Cape Town's Historical Archaeology Research Group.[3]

This chapter is primarily concerned with the social history of the Castle. Thus, it is chiefly concerned with its main inhabitants, soldiers. It examines their daily lives, their conditions of work, and their recreation. To a lesser extent, the chapter examines their relations with slaves, both inside and outside the Castle. Throughout, the Castle is seen as a site of struggle between various sectors of colonial society – between Company and colonists, between Company officials and soldiers and between soldiers and slaves. To a lesser extent the Castle was also a site of struggle between local officials and the metropolitan powers, as manifested in the events which led to the dismissal of Willem Adriaen van der Stel in 1707 and the Patriot Movement of the 1780s.

The Dutch settlement at the Cape of Good Hope was founded as a direct result of the extensive interests of the Dutch East India Company [hereafter VOC] in the East Indies. The Castle was built, first and foremost, as a military fortification as fears mounted that Van Riebeeck's dilapidated earthern fort would not be able to withstand an attack by a European enemy. Work on the Castle commenced in 1666. Eight years later it was occupied by the garrison. From the time that the Commander of the settlement occupied the Castle in 1680, until about 1811, the Castle served as the political nucleus of colonial society, being the headquarters of successive colonial governments.

Labour and coercion in the Castle

It is first necessary to examine the nature of the Company personnel. The typical soldier and sailor recruited for service in the VOC was German. People from all over Europe migrated to the Netherlands in the seventeenth and eighteenth centuries. Germans, fleeing the devastation of the Thirty Years War (1618 – 1648), came in particularly large numbers. The after-effects of this war lasted long after 1648.[4] One attraction was the higher wages offered in the Dutch Republic. In the eighteenth century foreigners accounted for nearly three quarters of those recruited into the VOC.[5] Scandinavians, Swiss and Danes also formed significant proportions of the Company personnel, including those at the Cape. Recent excavations at the Castle have revealed, *inter alia*, Danish coins and coins of various German states.[6]

Unemployment and poverty were in most cases the major factors prompting men to enter the service of the VOC. By far the most important contemporary source of the history of the Castle has been left – in two separate accounts – by Otto Mentzel, a German soldier in the service of the VOC.[7] Mentzel has left a detailed description of the manner in which soldiers and sailors were enlisted into the service of the VOC.[8] Immigrants to Amsterdam were bamboozled into the service of the VOC by the so-called *Seelenverkäufer* [soul-sellers].

Company servants were "encouraged" to work on the Castle by a combination of material and punitive inducements. When the first stones of the Castle were laid in 1666 the masons, carpenters and smiths collectively received a gift of 30 rixdollars from the VOC. In addition, they, as well as the soldiers who had worked on the Castle, were treated to 2 oxen, 6 sheep, 100 freshly baked wheaten loaves and 8 casks of Cape brewed beer. The food and drink were delivered and placed before them "well cooked ... with the hope that these sluggish fellows will by this benificence be henceforth better encouraged and made more willing to work".[9] This suggests that the 300 men who had for five months cleared the ground on which the stones were to be laid, had not been as fervent in their work as the Company officials would have liked.

On other occasions, too, the Company sought to obtain maximum productivity from labourers on the Castle by offering material rewards. On 20 January 1672, after the cutting through of the earthern wall of the new fortification had been completed, the men of the garrison were treated to a cask or two of beer and a few sheep. This was in lieu of a promise made to them by the governor.[10]

Rations were another way in which the Company induced men of the garrison to work. In 1678 the workers of the garrison were receiving a *dubbelde stuiver* per day for work on the Castle.[11] Then the sergeant of the garrison requested that a "solace" be added for their heavy work on the Castle. The men had been used to this but the practice was suspended one and a half years previously. The Council of Policy resolved to give them a *kelder* of brandy each to ensure a "happy day". In January 1679 it was decided to give the Company servants – soldiers, sailors and artisans – 20lbs rice and 10lbs hard bread per month as rations.[12] Another pound of bread was to be added weekly in "lieu of the hard work which has to be done on the fortifications". Previously Company servants had received an unvarying allowance of 40lbs of rice per month.

In addition to rations, Company servants also received money as payment for their work.[13] In May 1671 it was noted in the journal of the governor that the soldiers had complained from time to time that they could not subsist on the small food allowance, since the number of the garrison had considerably increased.[14] Then it was decided to "re-introduce the old custom regarding the slaughtering of cattle, that these poor people might be able to buy something for refreshment and their needs". The burghers would, by pro-rata shares, be allowed to kill 250 sheep weekly to be sold to the garrison at a fixed price. No connection is drawn in the journal between the fact that soldiers complained of lack of food and an entry of the previous day (5 May 1671), when it was noted that the "laziness and stubbornness of the soldiers in their daily occupations" had been overlooked "for some time", leading to an "abuse of our kindness". "In order to deter others" four of them had been sent to Robben Island to labour on the public works. This, it was hoped, would make them more tractable.[15] The journal entry of 18 June noted that the garrison men were "diligently" working on the fortification and on 20 June the four soldiers sent to Robben Island were sent back, with the hope that "they had been taught better obedience".[16]

Surely a direct connection is to be found between the soldiers complaining of lack of food and poor pay and their "laziness and stubbornness". There are at least two possible (though not necessarily exclusive) options: either the lack of food simply did not give the soldiers the bodily energy to carry out what must have been physically demanding work; or the soldiers simply refused to work for what they regarded as unjust remuneration. In 1672 it was noted that the building of the Castle was "successfully advanced ... as the daily wages make somewhat courageous workmen".[17]

The Company was not without help in getting soldiers to perform their duties eagerly. In December 1676 the Council of Policy noted that four sergeants of the garrison had in that year "provided such good service so as to encourage the *volk*." They had also performed other services without demanding payment so they were to receive one *schelling* per day as well as a flask of brandy per month for their good behaviour.[18]

It is clear that the soldiers of the garrison faced a considerable degree of insecurity as rations were added and removed at random. To cite another example, in January 1727 it was decided to give the garrison double their *Kostgeld* (ration money), namely 28 rixdollars, instead of their bread rations as a result of the shortage of bread.[19] A few days later, however, the Council of Policy was informed that the soldiers could not survive even on this double allowance. The earlier resolution was reversed and it was decided to give the soldiers 18 lbs of rice and 9 lbs of beans monthly instead of the double allowance.[20]

Lack of diligence on the part of the Company soldiers led to the Company experimenting with various forms of labour for the Castle. In 1672 the Company decided to employ Khoikhoi to carry earth for the building of the new Castle.[21] A few years later, in 1678, it was resolved to employ them to assist in building the moat in order to "remove all necessity for stealing".[22] In 1680 the Council of Policy noted that "the surrounding hottentots ... have been daily coming into the Castle" and received cash from Company servants, "for the smallest services" and no longer rice, tobacco etc. as they used to.[23] Also to be found working on the Castle were the slaves of the Company. In November 1680 it was noted in the governor's journal that the slaves were "diligently" working on the Castle moat on which significant progress was being made.[24] They were given, "as has been customary", spoilt tobacco and some money.[25] In 1689 the Council of Policy passed a resolution which compelled each burgher in the Cape District to lend one slave to work on the Castle moat.[26] Sailors, too, worked on the Castle. In 1680 it was noted that Company sailors were working daily on the bastion Leerdam.[27] They were also employed to remove the sewage from the Castle.[28] Thus, very early in the history of the Colony, Cape Town's labour demands were met by a diverse group of people.

Daily Life

By extensive reading of criminal records of the Dutch colonial period, much can be said about the daily lives of the soldiers and, to a lesser extent, the slaves in the Castle. Conditions of service for soldiers in the Castle were extremely harsh. The "Cape of Good Hope is indisputably the best place in the whole of the East Indies for military service. At the other stations ... the conditions are far worse, and the soldier is held in far lower esteem than at the Cape," Mentzel wrote. Even at the Cape, though, "military service is bad ...".[29] Soldiers arrived at the Cape impoverished. The money for Company uniforms was deducted from their pay.[30] Many of them also had to work off the cost of their transport from Holland to the Cape. This, according to an eighteenth century visitor to the Cape, took at least a year and a half "during which time they only receive a little subsistence and service-money".[31] All troops in the service of the VOC, according to Mentzel, received the same payment – 9 Dutch gulden per month, in addition to a monthly ration allowance or 6 lbs of salted meat and 40 lbs of rice.[32] The variations in ration and ration allowances have already been discussed. Mentzel's account is largely verified by archival sources and by historians of the VOC.[33] In addition to their ration allowances and pay, soldiers were also given 28 *stuivers (subsidiegeld)* per month. Mentzel calculated that a soldier had on average 1,86 stuivers per day on which to live, while he noted that even in the "meanest eating houses a little portion of meat costs two stuivers".[34] Soldiers received their pay every four months. In April 1781 the Council of Policy resolved instead that soldiers were to be paid monthly during the war (with England).[35]

It is possible that soldiers received even less than the rations stipulated. According to Mentzel, R. S. Allemann, who was the subject of his biography, had often to go without meat while he was on the *Nassau* bastion.[36] On this bastion "he knew, many days of Jewish fasting, on which he ate nothing at all ... now his best meals consisted of a piece of ration bread and a bowl of tea, two of which may be obtained from the garrison kitchen for a stuiver".[37]

Soldiers were to serve the Company for five years, exclusive of the time taken up by the voyage – which could last up to six months – and during this time they were not at liberty to return home.[38] Thunberg notes, however, that soldiers could obtain significant deductions from their service if they enjoyed the favour of their officers, and sometimes a soldier returned by the same ship with which he came.[39]

Many soldiers were able to supplement their incomes by being granted exemption from service, while remaining soldiers, and paying the Company 4 rixdollars per month in lieu of this. They received their full military pay together with their ration allowance and bread. These were the *pasgangers* and the money they paid in was divided amongst those doing military duty.[40] Others were able to earn extra money by practicing trades for individual burghers. Some also served as private servants to higher Company officials. For example, the governor was entitled to the use of twelve men in his private business without any cost; the *Secunde* (vice-governor) had three, while the fiscal (chief legal officer) and the vice-captain each enjoyed the labours of two members of the garrison.[41] In addition, there were those called the *lichten*, "who neither do duty, nor have any furloughs, nor receive any pay, and are always at their full liberty in time of peace; but when once they enter into the service again, they must serve their five years out, for which they agreed".[42]

Many soldiers were trapped in indebtedness. In 1779 the Council of Policy noted that many of the Company's ordinary servants were in debt – despite the *placaat* (proclamation) prohibiting the lending of money to Company servants – "and to pay this off they commit bad deeds".[43]

Mentzel estimated that in the mid-eighteenth century, the regular military force at the Cape consisted of 200 men. This included all those who actually wore uniform. He further estimated that about 400 did not do military service – 100 were *pasgangers* and *lichten* allotted by the Company to the service of officials; 100 were at work on the various outposts and 100 were in the service of burghers (*knegten*), while the remainder performed various trades.[44] In 1778 there were 354 ordinary soldiers at the Cape.[45]

The primary task of the soldiers was that of sentry duty. Thunberg, who visited the Cape in the latter half of the eighteenth century, noted that the soldiers had guard duty only every other or every third day, so they had a day or two to themselves. Guard duty, however, lasted for 24 hours.[46] Mentzel noted that a sufficient number of soldiers were always in service to allow each man to be free from duty for two nights out of three.[47]

Mentzel, in addition to teaching the children of a Company lieutenant, had the task of taking delivery at the Castle of goods from the country posts. This job he described as being

> a very convenient form of service, for I was not in any way responsible for the goods delivered, and all that I had to do was to make a note of them. Once this was done I was free for the rest of the day; so, since the wagons used to arrive at the Castle at dawn, and often only every other day, I had plenty of time to devote to teaching.[48]

As indicated, not all Company soldiers were restricted to the Castle. Some could escape the daily routine of the Castle by becoming *knegten* (slave overseers) on freeburgher farms. Others had duty on Company outposts. Theoretically, the years spent in the service of farmers did not count towards the five-year contract soldiers had with the Company, "but by making presents to the right people it is sometimes possible to secure exemption from this rule".[49] Company servants were released from duty in this way for a year at a time but Mentzel claimed that he had

> known men ... who had gone on for twenty years in this way, working for one settler after another, leading an extremely pleasant, care-free existence, gradually collecting a little hoard of money, and evincing not the slightest desire either to re-enter the Company's service or to return to Europe. The life of a school-master under these conditions is particularly happy. He can always go from one farmer to another as the children under his care grow up; reading, writing, arithmetic and the catechism are all that he teaches, and if only he is a man of sober habits, taking wine – of which there is a superabundance at the Cape – in moderation, and not frequently getting drunk, his life can be one of perfect contentment.[50]

The lives of *knegten*, however, were not always ones of carefree bliss. It is important to note that *knegten* remained under the control of the

Company.[51] Thus, the "Company knecht ... had two masters, the farmer and the Company".[52]

According to Theal, the Company was forced to reduce the number of men in the garrison in the 1780s as a result of the depletion of revenue.[53] As a consequence, he notes, more than a quarter of the garrison had been allowed to go into the employ of farmers, and it was "pretty certain" that many would never return to service in the military.[54]

Life for soldiers in the Castle was dominated by the clock. The average military day commenced at 5 am and lasted until 7 pm[55] Roll-call was read at 7 pm and "any man who (got) back too late (caught) it with the long (whip) from the corporal in charge of the barracks".[56]

Life was not nearly as hard for other ranks in Company military service. R. S. Allemann's personal fortune changed considerably when he was promoted to corporal of one of the Company's outposts. He was able to obtain money from which he bought rolls of tobacco and pipes which he sold to men under his charge. On these sales he made a profit of 33,3 percent.[57]

Drinking appeared to be the most dominant form of recreation of the Castle's inhabitants.[58] The "pipe and the bottle were the inseparable companions of the Dutch overseas ...", Boxer had written.[59] Drinking took place both within the Castle's walls and in Cape Town. The consumption of liquor was encouraged by the Company since it formed part of the soldiers' daily rations. The soldiers consumed far more than the Company intended and on occasion helped themselves to the Company's wine cellars. In 1696 Enog Colet, a soldier in the Castle, testified that he had on numerous occasions seen two coopers taking wine out of the cellar during the day and night.[60] He claimed that he had seen them taking it into the *kuyperswinckel* (coopers' workshop). He claimed that he did not know what they did with the liquor but that he had often seen strong drink on the bastions in the Castle. In 1742 Hendrik Schesser, a corporal in the Castle, took several flasks of wine to the puntsvolk (people of the bastion) of Nassau and told them that they could fetch more from him once it had been consumed.[61] In 1699, individuals who had been granted liquor licences (*pachts*) by the Company, complained that their profits were being undermined by the smugglers "who did not hesitate to convey their contraband liquor even into the Castle itself, and sell it there to the garrison and others".[62]

Drink was the downfall of many. Godfried Vergelly liberally handed out his money while intoxicated.[63] His constant intoxication led his fellows to remove money repeatedly from his wooden chest. On one occasion, Laurens Heyn, a *scheepscorporaal* (ship's corporal) took 21 rixdollars out of Vergelly's chest. Heyn, Simon Pieterz and Jan Werchformer each kept five rixdollars while the remaining six rixdollars were used for purchasing more wine. In 1685 the corporal Jan Tielmans was found drunk on his bed while he was supposed to have been on duty.[64] He was sentenced to sit on a wooden horse in the Castle for three days with twelve pound weights attached to his legs. He was also demoted to the rank of ordinary soldier and declared unfit for the post of corporal.

By using liquor to ensure complacency, the VOC authorities walked a delicate tightrope. Drinking led to rowdiness and violence. By 1699 the members of the garrison "were so slaves of drink that they even sold the clothing off their backs to satisfy their ruling passion".[65] In 1717 it was noted that since "wine and other strong drinks are fairly cheap, all workmen, drivers, and the lower classes are addicted to drink, and it is extremely difficult to restrain them and keep them at their duties".[66] It resulted in the corporal Andries Hansen refusing to obey the orders of his sergeant, Steckwey, and physically resisting him in order to acquire more wine.[67] This was clearly unacceptable to the Company. The prosecutor noted that Hansen was obliged to follow the instructions of his senior officer and that his behaviour was completely contrary to military discipline. Yet, the prosecutor noted, the sergeant had acted with excessive harshness against "people who had done no wrong, but were simply enjoying their drink with the knowledge of their officers".[68]

Despite the fact that the VOC encouraged drinking by the soldiers, they admitted as early as 1696 that the sale of drink to the garrison at night led to debauchery and that, in addition, it could lead to "misfortune" and even "mutiny and riot". They ordered all sergeants and lower officers to take note of liquor entering the Castle and to report this to their superiors.[69] Quite obviously, the use of drink continued. This was not the only time that the Company feared "mutiny". In 1682 the Council of Policy noted how the "Maccasaaren" were forming a community of their own and that this was affecting the soldiers of the garrison.[70] It was resolved to remove them from the Castle and place them in various different locations: Rustenburgh, Robben Island and Company outposts.

Card-playing constituted another form of soldier recreation. These sometimes turned into violent affairs. One evening in October 1699, for example, after an argument arose between two soldiers on the bastion *Nassau* over a card-game, one fatally stabbed the other.[71]

It was outside the Castle, in Cape Town, where soldiers spent most of their free time. Here they ate, drank, gambled and had sexual intercourse. Soldiers and sailors were the most frequent patrons of Cape Town's many drinking and eating-houses. Here they came into contact with sailors, free blacks, and slaves.[72] Cape Town's small Chinese population also had a share of the canteen industry and soldiers were to be found eating in their establishments.[73] One soldier of the Castle, Michiel Herda, also had a house in Cape Town.[74] Johannes Fick, a soldier of the Castle, went to the house of the widow of Johannes Pretorius of Table Valley for a period of ten months. There he made merry by playing the fiddle. His familiarity increased to such an extent that he enjoyed sexual intercourse with the eldest daughter of the widow.[75] Another soldier, Christiaan Lodewyk Clos, served as musician for Cape Town's burgher population, playing both for private individuals as well as his friends in one of Cape Town's canteens.[76] In 1781 the Council of Policy resolved to forbid gambling. Apart from forfeiting the money with which they played, offenders were to be fined 25, 50, and 100 rixdollars for first, second, or third offences respectively.[77]

Slaves and soldiers

Slavery was introduced early in the history of the Cape. In 1658 the first significant loads of slaves were imported into the colony.[78] The Company itself, Company servants and freeburghers were the three main slave-owning groups in the colony. In 1717 slavery was officially sanctioned as the main labour force of the colony.[79]

It cannot be determined how many slaves were in the Castle at any one time. Yet the fact that in 1736 a slave had been able to walk into the Castle "with insolent boldness ... in broad daylight" to pass a knife to his comrades incarcerated in the dungeon (Donckle Gatt) of the Castle, suggests that slaves were a common sight in the Castle.[80] Little is known, however, about the slaves actually there. In the criminal records there are only isolated references. For example, Adam van de Caab, a Company slave in the service of governor, entertained the latter by playing "comedie" (comedy/theatre).[81] Another slave of the governor, Araon, was suspected of attempting to poison his master.[82] Araon had taken a guava from a tree, poisoned it and thrown it on the ground beneath the tree, hoping, so he claimed, that the slave Bastiaan, with whom he had had an argument, would eat it and suffer a long illness before death. He told the governor that if this did not take effect he had resolved to poison Bastiaan's food. It is clear, however, that Araon was suspected of attempting to poison the governor, because he was asked under torture why he had thrown the fruit there if he knew that the governor often walked in the "orchard" and sometimes picked up the fallen fruit. He, however, insisted that his only intention was to poison Bastiaan.

Slaves had access to the money economy of the Cape. They expected to receive money from their owners. For example, Joseph, the slave of the *dispensier* of the Castle, stated that he had stolen goods in the city because his master had on a previous occasion refused to give him money when he had asked him.[83] He also claimed that he had given the cook several blows with the fist because the latter had refused to lend him money. Joseph was betrayed by another of his master's slaves to whom he had given a stolen gold buckle for safe-keeping.

It is of considerable significance that slaves and soldiers could not avoid contact in the Castle. They were found to be working side by side on the fortifications of the Castle and there is evidence of cooperation amongst them.

In 1677, for example, the Council of Policy noted, to its dismay, that the soldiers and other inhabitants of the garrison were wearing clothes which had been handed out to the Company slaves, which the latter had traded for tobacco or rice.[84] In September 1746, September, slave of the burgher Nicolaas Brommerd, purchased clothing to the value of eighteen *schelling* from a soldier.[85] The existence of such an informal market amongst the lowest members of Cape colonial society points to a much wider network of underclass culture. The roots of a vibrant underclass culture of early nineteenth century Cape Town which Andrew Bank has described, are to be found early in the history of the Colony.[86] It is also not surprising that, at times, the Company drew no distinction between slaves and Company servants. In 1686, for example, the Company prohibited Company or privately owned slaves, in addition to Company servants, soldiers or sailors, from being outside after 9 pm.[87] Clearly, the nightly activities of slaves and lower Company servants were regarded as a single danger.

Far more threatening to the Company was the fact that the slaves and soldiers made common cause. In 1680, for example, a privately owned slave deserted in the company of three "Dutchmen".[88] It is not clear who the "Dutchmen" were, but the fact that they deserted almost certainly suggests that they were lower Company servants. In 1712 two "white men" were hanged for desertion, sheep-theft and attempted murder.[89] A slave who accompanied them was sentenced to have his ears and nose cut off.

A few more details on relations between slaves and lower Company servants can be gleaned from the criminal records. On 17 February 1699 a big fire broke out in Cape Town.[90] Joseph of Batavia, slave of the *dispensier* Christiaan Stresen, went from the Castle to the house of Teunis van Schalkwyk where his master was assisting the family of Van Schalkwyk to salvage furniture from the fire. Joseph, pretending to assist in the salvaging, helped himself to a gold shoe clasp, gold buttons, a silver *meskokertje* (sheath), a silver *stoesje* and a silver *beeldje* (miniature).[91] He kept these goods with him until his master left the Castle the following Friday and sold the gold buttons to the *dominee* (minister) on the bastion *Buuren*.

What makes this case particularly interesting is that Pieter Pieterze van Tol, a baker in the Castle, went to the house of the freeburgher Marten Panssiven on that same day (17 Feb. 1699) and there also pretended to assist in salvaging furniture from the fire in Cape Town.[92] He then went to the house of the gardener Hendrik Bernhard Oldeland, where he also helped himself to goods. That a slave and a baker in the Castle should both have chosen to make the most of such a situation, in separate incidents, is of considerable importance. It is an apt demonstration of the similarity of their positions within the Castle society.

Another case also sheds light on the nature of the relationship between slaves and other members of the Castle population. One Sunday evening in 1688 the slave Samuel, who worked as a carpenter in the Castle,[93] came drunk into the guards' quarters on the point *Katzenellenbogen* where a group of masons was sitting.[94] Having lain on his bed for a while (and this suggests that he lived in close proximity to the masons), he began to vomit. He was ordered by the corporal to go outside. Instead he uttered "dirty words" at the corporal, calling him a "rascal" upon which the corporal gave him a number of blows with a cane. Siding with the slave Samuel, the carpenter Pieter Dirxe, who found Samuel crying, said: "This is a dog that has beaten you." A fight ensued between the corporal and Pieter Dirxe. Eventually the

Lieutenant of the garrison, Jacob Rootsteen, came to the aid of the corporal, telling Dirxe, "You rascal, are you the one who has beaten the corporal," at the same time hitting him with a cane.

How typical this incident is of relations between soldiers and artisans in the Castle is a matter of speculation. There are, however, a number of pointers. The close proximity between slave and artisan would almost certainly lead to a closer identity of interests. Furthermore, the slaves and artisans performed similar kinds of work. In the above case, conditions were such that an artisan supported a slave rather than a corporal.

Soldiers regularly enjoyed the company of female slaves in the Company slave lodge in town. Thunberg noted that many soldiers "ruin(ed) themselves by connexions with black women ...".[95] According to Mentzel the gates of the slave lodge were locked at 8 pm and re-opened at 9 am, "for no stranger is allowed to spend the night with the slaves".[96] Other soldiers enjoyed unions with slaves which were more than just sexual. One soldier had maintained a four-year relationship with Catryn van de Caab, a slave woman who had born his child.[97] He regularly gave her goods and money. This relationship could have been tenuous at best since he lived in the Castle whilst she lived in the town with her mistress. It was here that he was discovered sleeping one evening. Soldier Michiel Herda, who also had a house in Cape Town, had maintained a regular relationship with the slave woman Lysbet.[98]

Such relationships must have been fairly widespread for them to have come to the attention of the VOC. As early as 1681, the Commander noted disapprovingly that members of the garrison (as well as freeburghers) had not hesitated to have sexual intercourse with the Company slave women and commit all kinds of indecencies – such as "naked dancing" amongst slaves and Europeans. The Company slave lodge, it was noted, was the main centre for such activities so the Company decided to forbid soldiers entering the lodge during day or night.[99] Obviously this *placaat* was to little avail, for in 1718 the Council of Policy noted that soldiers and sailors (in addition to the burghers) had come to live lives of concubinage with Company slaves and others, and that they may even have fathered some of their children. This the Company found not only in direct violation of "good morals", but in violation of its published statutes.[100]

Those soldiers who deserted from the Castle were most likely to make common cause with the slaves.[101] Some deserters hid on Table

Mountain[102] where it is most likely that they would have made contact with slaves.[103] Table Mountain, Robert Ross has written, was "as it were, a liberated, unconquered zone, not within the city, but above it, beckoning or threatening the city dwellers".[104]

The potential for identity of interests between soldiers and slaves was severely circumscribed, however, when soldiers became *knegten* on freeburgher farms. The *knegt* was

> Janus-like – a man of divided loyalties. On the one hand, he had to establish a *modus vivendi* with the slaves, and on the other hand, to drive them to produce a good yield for the owner. It is not surprising therefore, that in the Cape ... overseers were dismissed as often for leniency as for cruelty. Ostracized from above, and forbidden by convention and statute from associating with those below, the Cape overseer lived in a social vacuum.[105]

One soldier who worked on a farm in Rondebosch obviously could not reconcile the ambiguities of his position. He claimed that he had "no rest in this land" and wanted to desert because the slaves on the farm would not obey him.[106]

The nature of relations between slaves and soldiers therefore, should not be seen as static. The likelihood of close cooperation amongst them may have changed as the nature of the slave society became more clearly defined and as the power of the burgher community expanded in the course of the eighteenth century. In 1746, for instance, the soldiers Jan Nicolaas Meutselaar and Jacob Josias van Rooyen, decided to desert because they claimed that they had to do the work of slaves (*slaafse dienst*).[107] Some soldiers became slave-owners themselves.[108] Pomade van Macassar, slave of the soldier, Nicolaas van Blerk, deserted in 1751 with numerous fellow slaves of the Castle.[109]

It would appear that slaves in the Castle were controlled in the same way as those in the Company lodge, namely, by the *mandoor* (slave headman/driver). A criminal case in 1699 refers to a *mandoor*, Christiaan van Wolle, who had control of the Company slaves in the Castle.[110] The slaves of the *oppermeester* of the Castle, Jan van Schoor, were under the command of the free black, Frans Lentz, a *mandoor* employed by his master.[111] In 1741 the slave Lapaey van Boegies, irritated at being threatened with punishment by Lentz, challenged Lentz to beat him. When Lentz smacked him he retaliated by stabbing him and chasing him across the yard of the Castle. Lentz managed to flee into the house of the minister Henricus Beck, whose door had been opened by the slave woman of Beck, Maria of Mallacka. The prosecutor requested that Lapaey be whipped, branded and work for ten years in chains on the public works. He noted that Lentz was a *mandoor* "under whom he [Lapaey] stands and whose commands he should fully obey".

There were other free blacks in the Castle. On Friday 26 December 1698 two schoolmasters, Johannes Kleyn and Daniel Rodrigo had an argument on the *kat* balcony, during which Kleyn beat Rodrigo with a cane.[112] Swellengrebel, a Company official who had arrived on the scene, grabbed Rodrigo by the hair, threw him to the ground and told him: "You black dog, how dare you lift your hands at a Christian."

Relations between soldiers and free blacks could sometimes be mutually beneficial. In 1700, for example, the free black Octavio came into the Castle to ask for assistance in opening a wooden chest in his house in town. He paid Sebastiaan Sigmund, a locksmith of the bastion *Oranje*, four *schelling* for doing so.[113]

Martin Hall has suggested that slaves made the grain store at the back of the *kat* their temporary quarters.[114] The dietary remains found there – mostly offal (particularly heads) and fish – together with the absence of utilitarian porcelain, is proof to him that this is the place where slaves spent a lot of time.[115] However, given the insecurity of diet of soldiers, it is perhaps doubtful whether such rigid divisions of diet existed amongst soldiers and slaves in the Castle. An entry in the day journal of the governor in 1677 noted that fish for the slaves *and garrison* was very scarce.[116] It would appear that the soldiers were regular consumers of fish. In the same year there is a reference to three soldiers fishing along the beach behind Table Mountain.[117]

While there exist accounts of a variety of relationships between Castle soldiers and slave men and women outside the Castle, the evidence concerning soldiers and Castle slaves is not as forthcoming. However, as can be gathered from the cases already cited, it would be difficult to conceive that similar relationships did not occur inside and outside the Castle. Because soldiers spent most of their recreational hours in town, this probably meant that opportunities for social mixing occurred mainly outside the Castle.

The Castle as symbol

It has been suggested that for Company officials "the Castle was a *symbol*: a testimony of their ability to stamp a colonial presence on the landscape".[118] The Castle was, however, of much more than symbolic value to the Company officials. It represented different things to different people in the colony. To the Company officials the Castle was the place where their power and authority rested; and that power was much more than just symbolic. It was very real, as the many who were confined in the *Donckle Gatt* and prison cells, and whose fate was decided by the Council of Policy and Court of Justice, must no doubt have discovered. The burghers showed their deference by removing their hats when entering the Castle.[119] They, too, felt its power when, upon bringing their produce into town, they had to pass the patrol in front of the Castle. In 1748 the burgher Jan Loose attempted to have elephant tusks smuggled past the toll.[120] For his crime he was fined 1 000 gulden. Burchell, who arrived in the colony, in 1810 noted that the Castle "completely controls the only road between the town and country".[121]

To the Khoikhoi the Castle was, perhaps above all else, the source of disintegration of their society. Increasingly it became the place from where power over them was exercised. In 1673 a military expedition was sent to the Khoi chief Klaas to acquire more oxen for work on the Castle.[122] In 1680 Cuyper, a Khoi "captain", appeared in the Castle with 50 sheep in part payment of his debt to the Company.[123] He was given "as has been customary" a piece of tobacco and a *soopje* (drink of wine). The following day Captain Schacher also appeared in the Castle with 50 sheep.[124] In 1690 Captain Dikkop was dragged to the Castle and the governor commanded him "to behave more decently and obediently in the future, and to follow the Company's orders exactly and without argument".[125] In 1702 the Khoi, Kuyper, complained that the "Bushmen" had attacked his kraal and taken all his cattle, had killed five of his wives and all his children.[126]

As early as 1700, Western Cape Khoikhoi chiefs were appointed by the governor. A staff with a brass knob bearing the VOC's emblem turned the Khoi chiefs into "captains".[127] In 1705 Khoi from the Swartland came to the Castle and reported that their "captain", Claas, had died. The governor then appointed his brother, Hoeza, to succeed him and presented Hoeza with a staff.[128] In 1716 three Khoi captains appeared at the Castle and complained that the Couquemas had robbed them of the canes which they have received from the Company.[129] They requested others which were given to them. It should be kept in mind, though, that the disintegration of the authority of Khoikhoi chiefs was a very gradual process "and one of which contemporary Khoikhoi and whites were probably scarcely aware".[130] Khoi life became so integrally linked to the Castle that the famous Khoi woman, Krotoa (called Eva by the Dutch), was buried in the Castle in 1674, six years before it was to be occupied by the Commander of the colony.[131]

Much later, in the nineteenth century, as most Khoi had lost their independence and some had been incorporated into a "Hottentot Regiment", the Castle still remained a source of authority. On 1 September 1795 about 170 of the Pandour Corps marched to the Castle with their arms and stated that they no longer wished to fight. Amongst their list of complaints was that their families had been ill-treated by the colonists during their absence and that they had not received the £40 which had been promised to them for good conduct, that their pay and wine rations were insufficient and that they were the object of abusive remarks by their superiors. The governor at the Castle, Sluysken, managed to pacify them with promises of pay and ration increases and that their families would not be abused.[132]

To slaves as well, the Castle represented a source of power. Some slaves of freeburghers made their way to the Court of Justice in the Castle to complain about their masters. More often than not, however, it was in the Castle that slaves faced the brutal arm of eighteenth century law. In 1797 Lady Anne Barnard exulted that the "days of torture are over, and the sad evidence of what was practiced by the Dutch Government only remain on a high ground hard by the entrance of the Castle".[133] On the days of execution the procession from the Castle "was an imposing one, guards, pikemen, prisoners, members of the Court of Justice, and those others who had as a punishment been ordered to witness the execution".[134] The instruments of the Company's power were therefore in very close proximity to the Castle. The road into Cape Town from the interior wound round the Castle but not "without bringing you close under the place of public execution, surrounded by a square wall, and where gibbets, wheels, and stakes of impalement are exposed to public view".[135] The slaves were acutely aware that power rested in the Castle. In 1808 an abortive slave rebellion led the Governor of the colony to report to London that the slaves had marched to Cape Town "for the purpose of demanding their liberty and in the event of refusal entertained the chimerical project of seizing the Castle and asserting by force of arms their own independence".[136]

The soldiers in the Castle were, of course, closest to the power of the VOC. Yet, many were able legitimately to escape its confines. Jacob Coetser, for instance, appears as a soldier in the documents in 1709. On 31 July 1714 he was granted his freedom. He married Susanna Snyman, daughter of Margaretha de Savoye from Drakenstein, and died in the colony in 1742.[137] Hendrik van Aarden of Antwerp remained a soldier from 1715 to 1725.[138] Hans Berlyn of Hamburg appeared as a soldier in 1703, was released in 1714 and died propertyless in 1748.[139] This is a small sample of a trend that requires further study and that remains to be quantified.

It would appear as if soldiers who had managed to leave military service attempted to put as much distance as possible between themselves and their military past. In 1729 Jan Bronkhorst appeared before the Court of Justice for harbouring a soldier, Jan Dirksz, for an entire year.[140] What makes this case particularly interesting is the fact that Bronkhorst, a farmer, was himself an ex-soldier.[141] He appears in the records as a soldier in 1699 and was released in 1711. On the surface it would appear as if Bronkhorst was assisting someone with whom he could sympathise. But the treatment meted out to Dirksz immediately suggests the contrary. Dirksz was compelled to work on the farm and on one occasion Bronkhorst gave him several kicks in the head. For this Bronkhorst was sentenced to be whipped, to work on the public works for five years and to have half of his property confiscated. He died in April 1740.[142]

Conclusion

This paper has attempted to show that there is more to the history of the Castle than simply being South Africa's oldest building. Housed within the Castle were a diverse group of people, ranging from the highest of Company officials to those lowest in the colonial order. Nowhere else did slaves, soldiers, Company officials, sailors, free blacks and possibly Khoi[143] live in such close proximity as in the Castle. Possibly also nowhere else in the Cape, during the seventeenth and eighteenth centuries, was the shared poverty of soldiers and slaves as pronounced as in the barracks of the Castle bastions. This constitutes the Castle's most important feature. The Castle thus occupies a special place in the history of Cape Town – as a place where the seeds of a variety of social relationships were sown.

Acknowledgements

I am deeply indebted to Jacqueline Lalou Meltzer for providing numerous references and assisting in every step of this work. The financial support of the Centre for Science Development is hereby gratefully acknowledged. The findings and conclusions expressed here are those of the author and do not necessarily reflect those of the CSD.

Endnotes

1. Foremost in such studies is the detailed study by A. Ras, *Die Kasteel en ander vroeë Kaapse vestingwerke, 1652–1713* (Cape Town, 1959). In addition, there is a chapter in A.J. Böeseken, *Simon van der Stel en sy Kinders* (Cape Town, 1964). See also E. Rosenthal, *Bastion of the South* (Cape Town, 1966); E. Rosenthal, *300 Years of the Cape Town Castle* (Cape Town, 1966); M.W. Spilhaus, *Company's Men* (Cape Town, 1973); H. Picard, *Masters of the Castle: a Portrait Gallery of the Dutch Commanders and Governors of the Cape, 1652–1795 1803–1806* (Cape Town, 1972).
2. For example, P.W. Laidler, *The Growth and Government of Cape Town* (Cape Town, 1939); P.W. Laidler, *A Tavern of the Ocean: Being a Social and Historical Sketch of Cape Town from its earliest days* (Cape Town, n.d.).
3. This work is ongoing. In the meantime, see M. Hall, "Towards an Archaeology of Slavery in the Cape: The Castle – Cape Town", Paper delivered at the "Cape Slavery – and After" Conference, University of Cape Town, 11–12 August 1989; M. Hall et al. "A 'Stone Wall out of the Earth that Thundering Cannon Cannot Destroy'? Bastion and Moat at the Castle, Cape Town", *Social Dynamics*, 16, 1, 1990.
4. J.R. Bruijn, F.S. Gaastra and I. Schoffer, with assistance from A.C.J. Vermeulen, *Dutch-Asiatic Shipping in the 17th and 18th Centuries*, 1 (The Hague, 1987), 155.
5. Bruijn, Gaastra and Schoffer, *Dutch-Asiatic Shipping*.
6. South African Numismatic Society Newsletter, no. 272, 1991.
7. O.F. Mentzel, *Life at the Cape in the Mid-Eighteenth Century: Being the Biography of Rudolf Siegfried Allemann, Captain of the Military Forces and Commander of the Castle In the Service of the Dutch East India Company at the Cape of Good Hope*, (Cape Town, 1919); *A Complete and Authentic Geographical and Topographical Description of the Famous and (All Things Considered) Remarkable African Cape of Good Hope*, 3 parts, (Cape Town, 1921–1944).
8. Mentzel, *Cape in Mid-Eighteenth Century*, 12–27.
9. H.C.V. Leibbrandt, *Precis of the Archives of the Cape of Good Hope: Journal, 1662–1670* (Cape Town, 1901), 2 Jan. 1666, 169.
10. H.C.V. Leibbrandt, *Precis of the Archives of the Cape of Good Hope: Journal, 1671–74, 1676*, (Cape Town, 1902), 20 Jan. 1672, 42.
11. *Suid Afrikaanse Argiefstukken: Kaap*, (hereafter SAA), 10 vols (Cape Town, 1957–1984), vol. 2, 14 July 1678, 258.

12. SAA, 25 Jan. 1679, 275.
13. G.M. Theal, *Abstract of the Debates and Resolutions of the Council of Policy at the Cape, from 1651 to 1687*, (Cape Town, 1881), 17 Aug. 1668, 104.
14. Leibbrandt, *Journal, 1671–74, 1676*, 6 May 1671, 14.
15. Leibbrandt, *Journal, 1671–74, 1676*, 5 May 1671, 14.
16. Leibbrandt, *Journal, 1671–74, 1676*, 18 June, 20 June 1671, 18.
17. Leibbrandt, *Journal, 1671–74, 1676*, 16 March 1672, 47.
18. SAA, II, 14 Dec. 1676, 157.
19. SAA, VII, 5 Jan. 1727, 305.
20. SAA, VII, 18 Jan. 1727, 313.
21. R. Elphick, *Kraal and Castle: Khoikhoi and the Founding of White South Africa* (New Haven and London, 1977), 176.
22. Theal, *Abstract*, 26 April 1678, 170.
23. SAA, II, 17 Nov. 1680, 338.
24. Cape Archives (hereafter CA), VC 9, 11 Nov. 1680, 153.
25. SAA, II, 14 Dec. 1676, 157.
26. SAA, III, 17 Feb. 1689, 203.
27. CA, VC 9, 16 Jan. 1680, 8.
28. CA, VC 9,18 June 1680, 85.
29. Mentzel, *Cape in Mid-Eighteenth Century*, 12.
30. C.P. Thunberg, *Travels at the Cape of Good Hope: 1772–1775*, (Cape Town, 1986), 29.
31. Thunberg, *Travels at the Cape*, 30.
32. Mentzel, *Cape in Mid-Eighteenth Century*, 24.
33. Bruijn, et al., *Dutch-Asiatic Shipping*, 210–211.
34. Mentzel, *Cape in Mid-Eighteenth Century*, 27.
35. K.M. Jeffreys, *Kaapse Argiefstukken lopende over het jaar 1778–1782*, 6 vols, (Cape Town, 1927–1935), vol. of 1781, Resolutions, 27 April 1781, 68.
36. Mentzel, *Cape in Mid-Eighteenth Century*, 42.
37. Mentzel, *Cape in Mid-Eighteenth Century*, 42.
38. Bruijn, et al., *Dutch-Asiatic Shipping*, 160.
39. Thunberg, *Travels at the Cape*, 30.
40. Mentzel, *Cape in Mid-Eighteenth Century*, 79.
41. Mentzel, *Cape in Mid-Eighteenth Century*, 4–5.
42. Thunberg, *Travels at the Cape*, 32.
43. Jeffreys, Kaapse Argiefstukken 1779, Resolutions, 4 May 1779, 55.
44. Mentzel, *Cape in Mid-Eighteenth century*, 149.
45. Jeffreys, *Kaapse Argiefstukken 1778, Uitgaande Brieven*, 10 Oct. 1778, 416.
46. Thunberg, *Travels at the Cape*, 30.
47. Mentzel, *Cape in Mid-Eighteenth Century*, 37.
48. Mentzel, *Cape in Mid-Eighteenth Century*, 98.
49. Mentzel, *Cape in Mid-Eighteenth Century*, 150.
50. Mentzel, *Cape in Mid-Eighteenth Century*, 150.
51. Shell, "Slavery at the Cape of Good Hope, 1680–1731", 2 volumes, (Ph.D thesis, Yale, 1986), I, 278.
52. Shell, "Slavery at the Cape", 279–80.
53. G.M. Theal, *History of South Africa: 1691–1795*, 2 vols (London, 1888), 2, 239.
54. Theal, *History of South Africa*, 2, 239.

55. Mentzel, *Cape in Mid-Eighteenth Century*, 157.
56. Mentzel, *Cape in Mid-Eighteenth Century*, 160.
57. Mentzel, *Cape in Mid-Eighteenth Century*, 45.
58. For a discussion of the role of drink and leisure in the early decades of nineteenth century Cape Town, see A. Bank, *The Decline of Urban Slavery at the Cape, 1806 to 1843* (Centre for African Studies, University of Cape Town, Communications 22, 1992), esp. pp. 120–121. It is clearly an overstatement to find in these decades a "burgeoning of a culture of leisure that gravitated around the canteens and streets of the city", ibid, 128.
59. C.R. Boxer, *The Dutch Seaborne Empire* (London, 1965), 208.
60. CA CJ 299, 13 Aug. 1696, 569.
61. CA, CJ 786, 22 Feb. 1742, no. 60, 395.
62. H.C.V. Leibbrandt, *Rambles through the Archives of the Colony of the Cape of Good Hope, 1688–1700* (Cape Town, 1887), 145.
63. CA, CJ 299, 13 April 1696, 225.
64. SAA, III, 26 July 1685, 110.
65. Leibbrandt, *Rambles*, 1688–1700, 146.
66. M. de Chavonnes, *Report of De Chavonnes and Van Imhoff on the Cape* (Cape Town, 1918), 88.
67. CA, CJ 339, 7 Oct. 1736, 339ff.
68. CA, CJ 339, 7 Oct. 1736, 339ff.
69. SAA, III, 17 April 1696, 303.
70. SAA, III, 26 Nov. 1682, 54.
71. CA, CJ 781, 17 Nov. 1699, no. 13, 113.
72. For example, CA, CJ 786, 31 Aug. 1741, no. 56, 366; CA, CJ 785, 20 Aug. 1733, no. 35, 291.
73. CA, CJ 790, 30 Sep. 1762, 235ff.
74. CA, CJ 344, I, 9 April 1739, 1.
75. CA, CJ 298, 5 Nov. 1695, 161.
76. CA, CJ 352, 14 Oct. 1745, 652.
77. Jeffreys, *Kaapse Argiefstukken*, Resolutien, 10 April 1781, 57.
78. J. Armstrong and N. Worden, "The Slaves, 1652–1834", in R. Elphick and H. Giliomee, (eds), *The Shaping of South African Society, 1652–1840* (Cape Town, 1989), 111.
79. De Chavonnes, *Report of De Chavonnes and Van Imhoff on the Cape*.
80. Mentzel, *Cape in Mid-Eighteenth Century*, 101.
81. CA, CJ 299, 25 Feb. 1696, 165.
82. CA, CJ 298, 23 Aug. 1695, 299.
83. CA, CJ 297, 28 Feb. 1699, 277.
84. SAA, II, 16 Dec. 1677, 216.
85. CA, CJ 354, 20 Sep. 1746, 630.
86. Bank, *Decline of Urban Slavery*, esp. pp. 120ff.
87. SAA, III, 3 July 1686, 139.
88. SAA, II, 12 Feb. 1680, 314.
89. H.C.V. Leibbrandt, *Precis of the Archives of the Cape of Good Hope: Journal, 1699–1732* (Cape Town, 1896), 16 July 1712, 255.
90. I have, however, not found a record of this in the day Journal of the governor.
91. CA, CJ 297, 28 Feb. 1699, 277.

92. CA, CJ 297, 27 Feb. 1699, 215.
93. There is no indication of whom the slave belonged to.
94. CA, CJ 290, 3 March 1688, 453.
95. Thunberg, *Travels at the Cape*, 51.
96. Mentzel, *Complete and Authentic*, I, 116.
97. CA, CJ 293, 5 March 1690, 269ff.
98. CA, CJ 344, I, 9 April 1739, 1.
99. CA, VC 9, 27 Nov. 1681, 451.
100. SAA, V, 1 Nov., 310.
101. Soldier desertion is the subject of a forthcoming paper.
102. CA, CJ 787, 27 March 1749, no. 45, 338ff.
103. R. Ross, *Cape of Torments: Slavery and Resistance in South Africa* (London, 1983), 76.
104. R. Ross, "Cape Town (1750–1850): Synthesis in the Dialectic of Continents", in R. Ross and G.J. Telkamp (eds), *Colonial Cities: Essays on Urbanism in a Colonial Context* (Dordrecht, Boston, Lancaster, 1985), 112.
105. R. Shell, "Slavery at the Cape", I, 284.
106. CA, CJ 787, March 1749, no. 45, 338.
107. CA, CJ 354, 10 Oct. 1746, 652; ibid, 611.
108. CA, CJ 340, 3 May 1736, 113.
109. CA, CJ 359, 20 Feb. 1751, 141.
110. CA, CJ 303, 17 Jan. 1699, 27.
111. CA, CJ 346, 19 Oct. 1741, 257.
112. CA, CJ 301, 29 Dec. 1698, 459ff.
113. CA, CJ 303, 25 Sep. 1700, 759ff.
114. Hall, "Archaeology of Slavery", 2.
115. Hall, "Archaeology of Slavery", 3.
116. CA, VC 8, 8 April 1677, 129, emphasis added.
117. CA, VC 8, 30 June 1677, 210ff.
118. Hall et al., "Bastion and Moat", 35–36, emphasis in original.
119. Lady Anne Barnard, *South Africa a Century Ago* (London, 1901), 66.
120. CA, CJ 356, 14 Nov. 1748, 266.
121. W.J. Burchell, *Travels in the Interior Parts of Southern Africa*, 2 vols (London, 1953), vol. 1, 55.
122. H.C. Bredekamp, *Van Veeverskaffers tot Veewagters: 'n Historiese ondersoek na betrekkinge tussen die Khoikhoi en Europeërs aan die Kaap, 1662–1679*, (Bellville, 1982), 42.
123. CA, VC 9, 30 August 1680, 118.
124. CA, CV 9, 31 August 1680, 118.
125. Elphick, *Kraal and Castle*, 191.
126. Leibbrandt, *Journal, 1699–1732*, 3 Feb. 1702, 47.
127. Leibbrandt, *Journal, 1699–1732*, 3 Feb. 1702, 191.
128. Leibbrandt, *Journal, 1699–1732*, 3 Feb. 1702, 26 Sep. 1705, 80.
129. Leibbrandt, *Journal, 1699–1732*, 3 Feb. 1702, 20 Nov. 1716, 270.
130. Leibbrandt, *Journal, 1699–1732*, 3 Feb. 1702, 188.
131. V.C. Malherbe, *Krotoa, called "Eva": A Woman Between* (Cape Town, 1990), 51.
132. J. de Villiers, "Hottentot-regimente aan die Kaap, 1781–1806", *Archives Year*

Book of South African History, 30, 2, 1967, 148; G.M. Theal, *History of South Africa Before 1795: The Cape Colony to 1705, The Korans, Bantu & Portuguese in South Africa to 1800: Being Volume Four of History of South Africa* (Cape Town, 1964), vol. 4, 337.
133. Barnard, *South Africa a Century Ago*, 79.
134. Laidler, *Growth and Government*, 103.
135. F.R. Bradlow, *Robert Semple's Walks and Sketches at the Cape of Good Hope* (Cape Town and Amsterdam, 1968), 23.
136. CA, GH, 23/2, Caledon to Castlereagh, 11 Nov. 1808, 32. For an account of the rebellion see Ross, *Cape of Torments*, 97–105.
137. CA, VC 56, unpaginated and undated.
138. CA, VC 56.
139. CA, VC 56.
140. CA, CJ 785, 13 Jan. 1729, no. 18, 150.
141. CA, VC 56, unpaginated and undated.
142. CA, VC 56.
143. A criminal case of 1699 gives the impression that some Khoi were in or near the Castle: CA, CJ 297, 28 Feb. 1699, 277.

2

Slave apprenticeship in Cape Town, 1834–1838

Nigel Worden

On 15 November 1834, two weeks before the implementation at the Cape of the *Act for the Abolition of Slavery throughout the British Colonies*, four retired army and naval officers landed at Table Bay.[1] Together with four others who arrived in the subsequent weeks, these men had been appointed as Special (or Stipendiary) Magistrates with the task of administering the apprenticeship system set up under the Act. None of them had experience of the Cape – in fact their lack of personal contacts in the colony was a major criterion in their appointment by the Colonial Office, which feared that social links with local slave owners would prejudice their judicial judgement.

D'Urban, the Cape Governor, complained bitterly at the inadequacy of the number of Special Magistrates allocated to the colony: only eight were appointed to administer a widely scattered population of apprentices and employers – the same number as those assigned for the small island of Barbados. Despite the intentions of Parliament, some local magistrates did have to supplement the work of the British appointees. The eight newcomers were sent to towns and villages in the regions where most apprentices were concentrated. Some lived in relative isolation and considerable loneliness surrounded by suspicious and sometimes overtly hostile farmers.[2] Others were more fortunate.

Major George Longmore was envied by his fellows, since he was placed in Cape Town. This chapter is an outline of some of the issues which arise from his records in relation to apprenticeship in the city.[3]

For four years the Special Magistrates attempted, with varying degrees of success, to mediate the transition between slavery and freedom. Their duties as laid down by the Abolition Act were extensive, if rather vague.[4] They were to adjudicate in any offence or dispute between employer and apprentice and they were to visit estates with more than twenty apprentices regularly to ensure that obligations and duties were carried out by both parties. There was lack of clarity over the precise division of authority between the Special and the Resident Magistrates in the adjudication of offences such as breaches of the peace or theft of goods by apprentices from anyone other than their employers. Each magistrate tended to follow his own policy. Longmore limited his brief strictly to cases where employers or apprentices brought complaints against each other and referred all other cases to the regular Clerk of the Peace.[5]

Each colony also passed its own legislation to define the duties of the Special Magistrates. At the Cape, Ordinance 1 of 1835 *For giving due effect to the provisions of ... An act for the Abolition of Slavery* copied the principle of the acts passed in Trinidad, St Lucia and Mauritius, and laid out the form of record books, monthly reports and forms of summons of apprentices and employers. It also specified the punishments to be given for each kind of offence. Whipping was the commonest form for male apprentices, with possible additions of imprisonment and hard labour. For females, whipping was forbidden, following the principle of the ameliorative slave legislation, but imprisonment, often with periods in the stocks and spare diet was prescribed. For employers convicted of neglecting or maltreating their apprentices, fines were imposed.[6]

Longmore certainly saw his main task as inflicting punishment on apprentices. His first action in Cape Town was to inspect the city jail, and to report on its inadequate accommodation for his purposes.[7] He maintained close association with the city's police force, one of whose major functions was to apprehend slave apprentices suspected of being deserters. And he had no qualms in imposing the maximum sentence on apprentices.

This, however, was not the only role of the Special Magistrate. Detailed procedures were also laid down enabling the purchase by apprentices of the remainder of their term of bondage, whereby valuations were to be made by the Special Magistrate but subject to appeal by the employer. Longmore was particularly involved in such valuations, since more Cape Town apprentices had acquired some money by casual or hired work with which to buy their freedom than was the case in rural districts. Even so, only twenty-seven apprentices in Cape Town made such claims during the four year period.[8] Freedom, as we shall see, was claimed by direct action rather than by purchase.

The task of the Special Magistrates was not an easy one and it was hampered both by the local situation and by problems caused by the Colonial Office. Before examining the situation in Cape Town specifically, some of these general issues need to be highlighted.

The very concept of slave apprenticeship was fraught with difficulty. Although slavery was formally ended on 1 December 1834, in practice only nomenclature had changed. 39 021 slaves and their owners now became "apprentices" serving their "employers" for an additional four years.[9] The Act had provided for two categories of apprentices, predial and non-predial workers, with the former serving a longer period of six years but receiving some remuneration for overtime work. At the Cape it was decided that the division between field labourers and other slaves was less clear than in the plantation economies of Mauritius and the Caribbean, and that a division of the two would cause dissent and unnecessary complications.[10] All Cape slaves were therefore categorised as non-predial, an arrangement which gave them a shorter term of apprenticeship, but also meant that they had no rights to overtime pay.[11] The apprentices were thus still bound to their owners, obliged to obey their orders and to work for them without remuneration until 1 December 1838.

The intention of Parliament in framing the apprenticeship system was to ease the transition from slavery. It gave owners a period of continued labour supply while providing time to prepare for wage or free labour. It was also intended to defuse more violent slave owner opposition which the Colonial Office feared in the wake of resistance to amelioration legislation in the late 1820s and early 1830s. For the slaves, Parliament hoped that apprenticeship would be a period of training in the habits and discipline of wage labour, marked by the overtime pay for predial apprentices. Evangelical abolitionists also stressed the use of the apprenticeship period for spiritual and educational "upliftment" which they believed the slaves required for a place in free society.[12] The very word "apprenticeship" evoked images of the training for a particular type of labour akin to the apprenticeship system in Britain, which "combined education and labour with the promise of eventual self-employment".[13]

In the colonies, both employers and apprentices saw the situation differently. Employers generally viewed apprenticeship as a continuation of slavery, more akin to the coercive indenture of the Khoi and "Bastaard-Hottentots" than to training in skills.[14] Although there were irritating interventions from magistrates brought in from abroad they saw this as a continuation of the process of government intervention in the master-slave relationship initiated in the 1820s.[15] And now that total emancipation was inevitable, owners viewed the remaining four years as part of the compensation due to owners for the imminent loss of their slaves. This was the last chance to extract the maximum amount of work from them without the cost of wages or other incentives. There was certainly little sense of any special obligation by employers to train their apprentices for a new life.

Most of the apprentices also experienced and viewed these four years as a continuation of their enslavement, sometimes with heightened resentment at the denial to them of their rightful freedom. The chains of slavery were all the more irksome when the hopes of freedom raised by the passing of the Emancipation Act in 1833 were so obviously postponed. Slave apprentices aimed for unconditional freedom, not continued slavery as envisaged by employers, nor "training" for a role as a subordinate wage labour force, as planned by abolitionists.

The system which the Special Magistrates were expected to administer was thus, in the words of one Caribbean historian, "an unhappy attempt at compromise between slavery and freedom".[16] Employers and apprentices had very different perceptions of apprenticeship, neither of which matched the goals of the Colonial Office as represented by the newly arrived magistrates. The tensions and contradictions inherent in such a situation were acute.

To add to this general difficulty, the efficient operation of the apprenticeship system was hampered by inadequate financing. The Special Magistrates were to be paid and supported entirely out of a Parliamentary grant made at the time of the Emancipation Act, which was an additional burden on top of the 20 million pounds to be paid out in compensation to slave owners.

The Treasury characteristically attempted to cut costs as much as possible. This was the reason for the inadequate number of magistrates appointed, and for the use of retired army and naval officers, already receiving a pension or on half-pay, who would only be expected to require a small additional sum to serve the Empire. £300 per annum was initially granted, plus £75 passage money. Much wrangling took place over the inadequacy of this stipend, and the inability of magistrates to pay for such necessary items as house rent, hire or purchase of horses for transport and employment of interpreters and clerks. Some adjustments were made but most magistrates felt aggrieved by financial restrictions. Thus Longmore complained soon after his appointment that he could not find a suitable clerk and interpreter, fluent in both Dutch and English, for the wages he was allocated.[17] Two years later he complained again that he could not afford to hire a horse for his interpreter if he needed to stay away overnight, although he admitted that he was less inconvenienced by this than his colleagues in the extensive rural districts.[18] Such issues were a considerable irritant to the Special Magistrates and impeded their ability to carry out the requirements of Ordinance 1, particularly in the rural areas.[19]

Longmore did not face quite such acute difficulties as many of his rural counterparts. But in his appeal for higher allowances soon after taking up his appointment he outlined several other issues which act as a pointer to the specific character of apprenticeship in Cape Town in contrast to the rest of the colony.

Longmore estimated that approximately 12 000 apprentices were under his aegis, which he claimed was equivalent to two or three other districts put together. This was certainly an exaggeration: only 5 702 were recorded in Cape Town in November 1838 at the end of apprenticeship, out of a total of 35 843 in the whole colony. Another 4 910 were living in the surrounding Cape District. But Longmore was not the only Special Magistrate in these areas; two others were located at Simonstown and Tygerberg. The Stellenbosch Special Magisterial district alone had 9 500 apprentices.[20] The fact that rural districts in the Boland had as high or higher numbers of apprentices than Cape Town is a reflection of the decreasing proportion of Cape slaves in the city between the 1810s and 1834, as the labour structure of the town changed from slave to free or hired workers, some were sold to rural districts during the wine boom, and manumission rates were comparatively high.[21]

Numbers alone are not the whole story. What was more to the point was that the apprentices and their employers in Cape Town lived much closer to the Special Magistrate's Office than their counterparts in rural districts. Longmore complained that they tended to bring all complaints, however apparently "trivial" to him.[22] In districts such as Worcester complaints were usually brought to the Special Magistrate by those living near Worcester village, or by farmers and their apprentices when he toured the district and came within easy travelling distance of the farm. There is no doubt that there was less direct intervention in the relationship of employer and apprentice in the countryside than in Cape Town.

This is apparent in the number of complaints brought to Longmore. For instance, in the first three months of 1835, he heard 103 cases in comparison to the 48 heard by his counterpart in Worcester. This level of activity continued in his office throughout the four years, during which time he heard over 1300 cases altogether.[23]

Some of these cases concerned apprentices who were not owned by Cape Town employers but who had taken refuge from the rural hinterland. Longmore was well aware of this, and vigorously attempted to prevent it:

> I have always thought it advisable that the Police Constables should take up any individuals seen loitering about, and suspected of being deserters as most of the apprentices who run away from the country districts take refuge in Cape Town, to elude the search of their employers, who are always willing to pay for the apprehension, it being the means of the apprentices being the sooner restored to labour.[24]

The reasons for rural apprentices coming into Cape Town and ending up in front of Longmore were varied. In the case which led to the comment above, the female apprentice Calister stated that she had not received justice from the Tygerberg Special Magistrate in a case of maltreatment brought against her employer. She therefore came to Cape Town to obtain redress, and was arrested for her pains.[25]

Calister's confidence in Longmore was misplaced, but her perception of the town as somewhere she could escape from the oppression of her owner was significant. A similar belief in the comparative shelter of the city was held by the many apprentices who ran away from farms to the town. Although records from the immediate hinterland districts do not survive, there are a number of such cases from the more distant Worcester district and it is likely that escape to Cape Town would have been just as prevalent from the farms which were closer.[26]

Conversely, the prospect of being moved away from Cape Town was enough to cause apprentices to desert their owners in order to stay in the city. And as in the period of slavery, the threat of being sent up-country was used by employers in an attempt to discipline their apprentices.[27]

Cape Town was thus seen by many apprentices as a refuge from the social controls of the countryside and as a more desirable place of employment than the farms. This was a contrast to the position in the eighteenth century, where Cape Town was a place to escape from, either by ship or more usually via the mountain ranges around the Cape Peninsula on the way to the maroon community at Hangklip or beyond the boundaries of the colony.[28]

The shift from the city as a place of control to a place of refuge reflects both the changing character of Cape Town and the changing perceptions of slaves and later apprentices. Until the later part of the VOC period the town was dominated by the militia and the authorities and any newcomer would have been immediately recognised. But by the 1830s Cape Town was large and diverse enough to offer refuge for runaways without immediate detection.[29] Furthermore, the network of the free black community, of casual workers and hired employees, meant that a complex fabric had emerged in which escaped apprentices could find employment. True, many of them were apprehended by the police, but many others went unnoticed, sometimes for as long as a year or more.[30]

Apprentices were thus now demanding the right to live and work on their own within colonial society, rather than running away from it. In one exceptional case, Philemon, apprentice of a Swartberg farmer, fled to the town with his employer's daughter whom he had "seduced", after the father and his neighbouring farmers had attempted to shoot him and had sent the girl to another district.[31] This elopement contrasts strikingly with a similar affront to rural racial taboos in the eighteenth century; David Malan and the slave Sara eloped by disappearing from the colony.[32] Philemon hoped to find a home in Cape Town, although he was ultimately outwitted by the intervention of Helena's uncle who followed them to the city and persuaded her to leave her lover.

It was not only rural slave apprentices who sought refuge from their owners in Cape Town. Urban apprentices also left their employers. Approximately two-thirds of the cases of complaint brought to Longmore were by employers against apprentices who had absconded from them.[33]

Cape Town provided many opportunities for apprentices to desert. Some such cases were of temporary absence, concerning those who had slipped away for a few hours, either to join their companions in the taphuis, down by the boats at Roggebaai or on the slopes of Signal Hill.[34]

Others were longer lasting. Many apprentices, particularly those with skills who were hired out by their owners, escaped to work for themselves or to hire themselves out by claiming that they were free. They worked in a variety of jobs, as masons, bakers' assistants, fishermen, carpenters, wood collectors and vendors. The development over the previous couple of decades of an urban work force which was a mixture of slave and free, gave the opportunity for such evasion.[35]

However, this was an option which was open primarily to men. Very few female apprentices were reported for desertion and those that were, were usually only temporarily absent. Casual labour or hiring out was predominantly a male activity, although there is one case of a female apprentice who escaped and survived by working as a prostitute.[36] Women were normally confined to domestic work in their owners' households, not only by the legal bonds of apprenticeship, but also by the lack of alternative economic options. There was no market for female casual labour until after the end of apprenticeship. As under slavery, the notion of social space and relative lack of control over Cape Town's apprentice population was confined to one gender.[37]

There was another common category of absentee apprentices, again primarily male. Moslems were often hauled before Longmore for absenting themselves on Fridays without permission, a clear indication not only of the importance of Islam amongst the Cape Town underclass but also of the assertion of the right to worship despite opposition of owners. Such actions included insistence on observation of the Ramadan fast, and the celebration of Eid in 1835, when many apprentices ignored the protest of their owners and went to the Moslem "priests" and houses owned by Free Blacks.[38] Certainly Islam was a marker of rejection of owner control. January, an apprentice who had constantly absented himself from his owner, Mr Jurgens, since 1 December 1834, was brought before Longmore in February of the following year because although he had been "brought up in the Christian religion ... [he had] latterly chosen to turn Malay". When refused permission to attend "the Malay Church" on Fridays, he replied defiantly that he would "run away instead and his Master might make a convict of him". The "spirit of insubordination", reported Jurgens, "was increasing".[39]

The growth of Islam as a marker of underclass identity, hiring out without the knowledge of the owner and male absconding into the city were continuations of processes which had existed under slavery. They were made possible by the specific structure of the urban economy and society, in which casual labour, a growing free black community and the space for religious and cultural independence existed.

But what was new was the resentment which many apprentices felt against their owners for keeping them in bondage after 1 December 1834 and the certainty of forthcoming freedom that both employers and apprentices possessed. It is this "spirit of insubordination" to which Jurgens referred. In several of the cases of desertion, apprentices argued that freedom was theirs by right, and they refused to accept the authority of either their owners or the Special Magistrate. Others refused to work under the same conditions as those of slavery, demanding wages, free time or a reduction of workload. Thus three apprentices who worked for the Wynberg farmer, Jan Munnik, deserted the farm for three days claiming that they had been made to work on Sundays and had the right to a holiday.[40] Isaac, an apprentice of Bertrand Daniel of Strand Street, left his owner's house on 1 December 1834, and "has been secreting himself about the city" for the following four months. When apprehended he had stated that he refused to stay with his owner.[41] And such "insubordination" applied equally to female slaves, even if they were less able to escape. Leentje, owned by Otto Landberg of Shortmarket Street, was brought to Longmore for her "insubordination" since emancipation day, and defiantly asserted that "she did not care for anyone, nor for the Tronk, nor for any punishment" and that "if she should [sic] stay in the Deponent's house a day longer she was certain she would hang herself".[42]

This frustration was clearly apparent at the beginning of the apprenticeship period, when hopes of true freedom were being curtailed. By the middle of 1838, the character of such "insubordination" was changing. Cases of desertion tended to be for longer periods than temporary absence, and some owners were content to be rid of troublesome servants so close to the end of apprenticeship.

Other apprentices were making preparations for final emancipation by staying where they were and extracting all they could from their owners. In an ironic reversal of the claims which had been dominant for over a century under slavery, some employers were now begging the Special Magistrate to free them of the burden of such troublesome apprentices. Thus Mrs Berstandig demanded that action be taken against her apprentice Elsie, who "despite every remonstration would not stir from her room ... [when] sent word that she must pack up her things and go she would not do anything nor quit the house". Clearly Elsie was going to continue holding on to her room until the very end and she only avoided punishment by Longmore on condition she quit her owner.[43] Sitie, a female apprentice of Mr Attwell, was more actively preparing for freedom. She stole handkerchiefs and cloth from her owner which she "intended to dispose of at a house of reception for stolen things", and she stated under cross-examination that "a Malay woman told her to bring her some handkerchiefs and any other things and that when she was free she could go and exchange these for clothing".[44] Such actions, unlike those of escape and self-employment, were made by both men and women.

These cases indicate that the period of apprenticeship in Cape Town heightened the tensions between the dominant classes of the city and a servile population with access to its own form of popular culture, perception of labour and freedom, and understanding of its rights. In many regards this was a continuation of the conflicts between master and slave that had existed since the seventeenth century and had taken more assertive forms in the courts during the period of amelioration. They reached new heights in the apprenticeship years.

There was one important difference between cases brought to the Special Magistrate in Cape Town and those brought earlier to the Protector of Slaves. The vast majority of cases brought to the Special Magistrate were by employers, complaining against their servants. Only a handful of complaints of apprentices against masters was made, and of these several were thrown out as unfounded and "malicious". This is in marked contrast to the position in Worcester, where almost 40% of the complaints were brought by apprentices. Perhaps Longmore acquired a reputation for lack of sympathy to apprentice claims. More likely, urban apprentices had a better means of dealing with their owners by linking themselves to the underworld of the city rather than relying on the appointee of the British government. This was an option unavailable to those who were confined to the isolated world of farms in the Worcester district.[45]

What became of Longmore? Despite his complaints of inadequate funding and overwork, he decided not to return to Britain, and along with four of his counterparts was taken into the magisterial establishment of the colony, where he was made the first Resident Magistrate of Wynberg. Prior to this appointment he had drawn the attention of the Colonial Secretary to the fate of children indentured to employers under the Emancipation Act: a loophole in the legislation which broke up slave families and led to bitter disputes between owners and apprentice parents.[46] In this, as in much else, the legacy of the slave apprenticeship system was to linger far beyond 1838.

In one sense apprenticeship did provide a period of preparation for freedom, although not on the terms envisaged by the framers of the Emancipation Act. It marked a strengthening of the bonds of the Cape Town underclasses, in which apprentices increasingly identified themselves with the free labouring poor of the city and rejected the control of its dominant classes. Apprentice deserters and "insubordinates" were learning to cope with an existence of precarious survival as free people at the bottom of Cape Town's social scale. The lines were clearly drawn up for the class divides of the city after 1838.

Endnotes

1. GH (Government House) 23/11, 64–5, D'Urban – Spring Rice, 22 November 1834. All archival sources used in this article are in the Cape Archives Depot, Roeland Street.
2. Although this paper is supposed to be about Cape Town, I cannot resist mentioning the hardships of Commander Thomas Sherwin, R.N., who earned the hostility of farmers by his apparent support for apprentices and of the Colonial Government by his complaints of low pay, inadequate allowances and his involvement in local law suits. At one stage he received anonymous warnings and threats from local inhabitants which eventually forced him to move from Uitenhage to Port Elizabeth. Major James Barnes of Swellendam faced not dissimilar problems.
3. This paper is part of a larger project on the operation of the slave apprenticeship system at the Cape. See N. Worden, "Between slavery and freedom: the apprenticeship system" in N. Worden and C. Crais, eds, *Breaking the Chains : Slavery and Emancipation in the Nineteenth Century Cape Colony* (Johannesburg, forthcoming).
4. A general outline of the duties of the Special Magistrates in the Caribbean is given in W.L. Burn, *Emancipation and Apprenticeship in the British West Indies* (London 1937), 203–13. This work is the classic study of the apprenticeship system, although by now rather dated and certainly prejudiced against the apprentices themselves. For a more recent view and one more sympathetic to the apprentices, see T. Holt, *The Problem of Freedom: Race, Labor and Politics in Jamaica and Britain, 1832–1938* (Baltimore 1992), 13 –122.
5. For instance Azor, an apprentice found in possession of a stolen telescope, 1/WBG Add 1/3/1, Wynberg Magistrate Records, Special Magistrate Reports, 10 April 1835; Adam whose attempt to "destroy machinery" was of "too heinous a nature" to be decided by the Special Magistrate, 1/WBG Add 1/3/1, 25 January 1836.
6. Ordinance 1 of 1835. The content and implications of this Ordinance is analysed more fully in Worden "Between slavery and freedom".
7. CO 441,2, Colonial Office, Cape Town, dispatches, Longmore to Colonial Secretary, 28 January 1835.
8. 1/WBG Add 1/3/1 Special Magistrate, Cape Town, Correspondence re valuations

of apprentices.
9. GH 23/11, 122, Statement of the number of slaves registered at the Cape of Good Hope on the 30th November 1834.
10. GH 23/11, 98, D'Urban – Spring Rice, 7 January 1835.
11. In the event, predial apprenticeship was also ended after four years following protest at the working of the system by the Anti-Slavery movement in Britain. See C. Wesley, "The abolition of Negro apprenticeship in the British Empire", *Journal of Negro History* 23 (1938) 155–99; I.Gross, "Parliament and the abolition of negro apprenticeship, 1835 – 1838", *English Historical Review* 96 (1981) 560–76; A.Tyrell "The "Moral Radical Party" and the Anglo-Jamaican campaign for the abolition of the Negro apprenticeship system" *English Historical Review* 99 (1984) 481–502.
12. For discussion of abolitionist and Parliamentary perceptions of apprenticeship and its aftermath, see the essays in J. Walvin, ed, *Slavery and British Society, 1776–1846* (Macmillan 1982).
13. This quotation is from S. Salinger, *"To serve well and faithfully": Labour and Indentured Servants in Pennsylvania, 1682 – 1800* (New York 1987), cited in C. Malherbe, "Indentured and unfree labour in South Africa: towards an understanding", *South African Historical Journal* 24 (1991), 6.
14. This tendency was also apparent in the ill-fated scheme of the Children's Friend Society to apprentice children from Britain to Cape employers in the 1830s and 1840s; whereas the Society anticipated that they would receive training for skilled wage labour, they were alarmed to discover that many of the employers were also slave owners and "their apprentices may have been looked upon much in the same light as slaves", GH 1/127, 132, Glenelg to Napier, 29 March 1839. On this scheme see E. Bradlow, "The Children's Friend Society at the Cape of Good Hope", *Victorian Studies* 27: 2 (1984).
15. J. Mason, "The slaves and their protectors: reforming resistance in a slave society: the Cape Colony, 1826 –1834", *Journal of Southern African Studies* 17,1 (1991); W. Dooling, "Slaves, slaveowners and amelioration in Graaff-Reinet, 1823 –1830" (B.A. Hons, University of Cape Town, 1989).
16. D. Hall, "The apprenticeship period in Jamaica, 1834 –1838", *Caribbean Quarterly* 3 (1953), 142.
17. CO 441, 121, Longmore to Colonial Secretary, 14 February 1835.
18. 1/WBG Add 1/3/1, Longmore to Colonial Secretary, 23 January 1837.
19. For instance the Swellendam Special Magistrate complained that he could not afford to visit farms with large numbers of apprentices or hold hearings in the remoter parts of his district when insufficient allowances were granted for transport, CO 465, 13 and 27 March 1837; CO 465, 23 Barnes to Colonial Secretary, 20 February 1837.
20. Editorial, *South African Commercial Advertiser*, 28 November 1838.
21. A. Bank, *The Decline of Urban Slavery at the Cape, 1806 to 1834* (Communications, Centre for African Studies, University of Cape Town, 22, 1991), 20–6 and 172–5.
22. CO 441, 121, Longmore to Colonial Secretary, 14 February 1835.
23. 1/WBG Add 1/1/1 – 1/1/16, Special Magistrate Reports, 1835–1838. These records, hidden in the Wynberg magisterial archive, are extremely rich sources for the social history of the Cape Town underclass, particularly in the absence of

regular magisterial records for the city before the 1840s.
24. CO 441, 48–9, Longmore to Colonial Secretary, 6 May 1835.
25. Ibid.
26. For instance, 1/WOC 19/27, Worcester Special Magistrate Record Book, cases of 8 February 1837 and 3 May 1837. These cases are taken from a four month sample of the Worcester cases, February–May 1837.
27. For instance, 1/WBG 1/1/1, 30 January 1835, Jan de Villiers vs Moses; 1/WBG 1/1/1, 12 March 1835, Dirk Breslau vs Mariana.
28. R. Ross, *Cape of Torments: Slavery and Resistance in South Africa* (London, 1983), ch. 5–7.
29. Ross believes that a "face-to-face community" had come to an end with the growth of population in the 1770s, *Cape of Torments*, 19. There is evidence however that it was only with the growth of the early nineteenth century that this was fully the case.
30. For instance 1/WBG Add 1/1/15, 144–5, Van den Bergh vs Marina, 27 August 1838. The male apprentice Marina had escaped almost two years previously and survived by collecting wood and selling it in the town. On the role of the police in capturing escaped slave apprentices, K. Elks "Crime, community and police in Cape Town, 1832–1850" (M.A., University of Cape Town, 1986).
31. 1/WBG Add 1/3/1, 5 April 1836.
32. CJ 795, Council of Justice, 56, Case of David Malan Davidsz, 5 March 1789.
33. This data is drawn from two samples of Cape Town apprenticeship cases; 102 cases between January and March 1835 (1/WBG Add 1/1/1) and 33 cases between August and November 1838 (1/WBG Add 1/1/15). In the first sample 67 cases (66%) were brought against deserters, in the second 21 cases (64%).
34. For example, 1/WBG Add 1/1/16, 3, Moore vs Dollie, 6 September 1838.
35. For example, 1/WBG Add 1/1/1, 28, 30, 59, 96; 1/WBG Add 1/1/15, 115, 140. The importance of the slave hiring out system and the ambiguities of slavery and freedom in Cape Town is stressed by A. Bank, *Decline of Urban Slavery*, 38–43.
36. 1/WBG Add 1/1/16, 15–16, Van Schoor vs Wilhelmina, 2 October 1838.
37. This is a point raised by Patricia van der Spuy, "Slave women and the family in Cape Town after the abolition of the slave trade", unpub. paper, Cape Town History Project Workshop, 11–12 November 1991, University of Cape Town. I am grateful to her for the insight.
38. For example, 1/WBG Add 1/1/1, cases 17, 25, 27.
39. 1/WBG Add 1/1/1 52, Jurgens vs January, 26 February 1835.
40. 1/WBG Add 1/1/1 9, Munnik vs Anthony, Carolus and Titus, 31 January 1835.
41. 1/WBG Add 1/1/1 95, Bertrand Daniel vs Isaac, 26 March 1835.
42. 1/WBG Add 1/1/1 54, Otto Landsberg vs Leentje, 27 February 1835.
43. 1/WBG Add 1/1/16 19, Mrs Bestandig vs Elsie, 23 October 1838.
44. 1/WBG Add 1/1/16, 5, Attwell vs Sitie, 10 September 1838.
45. See Worden "Between slavery and freedom" for discussion of these issues. The Worcester records are to be found in 1/WOC 19/26 – 27, Worcester Court Record Books.
46. For the issue of child indenture under apprenticeship see Pamela Scully's forthcoming chapter, "Liberating the family: private and public worlds of emancipation in the rural western Cape, c. 1830 – 1842" in Worden and Crais, eds, *Breaking the Chains*.

3

Leprosy and racism at Robben Island

Harriet Deacon

Introduction

Although much has been written on plague, syphilis, influenza and other diseases in Cape Town at the turn of the twentieth century[1], no specific attention has been paid to leprosy in the context of social histories of disease in South Africa. This is surprising because the social impact of the disease was considerable world-wide, especially in the last decade of the nineteenth century. The South African response to leprosy control lay on the extreme end of the spectrum, with compulsory legal segregation for all lepers. There is a growing body of comparative material on leprosy and its social ramifications in America, Australia, India, Sri Lanka, and Ethiopia, among others.[2] However, a more theoretical interest has been shown by some scholars in recent years.[3] Notwithstanding the historical importance of the disease, the only general work on South African leprosy in the nineteenth century is that by Sister Willies[4], formerly of the Westfort Leper Asylum in Pretoria. This chapter sketches the social history of leprosy in the Cape during the latter half of the nineteenth century, focusing on the Cape Colony's major leper asylum on Robben Island between 1846 and 1931. The chapter will discuss the way in which racism and the perception and treatment of those suffering from leprosy were linked during the nineteenth century.

The striking similarity between the negative stereotypes of the leper and the black person in the Colony forms a starting point for the discussion. Medical and popular aetiologies of leprosy were connected to negative characteristics associated with blacks. The particularly severe segregatory response to leprosy at the Cape was based on a recognition of the special colonial "problem" in having a large number of black lepers who were seen both as particularly susceptible and particularly irresponsible. The similarity between the negatively stereotyped leper and the black was thus not incidental to the form that the administrative and medical reactions to the disease took in the nineteenth century. Racism affected the colonial reaction to leprosy, as it also increasingly affected the position of black and white lepers on Robben Island. The use of segregation or quarantine for medical reasons (with racist undertones) was closely linked to the rising social segregation in Cape Town (on a racial basis).

The leprosy question must be seen in the light of concern about the spread of syphilis and leprosy in the Colony during the 1880s and 1890s, and the growing attractiveness and feasibility of quarantine as a means of dealing with contagious diseases such as leprosy, smallpox and plague. The link between racism and leprosy must be understood in the context of other interventionist health measures passed during the last few decades of the nineteenth century under the banner of Public Health. The model of urban racial segregation, conceived under the "sanitation syndrome"[5], fitted neatly into the segregation model provided by quarantine in medical science.

The Public Health movement, which equated sanitation with civilisation[6], provided the legal, intellectual and professional framework for the initial segregation, on a racial basis, of living areas and amenities in the Cape Colony and elsewhere at the close of the nineteenth century. Public Health legislation was used to effect forced removals to Ndabeni, Cape Town's first African location, which were not provided for in the Native Locations Act of 1899.[7] Although the plague itself played only a small role in justifying the location in 1901,[8] the "sanitation syndrome" had been deployed during the previous decade in pressurising the Cape Town Council to move Africans from racially mixed slum areas and from the docks. The notion was that Capetonians (the white dominant classes) had to be protected from contagious diseases emanating from the dirty, overcrowded areas inhabited by poorer (and blacker) classes, an idea already prevalent in middle-class Cape Town in the 1880s.[9]

Legislation such as the Leprosy Repression and Contagious Diseases Acts removed civil rights (such as the right to vote for lepers) from certain "contagious" groups, a selective interventionism which went beyond deprivation of freedom for medical reasons. Parallels may be drawn between this and the process of "social separation"[10] that gradually eroded black civil rights in Cape Town after the 1890s. In arguing for the potency of the "sanitation syndrome" over economic factors in the origin of racially segregated urban areas, Swanson[11] has rejected the notion that it was merely a justification for actions taken on economic imperative.

Some of the Public Health measures had racist undertones of their own. Van Heyningen[12] has argued that by focusing on the human factor in the transmission of plague in Cape Town at the turn of the century, doctors encouraged the targeting of "dirty" Indian and Chinese shops and overcrowded, unsanitary African dwellings in attempts to wipe out the disease. But the racism of the Public Health movement cannot simply be explained away as a justification for racial segregation. The extent of medical contributions to urban segregation must be measured against the racist content of medical metaphors. The analysis of debates and fears surrounding leprosy in Cape Town at the turn of the century provides some insight into the relationship between the content of racial beliefs and medical knowledge.

The biology of leprosy

As Rosenberg has said[13], "A disease is no absolute entity but a complex intellectual construct, an amalgam of biological state and social definition." Recognizing the importance of biological definitions, it is necessary to establish the current state of medical knowledge about the disease before examining its social ramifications and accompanying medical definitions in the nineteenth century.

Leprosy is a disease which affects the skin, the bones, the nervous system and the internal organs. Its onset is delayed, because of the weakness of the bacillus. The clinical symptoms are ulceration of the skin, contraction of the hands and feet, insensitivity of the skin, and gradual deformity of the face, with thickening of features. Today, two related types are recognised, the tubercular and the anaesthetic, which present with slightly different symptoms. A mixed or borderline form is a combination of the two. It has long been popularly believed that leprosy is highly contagious, but medical opinion fluctuated in the nineteenth century between this and the idea that it was hereditary, or in one line of thinking, caused by eating putrid or dried fish. Now the medical consensus is that leprosy is contagious to a very low degree, and that people generally have to be debilitated or have a hereditary disposition to the disease in order to be infected. Sixty percent of cases contract the disease as children.[14] But medical scientists still do not know exactly how it is transmitted, and have only recently been able to infect animals in order to observe the disease more closely. Infection through skin, gastrointestinal and respiratory tracts, and through the placenta, nasal mucous and insects has been suggested.[15]

In the 1940s the drugs Promin and Dapsone developed for tuberculosis treatment were first used for leprosy patients. Although various remedies were used before this, none were particularly successful. Leper asylums were centres for confinement rather than cure. In South Africa, Hemel-en-Aarde (1817) was succeeded by Robben Island in 1846 and other leper asylums sprang up after 1890. Institutional solutions were particularly favoured world-wide in the 1890s and after, especially in colonial countries. This was partly because of the perceived danger of contagion to the general public. In 1931, however, the League of Nations Health Organisation noted that it was "generally recognised" that "compulsory segregation" had drawbacks (such as concealment), and could be safely replaced by a more liberal "isolation policy", which distinguished between infectious and non-infectious cases.[16] Today, clinic-based out-patient treatment of the disease is more popular among doctors, but asylums are still used for badly disfigured and disabled cases who do not wish to leave. By 1968, there were only four leper asylums operating in South Africa.[17] Today, there is only one.

Cases at Westfort, near Pretoria, the major leper asylum in South Africa after 1931, peaked at about 873 in 1940.[18] Leprosy incidence began to decline world-wide in the twentieth century, a trend evident in South Africa: there are only about 50 lepers at Westfort today. After 1952, leper asylum accommodation was used for tuberculosis sufferers as well. Today, Westfort acts mainly as a mental asylum. The decline in cases is due to the use of antibiotics, and general improvements in diet and living conditions. Hunter and Thomas[19] have argued that African urbanisation, and concomitant changes have decreased incidence rates. They support the theory, first argued in 1905 by Calmette[20], that leprosy and tuberculosis give cross-immunity and that the rise of tuberculosis in Europe in the 15th century aided the decline of leprosy, and that a similar pattern is evident in Africa now.

The provision of distribution figures for disease is a political issue, and their interpretations are historical artefacts. The greater number of tuberculosis deaths among Africans in the twentieth century, for example, have been attributed either to the racial susceptibility of the South African blacks or to the Apartheid policies of the racist South African state.[21] In his recent book, Packard[22] rejects both as a total explanation. He suggests that prior to 1930, high tuberculosis susceptibility among Africans was due to the relative rarity of tuberculosis in South Africa prior to the nineteenth century, and hence also their relative inexperience of dealing with the disease. After 1930, adverse environmental factors tipped the balance for Africans. One could thus explain the higher incidence of leprosy among black people in contact with Europeans in South Africa during the nineteenth century by arguing that they were poor, often unhealthy, and had little acquired immunity to the disease.

The leprosy scare

Although it had been endemic in many countries since the beginning of the century, leprosy suddenly became a burning issue world-wide between about 1889 and 1900. The lepra bacillus now believed to cause leprosy had first come to light in 1874 under Dr Armauer Hansen's microscope in Norway. This, and the death by leprosy in 1889 of Father Damien, a white mission worker in Hawaii's leper settlement on Molokai island, was treated by most doctors and administrators as convincing evidence for the contagiousness of the disease. In particular, it was seen as evidence that Europeans, previously believed to be relatively immune, could contract leprosy. Although leprosy did not spread pandemically through the Western world, alarm and fear of leprosy "rode through Western nations on the tidal wave of the forces of racism and the yellow peril".[23] At the height of Western imperialism, leprosy was "discovered" in Asian populations emigrating to Australia, Hawaii and the United States, especially the Chinese. Other groups, such as Africans and Afro-Americans, were also identified as leprosy-prone populations.[24] In the United States, the leprosy question had been added to a long list of grievances against Chinese immigrants in the early 1870s. By 1882, when the period of free immigration was coming to a close, Chinese immigrants were alone in being specifically excluded from the country. The arguments for such exclusion were biological, economic and social, military, sexual and medical.[25]

The increasing use of segregation or exclusion in dealing with leprosy was related partly to an increasing medical consensus about its contagiousness. Because there was no certain cure for the disease during the nineteenth century, medical and administrative speculation in the Cape centered around whether segregation of lepers would help to stop them infecting others. There was little consensus on the mode of transmission of the disease in the early nineteenth century. Dr Wehr had plumped for infectiousness in 1826 in justifying the transfer of the lepers to a separate wing at Somerset Hospital.[26] The Colonial Medical Committee clearly thought the disease hereditary in 1842,[27] although they still thought Robben Island would be a good site for a leper colony. In 1846, the special Medical Board which recommended the removal of the lepers to the island, justified their segregation by saying that although the disease was not contagious, (a) Robben Island would be cheaper than Hemel-en-Aarde, (b) that the lepers' appearance was offensive, and (c) that if the disease was indeed contagious, that society would be protected.[28] Although weakly justified medically, the removal of lepers, and indeed paupers and lunatics, from the mainland at a time of increased social tension after emancipation and economic slump, made social sense to the colonists. This kind of concern papered over the gaps, equally evident later, between social/medical policy and medical theory.

Medical men distanced themselves increasingly from the "popular" opinion that leprosy was contagious during the 1850s. By 1861, the disease was generally thought in medical circles here to be transmitted by heredity. This view was vindicated by the reports of the Royal College of Physicians in 1867 and 1887 that leprosy was hereditarily transmitted. The important issue was thus to prevent sexual contact between lepers, and with healthy people. But there was in theory less urgency for segregation and, especially as many lepers were living free in the colony, some questioned the need for it at all.[29] The question of public stigma against lepers now arose as a rationale for segregating them from same-sex patients with other ailments, and even for their general segregation from society.[30] The "unpleasantness" of the disease often overflowed into this reasoning, despite admission of the fact that other diseases like secondary syphilis were as common and as ugly.[31]

In the early 1880s, compulsory segregation of all lepers became an issue as the Government and medical community became worried about increasing numbers of lepers, and the presence of the disease among whites. In 1882 a Circular requesting District Surgeons' reports for publication had thrown up large numbers of syphilis cases but no lepers.[32] The search for syphilis however, raised doctors' consciousness of other, clinically similar diseases such as leprosy.[33] Early in 1883, several districts sent representations to Government about the leprosy issue, possibly Caledon, Saldanah Bay and Malmesbury. The Medical Board also proposed steps against the disease, stressing the importance of segregation.[34] A Select Committee in August of 1883 reported that the disease was spreading, especially to urban areas and the white population, that it was dangerous, and required legislative action. The evidence labelled Kalk Bay, Wynberg, Hout Bay, Claremont (especially Malay traders there) and the Cape Flats as problem areas, as well as Caledon, Saldanah Bay, Malmesbury, Clanwilliam, Calvinia and the Frontier.[35] This notwithstanding the fact that the District Surgeons' reports in December that year showed no lepers in Calvinia and Clanwilliam.[36] In these first few years, in spite of the concern about leprosy spreading, numbers of reported lepers were not high, and usually less than ten (except in Herschel, where a possible 100 were suggested in the Reserve[37]). They were much lower than numbers of syphilis cases reported, although the Contagious Diseases Act was modified to deal with the syphilis problem a year later than the Leprosy Repression Bill was passed.

Because of this concern about the increase in the disease, a Leprosy Repression Bill, which allowed warranting and removal of any leper who might spread the disease by being at large, sailed through Parliament in June 1884[38.] Doubts were however expressed about the cost which compulsory segregation would incur for Government.[39] J. X. Merriman added during the debate in 1884 that if such steps were taken at all they must be carried through, and the lepers maintained for life.[40] These objections, and lack of finance, delayed the Act being promulgated until 1891.

By the end of the 1880s, medical arguments that leprosy was hereditary were waning. Leprosy was increasingly viewed as an incurable and contagious disease that could be easily transmitted (from blacks) to whites. Increasing pressure was put to bear on the Robben Island leper community, which had swelled by the number of female lepers sent back there from the Old Somerset Hospital in 1887. In a protracted battle with the lepers, starting in 1887, the Surgeon

Superintendent Ross and the Colonial Office managed (illegally, and because they controlled boats from the island) to prevent lepers from going on leave to the mainland. Ross, like so many of the other South African doctors, favoured strict segregation.[41]

A Commission in 1889 stressed the urgency of legislation to halt the spread into towns, the contagiousness of the disease, and the need to act quickly to reduce expense in the long run. District Surgeons of the "more populous districts" of the Cape and Paarl reported a marked increase in cases, and those in the outlying districts, except those of Stockenstrom and Alexandria, reported no cases, or no increase.[42] It was only then that the Colonial Government investigated the brass tacks of asylum organisation and other countries' records on the segregation question.[43] The Leprosy Segregation Act was finally promulgated in late 1891, and enforced in May 1892. It was felt that by strictly quarantining all of the small number as yet affected, it would be possible to "stamp out" the disease, with a strong focus on the towns.[44]

Among Cape doctors and administrators, therefore, there was a "segregation consensus" after about 1894 and legal segregation of all lepers after 1891. Few countries, even among the colonies, came out as early and as strongly on the contagion side of the transmission debate as South Africa did in the legislative arena. The difference between colonial policy for lepers and the laxer segregation laws of European countries, in particular, was explicitly justified in racial terms. In 1909, Dr Gregory, the Medical Officer of Health for the Colony, summed up the South African position by saying that "modified segregation", as practiced in Norway, was futile here because

> here you have a very different population to deal with. A people largely composed of native and coloured, unreliable, indifferent to the dangers of the disease, ignorant and devoid of the simplest knowledge of hygiene.[45]

The dimensions of the leprosy scare in South Africa give it the status of a "swart gevaar". In the 1890s Cape Town and Wynberg featured prominently among the regions providing the most cases for the island. Kimberley and Worcester were also heavily affected regions. There was even a reported "epidemic" in 1901 among miners in Kimberley.[46]

Action on the issue was not confined to the Cape, however. In the space of ten years between 1890 and 1901, 11 state-run leper settlements were established in the Cape, the Transvaal (the first at Johannesburg in 1893), Natal[47] and the Orange River Colony (the first at Bloemfontein in 1900). Nearly two thirds of all South Africa's leper colonies were established during this short period. The Cape Leprosy Repression Act and Amendment Act of 1891 and 1894 respectively, the Natal Leprosy Act of 1890, the Orange River Colony Leprosy Act of 1909, and the Transvaal Acts of 1904, 1907 and 1908 as amended in the Union's Leprosy Act no. 14 of 1914 were all passed within a similarly small period. Although numbers were relatively small, medical treatment non-specific, and direct cases of contagion rare, leprosy was treated as a special and separate disease, requiring specific, strict and intrusive legislation, between 1891 and 1977. The Department of Health was only responsible for control of the disease from 1923[48] and the Leprosy Act of 1914 was only subsumed under the Health Act in 1977.

The changing social face of leprosy

Leprosy had been known to Europeans long before the nineteenth century. It was, and is, a powerful metaphor for the outcast, the unclean. The long association between leprosy and segregation has been explained by some scholars whose argument relies on a form of biological determinism. Skinsnes[49] has argued that leprosy was a specific biological entity that produced stigma automatically because of its (a) visible and horrible effects, (b) progressive physical deterioration and prolonged course, (c) non-fatal and chronic nature, exposing the sufferer to secondary infections, (d) slow, insidious onset, (e) high endemicity, and limited epidemicity, (f) low incidence rate and association with poor living conditions, (g) apparent incurability and (h) long incubation period. Such arguments have some value in explaining the powerful metaphoric use of leprosy in the Western world, but have little power when it comes to the interpretation of the changing importance of leprosy as a social marker in South Africa. The term "leprosy" has in fact referred to different physical symptoms which have evoked different responses over time and space. And as Gussow[50] has argued, the minimal continuity demonstrated by the reaction to lepers (or the creation of lepers) is not due to anything intrinsic to the disease (as Skinsnes argues), but is re-created over time in particular socio-historical contexts, to exclude certain groups or justify prejudice against them.

"Lepers" in the Biblical sense referred to people suffering from several skin diseases, and not necessarily (tubercular) leprosy, a group not contiguous with (and not inclusive of) those we would call "lepers" today.[51] Neither was the term "lepra" used by Greek doctors in the same way as modern leprosy. The Greek/Egyptian term "elephantiasis" referred then to what we would call "leprosy" today, and was believed to originate from the melancholic black bile. The term "elephantiasis" is now used for an entirely distinct medical entity. Other Greek and medieval names for modern forms of leprosy were "Leo" (thickening of the face), "Satyriasis" (redness of cheeks and promiscuity), and "Heraclean" (strong, irresistible illness).[52] In early nineteenth century Ceylon, Heffner suggests that leprosy may have been confused with tinea versicolor, vitiligo, syphilis, lupus vulgaris and erythematosus, granuloma anmulare, cellulitis, erisipelas, diabetes mellitus and several other diseases.[53]

Symptoms that today would be indicative of leprosy were thus called by several different names. Some of these symptoms would today be evidence of other diseases, and not leprosy. In South Africa, criteria for admission to Robben Island seem to have shifted broadly from visible deformity or ulceration, and destitution, to these as well as more superficial skin problems, especially of the face (eg, one man was admitted with festering mosquito bites on his face in the early twentieth century) during the leprosy scare years (c. 1887–1910). After about 1896, but more consistently after 1901, the presence of lepra bacilli was used for confirmation of the diagnosis, which was very conservative[54] and based on superficial clinical presentation. The absence of bacilli did not however guarantee immediate discharge, as their reappearance was not unknown. In 1923, the South African criteria for discharge changed, and a large number were discharged from Emjanyana asylum, and probably from Robben Island too. This happened again in 1931. In the latter year, only cases which had negative smears for 12 months and no spread of skin ulceration were discharged.[55] It was suggested by Hansen in 1895, but only proven by Shepard in 1960, that some of the bacilli visible under microscope were in fact inactive.[56] So nowadays, some lepers are considered cured who have (dead) bacilli in their microscope smears.

Attitudes towards lepers have varied in different cultures. In England in the middle ages, lepers were often grouped with beggars, and old vagrant shelters became lazarhouses. European laws in 757 AD and on into the ninth century discriminated against lepers.[57] In spite of a general consensus in the mid- to late- nineteenth century that segregation was the only way of dealing with leprosy, partial segregation was implemented in most Western and colonial countries. In India, for example, only pauper lepers were put into the lazarettos. In Norway, home segregation was coupled with an asylum programme. In 1880, of the 1 382 lepers registered there, 617 were in asylums and 965 in their homes.[58] Leper contacts were followed up carefully, even in foreign countries. In India, lepers were only shunned by society in the latter stages of the disease, and in Africa there are examples of lepers mixing with the community without stigma.[59]

It has been shown that segregationist approaches are linked historically to increased social tension. Ginzberg[60] suggests that lepers were only fully segregated in lazarhouses outside the towns after the mini-inquisition of the fourteenth century. He advances the theory that in the middle ages, Jews and lepers were the targets for an early inquisition in France because of pressure on resources that was blamed on the wealth-seeking of the Jews, and the poor but "power-hungry" lepers. The Jews were accused of conspiring to take over the country with the lepers, who were to have poisoned the streams. Many lepers and later Jews were burnt at the stake, and the remaining lepers were then removed to settlements out of the towns. Although lazarettos were present in France in the eighth century, and then sprang up in Ireland (869 AD), Spain and England (eleventh century), Scotland (twelfth century) and Norway (thirteenth century)[61], they may have had varying importance in segregating lepers.

During the late nineteenth century leprosy scare, leprosy seems to have become a metaphorical repository for negative representations of the (largely racially identified) "other". The development of the leprosy scare was only partly related to the actual number of lepers and contact infections. For the historian, reactions to leprosy can indicate fault-lines in contemporary society. This paper will, following Gussow[62], explore social factors which influenced the timing and effects of the leprosy scare in South Africa. Most prominent among these are the dominant classes' fears of Malay independence and difference after the 1882 smallpox crisis, rising fears of a diseased black working class invading the towns in the late nineteenth century, and the fear of white degeneration through racial mixing among the lower classes which surfaced in the 1890s.

The social construction of disease

In order to examine leprosy historically, I shall use the theoretical perspective called social constructionism which has recently received particular attention in historically sensitive analyses of stigma, discrimination and institutionalisation. I define social construction as the creation of a social category through the selection and signification of physical features (eg, the creation of "race" or "disease") and/or behavioural features (eg, the creation of "madness"). More specifically, the notion of "disease" refers to a collection of real symptoms, but the specification of what symptom forms part of the collection, and the meanings attached to specific diseases are culturally and historically specific. There are two broad poles of social constructionism which I have called "minimalist" and "maximalist", referring to their degree of rejection of modern social constructions. I shall now briefly critique the two poles of this constructionist argument.

The minimalist pole of the social constructionist approach accepts the broad tenets for middle range differences but downplays the cultural and historical contingency of social definitions of extreme forms of deviance. It emphasises the naturalness of dividing our world in this way. Some people for example, "are just mad", and would be mad in any culture. In this line of thought (and the more conservative biological determinisms such as Skinsnes' theory), leprosy is so horrible that anyone in any culture at any time would shy away from a leper. For the social constructionists, this argument rests on the commonalities between the cultures we are conversant with, and does not explore the possibility that general agreement is distinct from general truth.

The maximalist argument that race, disease and madness do not exist "out there" is an attempt to unveil the social and non-natural aspect of deviance labelling by pulling the rug from under our feet. In an extreme sense, the modern disease is only thinkable within a modern political anatomy which allows for localised afflictions with organic causes. The argument tends, in its extreme forms, to downplay the existence of the physical/behavioural signs, rather than questioning the naturalness of classifications of, and meanings attached to, these signs. Some researchers on the maximalist side have emphasised the issue of power relations in the selection and treatment of socially defined deviants (in order to show the interests involved in attaching negative meanings to physical signs) rather than on the question of whether madness or leprosy, for example, exist outside culture or history. Gilman[63] says of madness that its importance lies in "the function of the idea of mental illness within the sign systems of our mental representations [which] shapes our 'seeing the insane'". Such an approach may become overly functionalist, unless we remain sensitive to the changing content of our stereotypes of madness and disease.

The idea of the stereotype, as proposed by Gilman, will be used here as a theoretical model that correctly recognises the connection between socially-defined signs picked out of real-life experience and the social constructions that are stacked onto such data. One cannot "create" a leper without these signs, just as one cannot "create" a blind man out of a fully sighted one.[64] Stereotypes, defined by Gilman[65] as "a crude set of mental representations of the world", are neither personal nor archetypal. They have very real historical and experiential roots and specific referents. Each culture has its own "tradition" on which it draws for the content of the stereotype, "a rich web of signs and references for the idea of difference [arising] out of a society's communal sense of control over the world". The patterns of association found in a stereotype are "most commonly based ... on a combination of (filtered) real-life experience and the world of myth". The stereotype is thus not random, as experience and the stereotype constantly interact. It is also not rigid and unchanging.[66]

One way of examining social constructions of leprosy is by establishing the historical dimensions of the stereotypical leprosy sufferer. The physical symptoms of leprosy clearly do exist: we just have to deconstruct the assumptions that group them together in the entity called the "leper" in varying forms at different times, and the different meanings attached to them. It is important to notice exactly what physical features are noted and signified, and thus to avoid detaching our discussions of social stigma from discussions of how people recognise the socially stigmatised "leper". Also, we need to relate this recognition and signification process to changing power relations in the society.

Leper stereotypes at the Cape, c. 1850 – 1900

It is necessary to note here that stereotyping is not in itself pathological, but rather necessary for our relations with the world. It is the content of such stereotypes, and their use in ordering the world, that, where associated with unequal power relations in a society, may produce systems disadvantageous to particular groups. Gilman[67] names three basic categories used in defining stereotypes of the Other and the self: our sense of mutability (eg, through illness), the central role of sexuality in our nature, and our relationship to a greater group (eg, by "race"). In this section I shall show that the negative leper stereotype (using illness as difference) and the racial stereotype (using "race" as difference) referred to a similar representation of the Other in nineteenth-century South Africa.

One could in fact speak about two leper stereotypes, the more positive "missionary" stereotype, which stressed suffering and stigma against the leper, and the negative "black" stereotype, which stressed that some culpability for contraction of the disease rested with the sufferer.

The missionary stereotype

This stereotype is sketched as a counterpoint to the racial stereotype, which is the central focus of the paper at this stage. The missionary leper stereotype drew from biblical mythology about the disease. Medieval leper asylums in Europe often had close connections with the church, and this association continued in the colonial era. Gussow[68] argues that the connections between the church and the leper are dependent on current circumstance. The reasons for missionary interest in leprosy sufferers, for example, changed over time, although they used the same biblical and spiritual justifications. He connects medical interest in eliminating leprosy with wider socio-political agendas. In the colonial period, medical care was a form of, and opening for, political and economic intervention. It also helped to get funding for proselytising in foreign parts. For example, the Leprosy Mission of 1873 funded its evangelical work through appealing for money to help lepers in India. And in the post-colonial period, leprosy treatment by mission organisations helped to justify their remaining in the newly independent colonies.

In the early years, Moravian influence at Robben Island stressed the pietistic ethic of suffering under affliction, but by the late nineteenth century, the "colour-blind" liberal humanitarianism of the Anglicans and others laid more emphasis on martyrdom and equality in the sight of God. These views were not uncontested. In the early years of Robben Island, the struggle between officials and the Moravian missionaries for control over the lepers certainly reveals some differences in their attitudes towards lepers. This conflict may bear some relation to colonial opposition to the missionary settlements for free Khoi earlier in the century. In 1853 the Commissioners of the Robben Island Inquiry remarked that

> the lessons of the Moravian brethren, as to patience under affliction, may... raise ideas in the mind of the facile Hottentot that, as a leper, he is one of a people particularly tried and set apart, thus leading naturally to a feeling akin to spiritual pride.[69]

The Moravians supported segregation, although not necessarily on Robben Island, and campaigned for better conditions on the Island. The other (Anglican and Dutch Reformed Church) chaplains before 1890 were less interventionist. Their Christian imagery becomes increasingly important, however, in representing the leper after the world-wide interest shown by missionary groups such as the Leprosy Mission (which still has a branch in the Transvaal today) in 1873 and the National Leprosy Fund in 1889 after the martyr-like death of Father Damien of leprosy in Hawaii. This contributed to the resurgence of a humanitarian feeling for the leper, at the same time as fear of leper contagiousness was escalating:

> it was the special fate of Damien not only to die of leprosy, but to have his death seen as somehow representative, so that he came to embody for the whole world what it was to be a "leper", his affliction signifying what the open sores of one man might mean to all men.[70]

In the missionary stereotype the leper is not culpable in any special way for his or her disease, and is a martyr in a Christian sense, suffering for the world's sins, especially that of stigma. Their salvation through Christ becomes of particular importance in reference to Jesus' cure of the sick man Lazarus. In Fish[71] a picture of a black leper with quite severe disfigurement is captioned "A Happy little Christian". This encapsulates the liberal paternalism that denied perceiving race and/or disease while affirming its vital importance. Fish deliberately illustrates the difference of the black leper by providing the photograph, in order to make his point that salvation is attainable by all, even those who are most horribly different. He thus affirms this difference.

In 1853 the lepers on Robben Island reportedly saw their affliction as imposed by the Hand of God.[72] However, there was also considerable resistance to biblical imaging by the Robben Island lepers. This resistance was probably more of a reaction to the use of the bible to condone segregation, and the biblical typification of lepers as "unclean", than a rejection of the missionary stereotype. Many lepers seem to have belonged to the Dutch Reformed Church (fewer were members of the Anglican church or other Christian denominations) and many converted to Christianity on the island (if we are to believe the ministers' reports). But in 1899 the lepers refused to hear from their minister about the biblical lepers.[73] In 1907, the white leper J.A. Botha wrote to the Colonial Secretary saying, "read the 13th chapter of Leviticus and you will see that I am not what God's Law describes".[74]

The black leper stereotype

The nineteenth century accounts of pathological female anatomy in the Hottentot (associated later with prostitutes), outlined by Gilman[75], underline the close associations made in the nineteenth century between anatomical difference and racial difference. Racial difference had to be "scientific", and thus increasingly it was assumed to be biological and unalterable. It is thus not surprising that leprosy and blackness were so closely related in South Africa in the nineteenth century, given also the relatively high incidence of the disease in the indigenous black population. The negative leper stereotype drew on many of the features of the Hottentot stereotype: idleness, unpleasant smell, promiscuous nature, dirty habits and nomadic lifestyle. In the first one-and-a-half centuries of white settlement at the Cape, the underdevelopment of the Hottentot in these respects was attributed to his idleness. This laziness was a "disease", said the missionaries of the Khoi in the nineteenth century, a disease which had to be cured by discipline.[76] The negative leper stereotype seems to be associated almost exclusively with the Hottentot from the 1840s until the 1880s, and then the small trader, most probably Malay, who sells vegetables or retails other food items, usually in Claremont or Wynberg[77], enters the picture alongside "mixed-breeds".[78]

It was believed that Khoi, "half-castes"[79] and later Malays[80], were particularly susceptible to leprosy. There were further suggestions that reactions to the disease were racially determined.[81] The contraction of the disease was linked to devalued activities, activities which were, especially in the years before 1880, associated with the Khoi. In 1861, a white leper called Julius Verreaux (the putative son of the French botanist) suggested that two Europeans he knew on Robben Island could have caught the disease through living in "excess", "roaming around the country with the very lowest", or "from women". Verreaux himself said that, as he was not of mixed descent (another causative factor), he must have caught the disease through his Hottentot wet nurse.[82]

Blacks in general were also especially prone to the disease because of their lifestyles: they were believed to be unhygienic and promiscuous, herding together in small living areas by choice. In 1848, Dr Hall remarked on the "promiscuous intercourse ... which forms so remarkable a feature of this intractable and hideous disease".[83] Other doctors in 1861 suggested that this was not the case, and that relatively few children had been born on the island.[84] Nevertheless, concern about the issue, and the fact that leper children were being born on the island, particularly when it was believed that leprosy was hereditary, prompted the complete removal of the female lepers from the island between 1871 and 1887. In 1883, evidence given before the Commission emphasised leper promiscuity.[85] By 1895, the Commission reported that lepers were not particularly promiscuous, contrary to previous beliefs.[86]

The Commission on leprosy in 1889 concluded that the disease was apt to spread quicker in a population where "races of the lowest type ... do not appreciate the dangers arising from contagion and have not the most elementary notions of cleanliness".[87] The 1894 Commission linked leprosy definitively to uncleanliness, citing the fact that more blacks than whites contracted it. The Resident Magistrate of St Marks noted that Hottentots and the Dutch were especially liable to leprosy which, he said, "may point to the fact that filth and dirt have something to do with it".[88] On visiting the Colony and Natal in 1902, Dr J. Hutchinson, who championed the idea that leprosy in Europe was not hereditary or contagious, but was transmitted in foods such as dried or rotten fish, wrote to Dr Black on Robben Island:

> Since I had the pleasure of an interview with you I have visited many leprosy foci in Natal and have encountered facts which compel me to modify my views as to communicability of the disease. Although it never spreads in England, France, Germany or the United States, it certainly does so in the Kraals of Kaffirs. Their careless method of feeding must, I think, be held to be the probable explanation.[89]

Under the contagion hypothesis, sexual contact with lepers was only one of many forms of contact that were considered dangerous. Fears about the contraction of leprosy from the urban small trader[90], or a black farm servant to the farmer or his children[91] arose increasingly after 1883. There was a more consistent but related contraction scenario for syphilis after 1882 in which the black nursemaid transmitted the disease first to the child and then, through the child, to the whole family.[92] The perception that blacks were "ignorant" of the danger of contagion, and did not have the same degree of stigma against lepers[93], played itself out in the policy arena, for example in justifying more white home segregation. The belief that some black groups did not share the negative leper stereotype thus formed one of the elements of the stereotype itself.

The hypothesis of increased social contact among blacks was used to explain uneven racial distribution later in the twentieth century. When visiting Westfort in 1940, Muir, the Indian leprosy specialist, speculated that the reasons for a higher incidence of the more severe lepromatous leprosy in whites were (a) that Europeans had less close contact with each other and thus only the more susceptible people contracted it in a severe form, and (b) that Europeans were at a climactic disadvantage in South Africa, or (c) that the disease produced in Europeans more mental and therefore more physical depression.[94]

Once diagnosed and segregated, lepers were seen as intrinsically problematic subjects, with little reference to the hardships of their enforced isolation on the Island. The Surgeon Superintendent on Robben Island in the late 1880s, Dr Ross, was particularly vociferous about the "filthy and careless leper nomads", "these sulky idle people" who would not work[95], "turbulent subjects" who smuggled drink and dagga onto the island.[96] Increasingly, too, the leper was represented as a recognisable type, not only medically, but also socially. This coincides with the representation of "race" as type in the late nineteenth century. Lepers were described in 1889 as "habitually torpid in movement and impassive in gestures", and as becoming "both mentally and physically a lower type" as the disease progressed.[97] In 1894, Impey stated that "moral suasion has no influence with this class of patients".[98] By the twentieth century, however, black lepers were to carry much of this burden alone.

Once contagion through a "germ" had been established as the major cause, blame could be shifted from the increasing number of "respectable" lepers to the "origin" of the germ: the black migrant or urban immigrant. Impey in his 1896 book, attributed the historical spread of leprosy in South Africa almost entirely to various black groups, most prominent among which was the "Bushman".[99] Increasing racial discrimination on Robben Island in the period after 1901 was associated with a state of affairs in which the white lepers' problems were seen as real problems. Black lepers were seen as simply "turbulent".[100] In an unfortunate outburst, Commissioner Chabaud noted in 1907 that unless (well behaved) "native" lepers were removed to the asylum at Emjanyana in Transkei they would "always be a festering sore on the Island"[101] because they resented the isolation of the Island.

The leper stereotype was never fully accepted among some groups. One mark of resistance to leper stereotypes is the refusal by leprosy sufferers to apply the derogatory term "leper" to themselves, calling themselves "people" or "sick people". Lepers in the Louisiana leper asylum, Carville, during the 1940s adopted the term "Hansen's Disease" in place of "leprosy"[102] to challenge stigmatisation. I have found few instances in which Robben Island lepers call themselves "lepers". In 1889, the author of the article noted that the words "leper" and "lunatic" were taboo on the island.[103] The Robben Island lepers often referred to themselves as prisoners instead, complaining that they were "imprisoned"[104], not "treated as ... free British Subject[s]"[105], "banish[ed]" to Robben Island[106], that they were "left on the island as people who are dead", and treated worse than convicts or slaves.[107] Here the negative associations of the leper stereotype are rejected as they assert their rights as free subjects.

The similarities between South African leper stereotyping and that in other countries during the leprosy scare years are striking. Here one can see that the contraction of leprosy was often linked to negative characteristics assigned to outgroups in each society.[108] Muir, the Indian specialist, believed the Chinese to have the highest incidence rates in Asia because they ate rotten fish and took no milk. He also noted that the incidence was generally higher in "primitive peoples".[109] The famed fish theorist, Dr Jonathan Hutchinson, said that leprosy used to be more common amongst Roman Catholics because of their fish-eating habits.[110] In Australia, a nineteenth-century historian reported that the Chinese "will continue to harbour and associate with lepers, provided the latter are either still able to work or have money".[111] Although miscegenation was not considered likely, the possibility that Chinese shopkeepers and businessmen would transmit leprosy to the white Australians was a major fear.[112]

Lepers in the Cape

The Dutch treated leprosy under the provisions of Batavian law which demanded strict segregation. The only evidence we have of application of this law is in 1756 when the Stellenbosch Council of Policy investigated four cases of leprosy: two local white farmers, one of their daughters, and a white woman, Maria Maree, who had become pregnant by a soldier. They were commanded to segregate themselves at home, and Maree's daughter was taken away from her. The soldier was sent away from the Cape.[113] In 1808 Dr Liesching wrote to the Medical Committee asking what to do with lepers he had found at the Hottentots Holland hills. At Genadendal Mission near Caledon, lepers were allowed to live within the settlement. At another Moravian mission, at Sunday's River, near Port Elizabeth, lepers were housed as early as 1786. There was also a lazar house near Uitenhage, on the Bakens River, and a small leprosarium at the Chavonnes Battery in Cape Town between 1821 and 1844.[114]

In 1813, "Hottentot lepers were put into quarantine in huts in [a] detached place" near Caledon's hot springs, and the Moravian station of Genadendal.[115] I have found no evidence that these lepers were separated from the rest of the Genadendal community. They were supported by "funds raised in the Swellendam District, where the scattered race of aborigines had been collected by missionary people".[116] Hemel-en-Aarde ("Heaven and Earth"), a farm between Caledon and present-day Onrust, was bought by Government in 1817 specifically for leprous "Hottentots, Bastards, Free Blacks and Slaves". In 1822 there were 150 persons at Hemel-en-Aarde, with "not more than two white women and 3 or 4 Mozambique slaves", and in 1827 there were 115 patients there.[117] Between 1817 and 1846, 400 lepers were admitted to Hemel-en-Aarde.[118] In 1842 there were 58 lepers there, most of whom were sent to Robben Island in 1846.[119]

Under colonial control, Hemel-en-Aarde was supervised by the Moravians, at Government request. In 1823 a Moravian, Rev. Leitner, was sent there as resident pastor. This underlined the interest that the Moravians had in the lepers, and the slow commitment of the colonial government to institutional control of the disease. In 1846 when these lepers were sent to Robben Island, they did so under the guarantee that their pastor, Rev. Lehmann, would go with them. He spoke for them (in Dutch) and fielded their complaints, but died soon afterwards. He was followed by a succession of Moravians (United Brethren) at Robben

Island, the last of whom was Rev. Kuster, in 1866. These men were sympathetic to the lepers, although Kuster does not seem to have visited them regularly in the 1860s. By this time, however, the government's favourable attitude towards Anglicans had finally forced the Moravians out.

Conditions were poor but not overly restrictive at Hemel-en-Aarde. The District Surgeons and the Medical Committee had however been complaining about the isolation of the settlement from medical attention since the 1820s. Dr Barry suggested removal to Simon's Town in 1823, and Dr Wehr of the Medical Committee suggested in 1827 that a new treatment be tried for six months and if unsuccessful, that the lepers should go directly to Robben Island, where they could receive medical attention and be "quarantined" at the same time.[120] The issue arose again in 1831 and 1842, when finally the Medical Committee stated that removal to Robben Island was essential. Concern about the number of lepers in Cape Town and Simon's Town, and about the proper site for the cure of such a disease fuelled the debate. Hemel-en-Aarde was criticised for its "dampness" and "lowness" while Robben Island was dry with fresh sea breezes. It was fortuitous for this plan that the island's convict population was soon needed elsewhere.

The move to Robben Island

In 1844 John Montagu proposed to utilise the "free" labour that able-bodied convicts could provide by sending them to convict road stations in the interior. Part of the same plan involved emptying the gaols of lunatics and the sick poor, emptying the (old) Somerset Hospital of lunatics (51 went to Robben Island) and chronic sick (17), protecting, perhaps, the expanding commercial wharf nearby, and also closing the Pauper Establishment in the Gardens (101 paupers) which was reportedly "a den of drunkenness" and a base for beggars.[121] These groups were all to be sent to Robben Island and housed in the old convict station buildings there. Montagu tied this in cleverly with the Medical Committee's original plan. But as the Medical Committee did not approve of putting lunatics and the sick poor on the island, Montagu appointed his own Medical Board to approve the scheme in its totality.

The placing of three quite different institutions together on the island at a time when institutions were being increasingly separated from each other in Europe, physically and ideologically, was a product of the polarisation of institutional populations into workers and non-workers that was brought about in the Colony in the early 1840s by the pressure for colonial expansionism and the need for cheap controlled labour. From the convict service perspective, the lepers, lunatics and chronic sick took the place of the banished prisoner on Robben Island once the prisoner's labour became the yardstick of his utility and identity as a convict in the 1840s. The lunatics and chronic sick, in particular, had become useless and non-curable elements in the institutional population that then overflowed into the gaols and convict road stations of the colony. Now nominally liable for specific treatments in separate buildings on the island, their removal from hospitals was also an indication of the embarrassment caused by the inability of the medical profession to treat leprosy or madness successfully. Essentially, the lepers on Robben Island were treated as a special subset of the chronic sick group under a workhouse-type ethic until the 1880s.[122]

The Robben Island leper

Before 1892, admission to Robben Island was legally voluntary, but in practice there was little opportunity for already institutionalised or destitute lepers to resist removal, or insist on their return once they were on the island. This was compounded by the fact that Robben Island was difficult to escape from. Some lepers were rejected by their families if they did return home.[123] The Commission of 1862 reported that there were many lepers still in the colony, "for it is known that the helplessly destitute leper alone resorts to the asylum on Robben Island".[124] An indication of this is the fact that leper numbers remained consistently below 100, until 1892, when they rose to 413. The number of lepers on the Island had risen to over 600 by 1915.

Most of the lepers at Robben Island in the first few years were sent there from Hemel-en-Aarde and Sunday's River. A cutter, the "Liaac", brought 31 lepers from Algoa Bay in January 1846[125] and by May 1847 there were 54 lepers on the island. These lepers were probably all in the final stages of their illness, and all but three of the Hemel-en-Aarde lepers had died or left by 1861.[126] The gaps caused by deaths or discharges from the leper wards were soon filled by fresh cases.[127] These were drawn from the convict stations and government offices, or, largely farm servants, through the request of magistrates and district surgeons. As late as 1887, lepers were being discharged from Robben

Island as time-expired convicts.[128] In this sense, prior institutionalisation was an advantage, as the term of the legal prison sentence took legal priority over the term of the disease.

The following example will illustrate the process of recognition and removal in the case of a farm worker's wife. In 1862 the leprous Khoi woman Roselyn Wildman was living with her aged husband in a field for common use near the prison and public offices at Worcester. They had a few sheep and a screen or hut of bushes to shelter them, but little else, and the husband used to beg for their keep. He also worked as a shepherd for a Dutch farmer in the town. Wildman was one of the lucky ones, as she elicited the sympathy of the local authorities when she refused to be separated from her husband to be taken to Robben Island. Also, the provision of transport and an attendant for her (she was very weak) on the way to Cape Town was giving the Resident Magistrate something of a headache. Instead, they now built her another hut on the commonage and supplied her with rations from the local gaol.[129] Remembering that no laws yet existed to justify forced removal, the fact that the officials arranged for Wildman's transfer to Robben Island in the face of her opposition, demonstrates the extent of the pressure exerted on these "voluntary" admissions.

In 1855, nearly three-fifths of the lepers on Robben Island were Khoi, two-thirds were men and three-quarters came from outside Cape Town.[130] At this stage, many of the Hemel-en-Aarde and Sunday's River lepers were still on the island. With black urbanisation, more leprosy cases came from the town areas, where they were more visible to the authorities and fears of contagion were most evident. Throughout the century, there were more men than women in the leper wards, but this was not just due to the medical contention that leprosy tends to affect men more easily. Over the period 1890 to 1892, during which compulsory segregation was introduced, the ratio of men to women dropped from an average of 3,4:1 in 1890 and 1891, to 1,9:1 in 1892, after the large intake of the latter year. The discrepancy was thus possibly also due to social factors, such as the more private nature of women's labour in the home, and their consequently greater invisibility to the authorities.

Lepers on Robben Island were also predominantly black. In 1859 there were only three white lepers there[131], with Khoi and "Africans" making up the balance of 47 lepers in nearly equal proportions. In 1868 there were 7 whites. Only two whites were named as lepers in the Census of 1875[132], but this was clearly a case of under-reporting. Numbers of whites at Robben Island had increased by 1878,[133] and in the 1880s there was also occasionally a leper of the "better class" there.[134] The ratio of white to black roughly doubled from 1:64 in 1857 to 2:46 in 1871, and tripled between 1871 and 1887, when there were 12 "European" lepers, but decreased slightly with compulsory segregation, halving between 1887 and 1894, while the actual number of white lepers increased to 30.

This was only partly due to immunity-related susceptibility to the disease (see above). Although black lepers were not all sent to the island, the more affluent white population had a better chance of avoiding it. The high proportion of foreign to South African-born white lepers on the island in the 1850s demonstrates the importance of family support in this regard.[135] It is not clear too, exactly how many white and black people with leprosy did stay out of the institution, in order to calculate the percentage institutionalised. Nineteenth century statistics will probably not be very informative on this question. The Colonial Medical Committee estimated the total leper population of the colony at 625 in 1891, which proved to be a gross under-estimation when lepers started pouring into Robben Island under the Leprosy Repression Act.

Lepers who were not on Robben Island

The changing visibility of "free" lepers in the primary sources reflects fluctuating concern about their dangerousness. Lepers were seen selling sweetmeats and washing clothes in Cape Town in 1853.[136] In 1861, Dr Ebden noted to the Commission on Robben Island that "in the upper parts of the town [Cape Town] there are many cases of ... lepers living with their friends".[137] In 1871, Ebden said he knew of "at least a dozen lepers" in Rondebosch who refused to go to the island. Lepers were also seen in the Cape Town streets in 1887.[138] The 1883 Select Committee took evidence on the existence of lepers in Cape Town, and some rural areas, many of whom were fishermen or small traders.[139] In 1889, Dr Wright noted that there were many cases among fishermen at Kalk Bay, and Dr Cox of the Free Dispensary said he had seen at least 10 mainly "poorer class" cases during his two-and-a-half years in Cape Town. White farming families were said to be harbouring several cases on the Boland.[140]

Even after the 1892 Act, some leper cases were concealed by

doctors[141], and others evaded detection by moving frequently, or absconding after being warranted for removal to the Island. In December 1897, 7 out of 19 cases had absconded[142], and in January 1898, 5 out of 14 warranted cases absconded.[143] By June 1899, out of the 2 004 cases warranted since 1892 in the Colony and Transkei, 1 280 had been sent to asylums, 98 had died, 22 were discharged, 4 were segregated at home and 84 had absconded. The rest were awaiting removal.[144] Some lepers escaped from the Colony and the Orange Free State altogether, and hid in Lesotho. Some richer people left for England, where the disease was rare and not notifiable.[145] The upheavals caused by this subterfuge can be well illustrated by one example. In 1909, near Muizenberg station, a woman was spotted hiding behind a newspaper on her verandah by the Medical Officer of Health, Gregory, who happened to be passing by. He made inquiries and her doctor admitted her affliction could be leprosy. But by the time they went to her house again to examine her, the whole family had left the area without a trace.[146]

Legal home segregation became possible in the 1890s but its application was racially skewed. In mid-1892 some 70 Cape Muslims signed a petition asking that they be allowed to segregate Muslim lepers in an institution on the Macassar Downs.[147] They met with the Colonial Secretary, but were told that the cost to them would be very high, so were forced to ask instead that Muslim lepers on the island be given halaal food and proper burial rites. Because of the expense, opportunities for home segregation (which became legal after 1892) were more favourable for the better-off whites. The patient's family had to bear the substantial costs of separate amenities, clothing and utensils.

Cases which were believed to be less severe and possibly "arrested" or "burnt out" were more readily allowed home segregation. Before consistent bacteriological tests, this was difficult to ascertain with certainty. Even then, anaesthetic cases sometimes had few bacilli in nasal or blood smears.[148] It was only after 1901 that concern about non-lepers on the Island prompted a Board who inspected doubtful cases every six months, and discharged a relatively large number of them. Many of the doctors believed that lepers were less stigmatised in the coloured community, or the less educated classes, and would be treated just like other members of the family. This, and the concern that home segregation was generally unreliable, meant that very few applications were ever successful. Numbers were never large: by 1894 only 5 cases were officially segregated at home, and in a debate in the

House of Assembly, Mr Schreiner reported in 1899 that there were only 7 whites and 3 blacks who were segregated at home.[149]

Enforcing the Leprosy Repression Act, 1891

For some, such as Ross in the late 1880s, control of the disease necessarily involved the removal of all "civil rights" from the lepers.[150] Indeed, after 1892, and the Amendment Act of 1894, lepers were no longer allowed to leave the Island, to vote (even by 1899[151]), to kiss or otherwise touch their visitors, or to prosecute adulterous wives under colonial law. In the eyes of the law, they became as dead people. But there was a tension between this attitude and the humanitarianism required both by current "missionary" stereotypes of the disease, and by government. The Robben Island leper settlement had been severely criticised in an article in the *Blackwoods Edinburgh Magazine* of 1889 which provoked criticism from England as well as by Capetonians of the Robben Island administration.[152] The 1891 Act, and government concern to avoid bad publicity about treatment of lepers on the island, thus prohibiting punishment except by withdrawal of privileges, in fact gave the lepers more power over island administration than they had ever had before. This was exaggerated by the lack of regulations, which had been provided for in the Leprosy Repression Act Amendment Act of 1894 but were only finalised in 1902.[153]

The lepers used their new-found power when they realised that the 1891 Act had in turn divested them of their rights to leave the island on visits to family and friends. In September 1892, under the leadership of a "coloured" leper called Franz Jacobs, they struck against the introduction of female nurses (from Kimberley) in the wards, and threatened to combine forces with the convicts, and to rape the women on the island. Jacobs wrote a petition to the Queen, saying they were treated like convicts. They demanded table napkins and beer, table cruets and extra sugar in an attempt to push the humanitarian veneer of the Act to an unworkable limit. The response came swiftly: extra men were brought over as leper police and Jacobs was exiled from the island community to Somerset Hospital until he "repented" in November of the same year. But in the following year, free passes were granted to families of lepers, and postage costs for parcels sent to them were waived.[154] The resistance continued. In 1895, 6 lepers escaped in a boat, and two of them were never recaptured. Some male lepers later set fire to pavilion no. 5. At the end of the year, additional attendants and leper police were taken on. Pavilion five had been rebuilt by 1897, and a lock-up in the male leper settlement was half complete.[155]

The women lepers were not silent during this time. In his report for 1893, Dr Impey mentions that the female lepers would not "assist in any kind of sanitary work; they will not clean their own wards, or scrub, they will not sweep in front of their rooms ... although I have offered to pay them". He had to employ convicts to do this work, and to clear the yard and enclosure of the "filth which they persist in throwing there".[156] They also refused to send all their washing to the new leper laundry. This resistance was an extension of their refusal to wash clothes on their return from Somerset Hospital in 1887.[157]

Off the island, the Act intensified a minor hysteria that had been developing against lepers since the 1880s: relatives of lepers had found it difficult to get jobs[158], and mail steamers refused to carry leper passengers in 1899.[159] When a missionary woman, Von Blomberg, visited the island in about 1888, she found that visitors refused to shake hands with the leper patients.[160] In 1892 shipping companies refused to transport lepers, road transport was fraught with difficulties, and a special railway carriage had to be used.[161] Some families were evicted from their homes or found it difficult to get accommodation.[162] At King William's Town in 1894 doctors had to give certificates to black patients with leucoderma, a similar-looking skin disease, to protect them against neighbours suspecting them of having leprosy.[163] On the other hand, however, families of many lepers continued to hide them at home to forestall removal to the island.

Racial segregation on the island and in town

As we have seen, there was a close relationship between views of the leper and of the black man. Segregationist ideology in the Cape owed something to the use of segregation to combat contagious diseases, of which leprosy became an example in the 1890s. But racial segregation among lepers on Robben Island was in turn directly influenced by the development of exclusionary and later segregatory practices in Cape Town. The Robben Island material can thus cast some light on timing and process in the development of exclusionary racist practice, as sketched by Bickford-Smith for the 1870s, and its gradual supersession or incorporation by racial separation after 1890.

The emergence of racism and racial segregation has been a subject of much discussion over the last twenty years. The current view is that racism emerged well before the mineral revolution, and had important roots in racial slavery in the South Western Cape.[164] It has been suggested that there was a hardening of racial attitudes in the 1830s, over the period of emancipation.[165] The frontier wars, the struggle for representative government and the anti-convict crises of the 1840s and 1850s contributed further to the racial polarisation of Cape society.[166] In the 1870s, there was informal racial segregation in Cape Town, which Bickford-Smith calls "exclusion", that confined most blacks to the poorer schools and the back benches of churches and did little else.[167] The 1875 Census demonstrates the existence of a race-class relationship by this time: whiteness correlated positively with higher rates of pay.[168]

By the 1880s, large numbers of Africans were moving into Cape Town and fears that the dominant (white) class were threatened fuelled the election in 1882 of "Clean Party" candidates for the Town Council. These men failed to produce the sanitary city which was becoming increasingly desirable in the eyes of middle-class Cape Town by the end of the decade. The dirtiness of the slum areas of the city was associated with the spread of disease by the undeserving and immoral poor, ie the black poor.[169] In the 1890s, an economic boom and extensive immigration both from the Colony and from England provided a suitable background for the "social separation" of the races, by now the general ideal of the dominant classes.[170]

The 1891 Clean Party candidates, who were modern-style merchants and businessmen, were prepared, and able, to initiate the ordering of the city along the lines of race and respectability and to take steps improving sanitation.[171] The 1894 Act providing for compulsory registration of births and deaths, and the 1897 Public Health Amendment Act, which gave Government absolute powers in dealing with epidemic disease, were products of the new regime. The new Council was interested in ordering the city to make it commercially viable, but also in retaining the status quo. The position of poor whites, who were really the only whites mixing with other "races" in Cape Town[172], now became an issue. They were seen as the deserving poor requiring upliftment, especially through preferential education.

Although a labour hostel for Mfengu dockworkers was built in 1892 and another male hostel, the Salvation Army Metropole, was built in the town in 1897, the Council was reluctant to undertake further expensive measures for residential segregation that might remove useful labour far from their workplaces.[173] In 1898 there was much agitation for locations because of increased African immigration on account of the rinderpest in 1895, and revival of the poor white issue, first contested in the early 1890s. At the same time, the *de facto* racial segregation of prisons, hospitals, schools, and better class hotels and sports clubs was coupled with legal restrictions on the franchise in 1890 and 1893 that effectively eliminated much of the "coloured" vote.[174] The exclusion of non-whites from some residential areas was envisaged after 1900, and calls for segregation of sidewalks and trams were made during the war.[175] Racial segregation of education was legislated for in 1905. The exclusionary racial separation of the middle classes in the 1890s was thus overflowing, albeit slowly, into the more racially integrated lower classes in the 1900s.

Systematic racial segregation of lepers at Robben Island happened in 1893, much later than racial classification on paper (which began in the late 1850s), and racially discriminatory treatment (which began in the 1850s). The general distinctions in treatment within the Robben Island institutions recognised only two divisions: white versus non-white and better-class versus the rest. The racial division became increasingly dominant after 1904.

The Medical Committee had suggested as early as 1854 "as a great improvement to this establishment [on Robben Island], that white inmates whether insane or lepers, should be kept separate from the blacks, as the intermixing of the two classes without distinction is undesirable".[176] At the same time, one of the only white lepers, called Julius Verreaux, was allowed to move from the general ward into a separate room even though he was a non-paying patient.[177] And further differentiation in treatment seems to have crept into Robben Island practice with the arrival of Minto as Surgeon Superintendent in 1855. White patients got sheets, new clothes, less work or less heavy work and coffins rather than blankets for their dead by 1861.[178] White lunatics got white bread, on Minto's orders, and some male lunatics were put in a separate ward in the late 1850s by their keeper, Roach, because they were white.[179] Some of these privileges were removed during the 1860s.

The only paying patients on the island (7 or 8 in number) were lunatics before 1861, and Minto tried to separate the social classes "when our wards will afford it".[180] In 1860 he suggested that new buildings for the lunatics could effect a clear racial segregation with one further division on the basis of tractability within each racial group. This did not happen quite as he proposed although the male and female lunatics were each divided into two groups at some stage between September 1860 and November 1861.[181] By 1861, especially for the male lunatics, an exclusionary racial division seems to have been in operation. For better control, however, the most violent white male lunatics were put in the predominantly black "asylum" or "kraal" section, while some "respectable" black men were put in the predominantly white "lunatic square".[182] In one of the two female sections there were some rooms used for the more "respectable" patients, and the paying patients received better food.[183] A further medical-behavioural classification, delineating three rather than two groups for both sexes, continued the exclusionary trend in the later 1860s by keeping one section largely white. Allocation of chronic sick accommodation in front rooms and back rooms was made on a linguistic basis by 1869[184], and in different wards on a racial basis by 1878.[185]

In 1889, the *Blackwoods* author described one leper ward as "occupied by a race part Hottentot and part Malay, with an infusion of white blood".[186] Such mixing was seen as undesirable, but racial exclusion or separation was not formally instituted. But as an influx of better-class white lepers loomed in 1892, concern grew among doctors and officials about their position. The Rules for 1866 had not prescribed racial separation for lepers on Robben Island. In 1892, however, the "Rules of the Leper Hospital" insisted on first, racial segregation and then "if possible", the separation of lepers according to the stage of their disease.[187] In line with other institutional segregation on the mainland at the time, the pavilion system introduced in 1893 divided the white and black lepers.

Racially discriminatory treatment for lepers was systematised in practice after 1892, although it was not yet formally provided for in legislation.[188] Discriminatory treatment was exaggerated as public concern for the lepers increased. In 1895 Cecil Rhodes donated a bath chair for the female European lepers[189] and in about 1908 or 1909, two horses and a cart were made available for the male European patients.[190] The European lepers by 1901 got better clothes than the rest[191], a different diet with "medical extras" such as tinned sardines[192]; by 1907, they got better coffins with name plates[193], and by late 1910, free 2nd rather than 3rd class tickets for relatives travelling by train.

The relationship between paying and non-paying white patients is an informative one. Four semi-detached cottages for paying lepers were built between 1892 and 1893, and by 1904 there were about 10 similar cottages.[194] Special new wards, rather than the ordinary pavilions for men and wards for women, were occupied by non-paying "European" lepers in 1904.[195] Some non-paying white lepers of a "better class" received the privileges of the paying patients because the staff on the island clearly felt more comfortable with this arrangement.[196] When the paying system was abolished in 1904, this anomaly fell away, as all whites were treated equally (except that those who had been paying patients retained some privileges) and now paid for extras out of their own pockets.[197] The paying patients were subsumed into the general white category. In 1910, Commissioner Magennis allocated the private quarters carefully on the basis of conduct rather than financial ability so that the occupant could be censured by removal.[198] He also refused an application for private quarters by the mortuary attendant, Jantjies (who said the others in his ward made offensive remarks about his job), saying that he "was averse to coloured patients having private quarters".[199] The "paying category" was thus explicitly white, and not dependent on financial status within the white category. It thus became contiguous with the white category.

Conclusion

This paper has explored the racist content of the response to leprosy in South Africa in an attempt to contribute to the growing body of social histories of medicine, as well as the segregation literature on Cape Town in the late nineteenth century. The South African response to leprosy was part of a general concern about syphilis and leprosy in the rural areas in the 1880s and in the towns in the 1890s. This concern gave rise to the Contagious Diseases Act of 1884 and the Public Health Acts of 1883 and 1897. Concern about the spread of smallpox (by unvaccinated Malays in particular) and leprosy (by blacks) fuelled segregatory responses to disease and increasingly also to what were seen as harbingers of disease: black people and their slums. The particular viciousness of the responses to these contagious diseases, and to the people who suffered from them, was justified medically by the perceived origin of the diseases in black uncleanliness and prostitution.

The South African response to leprosy during the crucial years between 1890 and 1910 was swift and segregatory, like Australia's response (which labelled the Chinese as the culprits). India, which had a very small white leper population, segregated only the (black) pauper leper. Other countries, such as Norway, opted for segregation of only a small proportion of lepers. In the colonial context, the "dirty" native was guilty of contracting leprosy both in his lack of stigma against the disease, and in his choice of lifestyle. Segregation drew him out of this unhealthy environment, enforcing stigmatisation where his culture refused to do so. Home segregation was thus seen as an especially risky policy when dealing with black lepers. The British and colonial delegates at the Bergen conference on leprosy in 1909 drew up a special resolution along these lines.[200]

Although the timing of the final promulgation of the Leprosy Repression Act (1891) was related more to the world-wide leprosy scare following the death of Father Damien in 1889, its strict segregatory content was related to the meshing of the black and leper stereotypes during the nineteenth century that served to label the typical leper as black, with pathological social habits of overcrowding and poor sanitation which had caused their leprosy. This meshing, it is suggested, had an effect, not directly on the segregatory movement then happening in the Colony, and Cape Town in particular, but on the metaphors surrounding Public Health legislation that allowed for the segregation of black uncleanness from white purity.

On the Island itself, the emergence of racial segregation among the lepers was closely tied to emerging segregation in Cape Town. The differences between the implementation of exclusionary practices for lunatics or chronic sick on Robben Island and for lepers illustrate possible differences in the perceived usefulness of separating the races or classes, and the importance of numbers in influencing perceptions of the need for exclusionary class separation or full racial segregation. The number of white lepers was too low before 1890 to require anything more than an ad hoc system of racial differentiation in treatment. By 1892, racial segregation in different wards was made feasible for the first time, because of the larger number of white lepers, and desirable in terms of the broader segregatory ethic emerging in other state institutions in Cape Town. By the 1890s, the dominant classes in the Colony had accepted social separation of the races as an important ideal.[201] Class segregation (perhaps better labelled "exclusion") survived alongside racial segregation for lepers on the Island for some years but was treated as an anomaly within the system by 1904.

Legal institutionalisation under a humanitarian banner forced the Government to promise maintenance "in the manner to which they have been accustomed" rather than treating lepers as paupers under the workhouse ethic of the 1860s. Ironically, with vast increases in leper numbers, and rising stigmatisation of contact with lepers, this was the first time that the patients had to undertake a significant proportion of the island workload. But white lepers were increasingly channelled into supervisory and artisanal work.

Endnotes

1. A. Davids, "The Revolt of the Malays: a Study of the Reactions of the Cape Muslims to the Smallpox Epidemics of 19th-Century Cape Town" *Studies in the History of Cape Town* (hereafter *Studies*), V. (1983); K. Jochelson, "Environmentalism versus Hereditory: Explanations for Poor White People in South Africa" Paper delivered to the 16th Annual Conference on "Research in Progress" at the Centre for African Studies, University of York, 1991; H. Phillips, "Black October: Cape Town and the Spanish Influenza of 1918" *Studies*, I, (1979); M.W. Swanson, "The Sanitation Syndrome: Bubonic Plague and Urban Native Policy in the Cape Colony, 1900 – 1909" *Journal of African History* (hereafter *JAH*, XVIII(3), (1977) 387–410; E.B. van Heyningen, "Cape Town and the Plague of 1901", *Studies*, IV, (1979) ; E.B. van Heyningen, "The Mysteries of the Scarlet Phial: Spies and Plague in Cape Town in 1907", *Quarterly Bulletin of the South African Library* (hereafter *QBSAL*), 34(2), (1981); E.B. van Heyningen, "Public Health and Society in Cape Town, 1880 – 1910" (Ph.D. thesis, University of Cape Town, 1989); E.B. van Heyningen, "The Social Evil in the Cape Colony 1868 – 1902: Prostitution and the Contagious Diseases Acts", *JSAS*, 10(2), (1984) 170–197.
2. Z. Gussow, *Leprosy, Racism and Public Health* (Westview Press, 1989); W.B. Davidson, *Havens of Refuge: A History of Leprosy in Western Australia* (Perth, 1978); J. Maguire, "The Fantome Island Leprosarium" Australia, (draft chapter of thesis 1991); L.T. Heffner, "A Study of Hansen's Disease in Ceylon", *Southern Medical Journal*, 62, (1969) 979–85; M.W. Dols, "Leprosy in Mediaeval Arabic Medicine", *Journal of History of Medicine and Allied Sciences*, 34, (1979), 314–333; R. Giel, and J.N. van Luijk, "Leprosy in Ethiopian Society", *International Journal of Leprosy*, 38, (1970) 187–98.
3. I.J. Volinn, "Issues of Definition and their Implications: AIDS and Leprosy", *Social Science and Medicine*, 29(10), (1989), 1157–62; N.E. Waxler, "Learning to be a leper" in E.G. Mishler, et al., *Social Contexts of Health, Illness and Patient Care* (Cambridge, 1981); G.A. Ryrie, "The Psychology of Leprosy", *Leprosy Review*, 21(1), (1951), 13–24; Z. Gussow, and G. Tracy, "Status, Ideology and Adaptation to Stigmatised Illness", *Human Organization*, 27, (1968), 316–25.
4. E. Willies, "A History of the Development of Leprosy in South Africa", unpublished work, Westfort Leper Asylum, 1984. Studies are currently being done on Zululand leper colonies and on leprosy in the Eastern Cape.
5. Swanson, "The Sanitation Syndrome", 387–410.
6. Van Heyningen, "Public Health and Society in Cape Town" 13.
7. C. Saunders, "The Creation of Ndabeni: Urban Segregation and African Resistance in Cape Town", *Studies*, I, (1979), 138.

8. Africans were in fact targeted in spite of a low medical threat. "Coloured" people were not permanently removed even though plague incidence was three times higher in that group than among Africans: Saunders, "The creation of Ndabeni", 142–3. The establishment of the location in fact protected many Africans from contraction of plague, rather than protecting the town: Van Heyningen, "Cape Town and the Plague of 1901", 12.
9. V. Bickford-Smith, "Dangerous Cape Town: Middle Class Attitudes to Poverty in Cape Town in the Late Nineteenth Century", *Studies*, IV, (1981), 40.
10. V. Bickford-Smith, "Cape Town's Dominant Class and the Search for Order, 1891 – 1902", Western Cape Roots and Realities Conference, U.C.T., (1986) 4.
11. M.W. Swanson, "The Asiatic Menace: Creating Segregation in Durban 1870 – 1900", *International Journal of African Historical Studies*, 16(3), (1983), 401–2.
12. Van Heyningen, "Cape Town and the Plague of 1901", 8.
13. Quoted in R. Packard, *White Plague, Black Labour: Tuberculosis and the Political Economy of Health and Disease in South Africa* (Pietermaritzburg, 1989), 32.
14. W.H. Jopling and A.C. McDougall, *Handbook of Leprosy*, 4th ed. (Oxford, 1988), 1.
15. Jopling and McDougall, Handbook of Leprosy, 1–2.
16. First General Report of the Leprosy Commission, April 1931.
17. E.J. Schultz and H. Pentz, "Leprosy Control in South Africa", *Leprosy Review*, 41(1), (1970), 16.
18. E. Muir, "Report on Leprosy in the Union of South Africa", *Leprosy Review*, 11, (1940), 43.
19. J.M. Hunter and M.C. Thomas, "Hypothesis of Leprosy, Tuberculosis and Urbanization in Africa", *Social Science and Medicine*, 19(1), (1984), 27.
20. Hunter and Thomas, "Hypothesis of Leprosy", 32.
21. Packard, *White Plague, Black Labour*, 5.
22. Packard, *White Plague, Black Labour*, 31.
23. Gussow, *Leprosy, Racism and Public Health*, 115.
24. Gussow, *Leprosy, Racism and Public Health*, 111.
25. Gussow, *Leprosy, Racism and Public Health*, 116.
26. Cape Archives (hereafter CA), MC 19, Medical Committee: Miscellaneous – Somerset Hospital, 1826 – 1850, 25 March 1826.
27. G 4–1895, *Commission of Inquiry into the General Infirmary and Lunatic Asylum on Robben Island*, 1861, 129.
28. G 4–1895, xix–x.
29. G 4–1895, 251.
30. G 4–1895, 240.
31. G 4–1895, 240–1.
32. See CA, CO 4526, G 91–1883, *Reports of Civil Commissioners etc.* for 1882.
33. CA, CO 4736, Replies to Circular re Prevalence of Leprosy, Bedford District Surgeon (hereafter DS) to Under Colonial Secretary (hereafter UCS), 4 Oct 1890, CO 4736.
34. CA, CCP 1/3/1/8, Debates in the House of Assembly, Scanlen's reply to Louw on 3 July 1883.
35. SC 23–1883, *Report of the Select Committee on the Spread of Leprosy*, 1883, minutes of evidence, 20,29 and appendix, xiii ff.
36. G 67–1884, *Reports of District Surgeons for 1883*.

37. G 19–1885, *Reports of District Surgeons for 1884*, 20: only 31 lepers were reported for that district in 1889, however. See CA, CO 4736, Replies to Circular re Leprosy, 1889.
38. It was not extensively debated and few changes were made in Committee. The Governor sanctioned it in June 1884. CA, CCP 2/3/1/8, Debates in the Legislative Council, 1884, 177.
39. On the question of depriving persons of their liberty. Upington, CA, CCP 1/3/2/1, Debates in the House of Assembly, 1884, 123. And Scanlen on 16 June 1884, 184.
40. CA, CCP 1/3/2/1, J.X. Merriman, 16 June 1884, 184.
41. Public Record Office (hereafter PRO), GH 23/39, 1888 no. 8 and 1889, no. 138, Government House – general despatches, 1886 – 93. Minutes from Ministers re the Spread of Leprosy, Ross to UCS, 17 Jan 1888.
42. G 3–1889, *Select Committee, inquiring into the Spread of Leprosy*, 1889, 2.
43. Pressure was exerted by district surgeons and the Medical Committee during this time: see G 15–1888, *Medical Committee Report for 1887*, 3. The UCS corresponded with the Cape Town Council on the funding of leprosaria in December 1889: see CA, CO 4737, Replies to circulars of 1889 and 1891. In about 1890 the Cape Colonial Office documented leprosy incidence and treatment in other parts of the world: see "Notes on Leper" in CA, CO 4530, Correspondence re Leprosy. Dr Dodds drafted some "Notes on Leprosy", detailing legislative needs, which were circulated among the medical fraternity in 1890: CA, CO 4736, Replies to Circular re Leprosy, at end of volume.
44. G 3–1889, *Report of the Select Committee inquiring into the Spread of Leprosy*, 1889, x and Impey, in Robben Island Report, Annexures 1892; G 36–1892, *Reports of the Medical Committee, the Vaccine Surgeon, the Inspector of Asylums, and on the Government and Public Hospitals and Asylums for 1891*, 32–3.
45. A 12–1909, *Report of the Select Committee on Robben Island Lepers*, 1909, 22.
46. G 36–1892, *Reports of the Medical Committee, the Vaccine Surgeon, the Inspector of Asylums, and on the Government and Public Hospitals and Asylums for 1891*, 30–1.
47. The first leper asylum had already been established at Greytown in 1878.
48. Schultz and Pentz, "Leprosy Control in South Africa" , 16.
49. O.K. Skinsnes, "Leprosy in Society III: the Relationship of the Social to the Medical Pathology of Leprosy", *Leprosy Review*, 35(4), (1964), 181.
50. Gussow, *Leprosy, Racism and Public Health*.
51. Dols, "Leprosy in Medieval Arabic Medicine", 314.
52. Dols, "Leprosy in Medieval Arabic Medicine", 315.
53. Heffner, "A Study of Hansen's Disease in Ceylon", 980.
54. That is, doctors were unwilling to discharge subjects that had been diagnosed leprous by other doctors.
55. A.R. Davison, "Anti-Leprotic Treatment at the Emjanyana Leprosy Institution", *Leprosy Review*, 2, (1931) 147–9.
56. J.K.A. Clezy, "Hansen and his Bacillus", *Papua New Guinea Medical Journal*, 16(2), (1973), 72.
57. "Jadroo" [pseud.] *Disease and Race* (London, 1894), 10.
58. H.V. Carter, *Observations on the Prevention of Leprosy by Segregation*, (London, 1887) 2.
59. J. Iliffe, "Leprosy in India and Africa" , unpublished seminar at University of

Cambridge, 1991.
60. C. Ginzberg, *Ecstasies: Deciphering the Witches' Sabbath* (London, 1990).
61. "Jadroo", *Disease and Race*, 10.
62. Gussow, *Leprosy, Racism and Public Health*.
63. S. Gilman, *Difference and Pathology: Stereotypes of Sexuality, Race and Medicine* (Ithaca, 1985) 23–4.
64. This refers to the work of R.A. Scott, *The Making of Blind Men* (New York, 1969).
65. Gilman, *Difference and Pathology*, 17.
66. Gilman, *Difference and Pathology*, 20.
67. Gilman, *Difference and Pathology*, 23.
68. Gussow, *Leprosy, Racism and Public Health*.
69. SC 37–1855, *Report of the Select Committee upon, and Documents Connected with, the Robben Island Establishment, 1855*, 69.
70. G. Daws, *Holy Man: Father Damien of Molokai* (Honolulu, 1973), 5.
71. J. Fish, *Robben Island* (Kilmarnock, 1924).
72. SC 37–1855, 94.
73. P.D. von Blomberg, *Allerlei aus Süd-Afrika* (Gütersloh, 1899) 56–7.
74. CA, RI 69, Letters despatched, Robben Island, 1 April 1907.
75. Gilman, *Difference and Pathology*, chapter 3.
76. J.M. Coetzee, *White Writing*, (Yale University Press, 1988) 25, 26.
77. See SC 23–1883, 22, on number of Malays with leprosy. And G 3–1889, 4 on the prevalence of petty traders in Wynberg with leprosy.
78. SC 23–1883, 11 and 33, for example.
79. G 31–1862, *Report of Commission of Inquiry into the General Infirmary and Lunatic Asylum on Robben Island, appointed 25 October 1861*, 161, evidence of leper Verreaux.
80. Especially those with low morals, J.W. Matthews, *Incwadi Yami or Twenty Years Personal Experience in South Africa* (New York, 1887) 350.
81. G 2–1865, *Report on the General Infirmary, Robben Island for 1864*, 8 on the severity of the disease in Europeans.
82. G 31–1862, 161, evidence of leper Verreaux.
83. G 31–1862, 134.
84. G 31–1862, 239.
85. SC 23–1883, 25, 35.
86. G 4a–1895, *Final Report of Leprosy Commission appointed 1894*, 51.
87. G 3–1889, x.
88. G 4–1895, 143. The Dutch were included in only one such typification of the leper that I have found.
89. CA, CO 7663, Health Branch, letters received from Robben Island re Leprosy Commission, 1893 – 1903, 6 Feb 1902.
90. For example, G 3–1889, x.
91. G 4–1895, 89; G 3–1889, 8 (Dr Simons).
92. See, for example, G 67–1884, *Reports of District Surgeon for 1883*; and CA, CO 4526, G 91–1883, *Reports of Civil Commissioners, Resident Magistrates and District Surgeons for 1882*, especially those for Aberdeen and Caledon.
93. It is not clear whether there was in fact less stigma attached to leprosy in some indigenous communities. If this was so, it is possible that resistance to stigmatisation may have become an anti-colonial statement, like the

anti-vaccination campaigns (in which, incidentally, leprosy transmission was used as a weapon). Gussow, *Leprosy, Racism and Public Health*, 96–7 has suggested that the open non-stigmatisation of lepers by Hawaiians may have been part of the broader anti-colonial movement.
94. Muir, "Report on Leprosy in the Union of South Africa" 43.
95. CA, CO 1438, Letters received from Robben Island, Jan to June 1889, Ross to UCS, 7 Jan 1889. 19 Feb 1889.
96. G 15–1888, *Reports of the Medical Committee, the Vaccine Surgeon, and on the Government and Public Hospitals and Asylums for 1887*, 10.
97. G 3–1889, 6–7.
98. G 70–1994, Impey to Leprosy Commission, 30 July 1894.
99. S.P. Impey, *Handbook on Leprosy* (London, 1896), ch. 1.
100. CA, RI 73, Magennis to Under Secretary for the Interior, 18 Oct 1910.
101. CA, RI 29, Chabaud to UCS, 3 May 1907.
102. Gussow, *Leprosy, Racism and Public Health*, 13.
103. "Lepers at the Cape: Wanted, a Father Damien", *Blackwoods Edinburgh Magazine*, (September 1889), 298.
104. SC 37–1855, 4.
105. CO 1384, Ross to UCS, 22 March 1887.
106. PRO: GH 23/40, Minute re disturbances at Robben Island 1892. Leper complaints.
107. PRO: GH 23/40, Petition of leper Franz Jacobs to the Queen, August 1892.
108. The higher incidence among men was not generally commented on.
109. E. Muir, "Some Factors which Influence the Incidence of Leprosy", *Indian Journal of Medical Research*, 15, (1927–8), 10.
110. Muir, "Some Factors which Influence the Incidence of Leprosy", 7.
111. J. Thompson, "A Contribution to the History of Leprosy in Australia", in *Prize Essays on Leprosy* (London, 1897), 97.
112. Thompson, "A Contribution to the History of Leprosy in Australia", 65, 50.
113. It has been suggested by Willies, "A History of the Development of Leprosy in South Africa", 41, that a lazaretto was started in 1750 at Caledon or Groot Drakenstein probably for "Hottentots" or slaves, but I have not been able to verify this yet.
114. Willies, "A History of the Development of Leprosy in South Africa", 41.
115. G 31–1862, Colonial Medical Council, in litt. 27 June 1842.
116. 31–1862, Colonial Medical Council, in litt. 27 June 1842.
117. G 4–1895, xx, xxi, Annual Medical Report Dec 1821–1822.
118. Impey, *Handbook on Leprosy*, 3.
119. G 4a–1895, 8.
120. G 31–1862, 127, 128.
121. G 31–1862, 267.
122. G 19–1870, *Report on the General Infirmary, Robben Island, for 1869*, 17.
123. G 31–1862, 61.
124. G 31–1862, ix.
125. *Cape Town Mail*, 14 Feb 1846.
126. G 31–1862, Evidence of leper Gerts.
127. G 6–1861, Report on the General Infirmary, Robben Island for 1860, 1.
128. G 15–1888, Reports of the Medical Committee, the Vaccine Surgeon, and on the Government and Public Hospitals and Asylums for 1887, 10.

129. CA, CO 4126, document L 61, 13 October 1862.
130. J. Iliffe, *The African Poor: a history* (Cambridge, 1987) 103.
131. G 11–1860, Report on the General Infirmary, Robben Island for 1859, 3.
132. G 4a–1895, 8.
133. CA, CO 1067, Colonial Office from Medical Committee, Robben Island and Somerset Hospital, 4 Jan 1878.
134. G 29–1883, *Report on the General Infirmary, Robben Island for 1882*, 6.
135. Although perhaps this is too small a sample to tell.
136. *South African Commercial Advertiser*, 6 September 1853, De Kock to the editor.
137. G 31–1862, 252–3.
138. J.S. Little, *South Africa: A Sketch Book of Men, Manners and Facts* 2nd ed. (London, 1887), 270.
139. SC 23–1883.
140. G 3–1889, 5, 27, 9.
141. Impey, the ex-Superintendent of Robben Island was accused of doing this in 1908. CA, MOH 353–C121A vol. 5, MOH to UCS, 16 July 1908.
142. CA, CO 7210, Piers to Col Sec, 10 Jan 1898.
143. CA, CO 7210, Piers to Col Sec, 22 February 1898.
144. Mr Schreiner, House of Assembly Debate c. 15 August 1899.
145. *South African Review*, 12 October 1908, "Lepers in Name only".
146. SC 12–1909, *Report of the Select Committee on Robben Island Lepers*, 1909, 15.
147. CA, CO 4280, Memorial n.d.
148. CA, CO 7864, Sanders to Magennis, 14 March 1910.
149. CA, CO 7509–635, Copy of statistics given in the House of Assembly, August 1899.
150. PRO, GH 23/39, 1888 no. 8 and 1889, no. 138, Ross to UCS, 17 Jan 1888.
151. CA, RI–59, Piers to UCS, 5 Jan 1899.
152. "Lepers at the Cape: Wanted, a Father Damien" *Blackwoods Edinburgh Magazine*, (September 1889), 292–299.
153. CA, CO 7659, UCS's Memo, 1 May 1902.
154. See PRO, GH 23/40, Correspondence 1892–3 re lepers on Robben Island.
155. G 20–1897, *Reports on the Government and aided Hospitals and Report of the Inspector of Asylums for 1896*, 83, 86.
156. G 24–11894, *Reports on the Government and Public Hospitals and Asylums and Report of the Inspector of Asylums for 1893*, 88.
157. CA, CO 1414, Ross to De Smidt 12 March 1888.
158. CA, RI 59, 3 March 1889 and PRO, GH 23/40, Correspondence 1892–3 re lepers on Robben Island.
159. G 3–1889, evidence of Dr Dixon, 17.
160. Van Blomberg, *Allerlei aus Süd-Afrika*, 56–7.
161. PRO, GH 23/40, Correspondence 1892–3 re lepers on Robben Island.
162. CA, RI 59, 27 March 1899.
163. G 4–1895, 89.
164. See V. Bickford-Smith, "The Background to Apartheid in Cape Town", Paper presented to the University of Witwatersrand History Workshop, February 1990.
165. S. Judges, "Poverty, Living Conditions and Social Relations" (M.A.thesis, University of Cape Town, 1977) 165–6.
166. D. Warren, "Merchants, Commissioners and Wardmasters", (M.A. thesis,

University of Cape Town, 1986) 44.
167. Bickford-Smith, "The Background to Apartheid in Cape Town", 6.
168. Bickford-Smith, "Cape Town's Dominant Class".
169. Bickford-Smith, "Dangerous Cape Town", 36.
170. Bickford-Smith, "Dangerous Cape Town", 4.
171. Bickford-Smith, "Cape Town's Dominant Class", 1.
172. Bickford-Smith, "Cape Town's Dominant Class", 31.
173. Bickford-Smith, "Cape Town's Dominant Class", 24.
174. Bickford-Smith, "Cape Town's Dominant Class", 34–5, 30–1, 12.
175. Bickford-Smith, "Cape Town's Dominant Class", 33.
176. G 4–1895, 1861 Commission, 148.
177. G 4–1895, 1861 Commission, 158.
178. G 4–1895, 1861 Commission, 73, 96, 77, 54. Some of the cleaner and more "respectable" coloured patients also got newer and better clothes.
179. G 4–1895, 1861 Commission, 89.
180. G 4–1895, 1861 Commission, 8.
181. G 4–1895, 1861 Commission, 77.
182. G 4–1895, 1861 Commission, 72, 223, 97–8, 100.
183. G 4–1895, 1861 Commission, 206.
184. Chaplain's Diary, 14 May 1869.
185. Chaplain's Diary, 1878.
186. "Lepers at the Cape: Wanted, a Father Damien" 274–5. This comment may just have been sensationalist.
187. GN 520, 1892. ARCH-73
188. Rules drawn up before 1894 were not provided for in Law. The 1894 Amendment Act was intended to provide for such regulations, which were finally passed in 1902.
189. Official Report on Robben Island for 1895, 86.
190. CA, RI 75, 12 Sept 1910.
191. CA, RI 61, 15 Oct 1901.
192. CA, RI 61, 27 Sept 1901.
193. CA, RI 69, 22 May.
194. CA, CO 7862, 27 August 1904.
195. Official Report on Robben Island for 1904, 100.
196. CA, CO 7862, Engleheart to Commissioner, 3 Sept 1904.
197. CA, CO 7862, 10 August 1904.
198. CA, RI 73, 8 September 1910.
199. CA, RI 73, 11 November 1910.
200. SC 12–1909, Appendix A.
201. Bickford-Smith, "Cape Town's Dominant Class", 4.

4

Protest, organisation and ethnicity among Cape Town workers, 1891–1902

Vivian Bickford-Smith

In the eleven years between 1891 and 1902, Cape Town underwent rapid economic and demographic growth and change. This was a delayed result of the discovery of gold on the Rand, which had taken place in 1886, as well as the mini-boom brought by the war years from 1899 to 1902.[1] This chapter examines the consequences of such economic and demographic growth and change for worker militancy and ethnic consciousness in the city. It seeks to explore the motivations behind the protest and organisation of workers, and to reveal what factors enhanced, or limited, their likelihood of success in these endeavours. In the process the chapter explores the relationship between ethnic and occupational or trade union consciousness. It attempts to demonstrate that the unpredictable nature of this relationship in Cape Town, most specifically among skilled workers, was the result of complicated and precise historical circumstances.

The expansion of economic activity in Cape Town between 1891 and 1902 did not automatically mean that the position of labour was dramatically strengthened. Employers of labour, with the aid of central government, were able to find new sources of labour in this period in their attempt to minimise wages. This was the background to the establishment of a migrant labour system between the Eastern Cape and the docks and the employment of greater numbers of women, particularly in the new factories and workshops. Rising demand for skilled labour was largely met by the importation of artisans from Britain and Australia.

Moreover, the slow growth of mechanisation and industrialisation took time to change the characteristics of the labour market that had prevailed since 1875: seasonality, casualisation and a less than rigid division of labour. Together with the artificial stimulation of the labour pool, these factors ensured that the position of workers in Cape Town remained weak and most workers remained unorganised. Only in the mid-1900s, thanks largely to the efforts of the Social Democratic Federation, did considerable numbers of skilled or semi-skilled Cape Town workers form unions and take part in industrial action. However, these organisational efforts took place in the depths of a depression which virtually ensured their failure given the larger number of potential strikebreakers amongst the unemployed. When the SDF tried to politicise the latter and organise demonstrations, the result, paralleling what happened after similar efforts by London's SDF, was riot and suppression.[2]

Despite the continued weak position of labour, the 1890s and early 1900s was not a period devoid of conflict between workers and their employers. Individual workers, as well as groups of workers, showed on numerous occasions that they would not accept, or wished to improve, the conditions of their employment. Such instances of worker action may not have amounted to displays of working class consciousness or consciousness of being part of a class acting for itself. But these displays did range from instances of what Phimister and van Onselen have dubbed worker consciousness to the group and trade union consciousness of dock workers and skilled artisans respectively.[3]

Worker consciousness has become a controversial term. Van Onselen has argued that it can be expressed by individual workers in their "day-to-day responses in the work situation" and by judging their "strategy in the context of the overall functioning of the political economy".[4] Thus a range of worker activities from deliberately sloppy work to desertion could be examples of such consciousness. Goldberg, and later Dubow, have argued in contrast that a "distinction must be made between individual consciousness on the one hand and collective consciousness on the other". The term "worker consciousness" should only be used to describe examples of the latter as they are "manifested primarily in economic struggles" in the early phases of the capitalist mode of production.[5] While accepting Goldberg's and Dubow's concern to distinguish between individual and collective action, it would still seem appropriate to use a term, worker protest, to reflect the strategy and responses of an individual member of the working class to that individual's conditions of employment. Dubow might object to this term, apropos migrant labourers, because they were only "partially proletarianised".[6] In other words, they were part-time peasants. Yet in attempting to reject certain conditions of employment by, say, deserting, African dock workers in Cape Town were adopting the same strategy as many domestic servants or other fully proletarianised workers. Moreover, Mfengu dock workers in the 1890s had apparently been recruited because of their rural poverty. Certainly the fact that African dock workers were only semi-proletarianised is important. It helps to explain something of their bargaining strength with employers as well as the development of group consciousness amongst them. However, it would still seem appropriate to use the term worker protest to describe the responses and strategies of individual workers to their work, be they semi- or fully-proletarianised.

Worker protest and group consciousness

Examples of worker protest in the period 1891 to 1902 are legion. They range from the boycotting of certain occupations through desertion, because of bad conditions or unfair treatment, to changing employment to seek better pay. Two types of occupation stand out because of their unpopularity and the continual conflict they provided. The first concerned dock workers and involved carrying coal to steamships. According to McKenzie, "Cape Boys" refused to do this work, or refused to do it at the requisite wage, which forced him to employ Africans.[7] Yet less than a month after McKenzie had brought in Mfengu migrant workers as coal carriers, several had deserted because it was "too hard work".[8] The unpleasantness and unpopularity of working with coal, together with the low wages before 1896, poor food and awful accommodation, helps to explain the high rate of desertions of Africans involved in this work during these four years.[9] It might also help to explain why Africans employed in this capacity were accused of sloppy work in 1892: throwing the bags into the bunkers with the coal instead of pouring the coal in separately and saving the bags.[10] In the early 1900s Africans at the docks still attempted to avoid certain kinds of work such as carrying quarters of beef weighing from 150 to 180 pounds.[11]

The other occupation that was most unpopular was domestic labour. The major reason for this was probably the lack of freedom it involved. According to witnesses to the Labour Commission of 1893, women preferred to accept lower wages in factory jobs or as shop assistants rather than the restrictions of domestic labour.[12] The expansion of employment opportunities for women in this period gave some the chance to make this choice.[13] This was one of the reasons why such labour was imported from Britain and St Helena in the 1890s. Certainly many of the conflicts between Madams and Maids in the course of this decade involved the latter staying out late, overnight or being visited by men.[14] A rare letter to a newspaper from a domestic servant complained that domestics were often not given a single day off in the month but told to ask for one when wanted. When they did they were informed that "it was not respectable to go out in the evening".[15] The lack of privacy, loneliness, long hours and low pay involved in domestic work are evidenced by extant contracts as well as the correspondence on "The Servant Problem" in the local newspapers.[16] Such conditions were the background to recurrent cases of work done reluctantly, or even theft, on the part of the domestics.[17] The latter were not without the ability to get their own back on particularly bad employers, or ones who had been forced to dismiss recalcitrant workers. A letter to the *Cape Argus* said that particular employers might be boycotted if they dismissed a servant: "her version" would be told to acquaintances and a new servant would be obtained only with the "greatest difficulty".[18]

Closely tied to the question of workers disliking or boycotting particular kinds of work is that of their complaints of unfair demands or bad treatment by employers, and the workers' attempts to resist them. Thus a cook left her job in 1895 when she was asked to take on other duties.[19] The letter writer of 1896 suggested that this was a common problem facing domestic servants and an additional reason for their unhappiness. Dock labourers who deserted in 1892 argued in court that they had done so because they had been made to labour when sick.[20] This argument was also used by dock workers deserting in 1896 who, in addition, complained that the food they had been given was insufficient.[21] The latter point was made, also in 1896, by four domestic servants from St Helena who refused to work at a boarding house in Sea Point shortly after their arrival.[22] Three years later a coloured domestic servant said that she had deserted because her mistress had treated her badly. Without questioning the charge, the Magistrate said that she was not allowed to leave. He gave her the option of a fine or seven days imprisonment.[23]

The fate of this last worker, and indeed many of the workers cited above, was to run foul of the Masters and Servants Act of 1873. Its punitive clauses allowed for fines ranging from £1 to £5 and/or imprisonment with or without hard labour from one to three months. These penalties could be incurred for "refusal to obey", "bad language", "neglect" as well as absence from work.[24] They may have been the reason why some workers pleaded sickness or unfair treatment when in fact they were deserting in favour of better employment. The *Lantern* had complained in 1881 that this had been the reason for Delagoa Bay labourers deserting in large numbers.[25] Eight years later it was the motivation for street cleaners to leave their employer and seek work at the docks where a strike had raised the level of wages.[26] In 1892 it was the turn of 100 dock workers to gain higher wages by working for the Cape Government on the Guano Islands.[27] Ten years later the same reason motivated Africans to leave the docks for employment at the military camp in the city.[28] In a period of economic expansion it was actions such as these, as well as the realisation by employers that they faced competition in the labour market, that raised the level of wages of unskilled workers unable to organise general strikes. One correspondent to the *Cape Times* wrote in 1901 that the "Natives" first question was "Work Boss?" Their second was "How much?" He said that Africans understood the laws of supply and demand, prerequisites of effective collective action.[29]

Group consciousness was evidenced most strongly, but not exclusively, by dock workers in our period. Indeed a case could be made for the existence of such consciousness amongst the St Helena domestic servants who had first refused to work and then planned to desert from their boarding house employer in the course of 1896 – 1897.[30] The shared origins of these workers, as was the case with African dock workers and British artisans, undoubtedly served to strengthen their group identity. Striking labourers at the Salt River railway works in 1896 who tried, but failed, to force a wage rise of 6d per day, would also appear to have evinced group consciousness. However, more research is required on this group of workers.[31] The same could be said of the 100 Africans working on the construction of the Table Mountain Reservoir in 1901 who were equally unsuccessful in their bid for higher pay.[32]

What the last two groups had in common with dock workers was the fact that they were working together in fairly large numbers compared to most labourers in Cape Town. Moreover, the isolation of construction workers on the top of Table Mountain doubtless added to their sense of mutual identity and aided their ability to combine. Similarly, so did the fact that African workers were housed in barracks or a location in the mid-1890s or early 1900s. Ethnic identity and shared migrancy could only strengthen, rather than undermine, the group consciousness of such African workers. This group consciousness was, by 1903, reinforced by participation in communal dances and expressed in songs that talked not just of rural life, as in 1893, but now also of life in the docks and the hard lot of Africans in Cape Town.[33]

Before the introduction of Eastern Cape migrant labourers in 1892, dock workers had managed two successful strikes. The first was in 1889, just as the discovery of gold was beginning to lift the depression and before the mini-depression of 1890. Although details of the strike are scanty, the dock workers had apparently demanded and received an increase in pay. The *Excalibur* commented that the strike was "more evidence of advance amongst our coloured classes than appears on the surface".[34] Almost three years later this advance was confirmed when 200 to 300 dock workers struck again for increased pay, this time setting out their demands to A. R. McKenzie in "a lengthy document". The dock workers had chosen their moment well. They struck at a time when there was an "unusual" number of ships in Cape Town harbour, a sign of Cape Town's recovery from the mini-depression. They succeeded in winning a rise in pay from 3s 6d to 4s 6d. It was this success that prompted McKenzie to experiment with migrant workers from the Eastern Cape in the following year, who were paid between 30s and 50s a month (see table below).[35]

Wages of lowest paid labourers at the Cape Town docks, 1860 to 1902[36]

1860 – 1867	2s 6d per day
1867 – 1889	3s 0d per day
1889 – 1891	3s 6d per day
1891 – 1892	4s 6d per day
1892 – 1896	30s 0d per month
1896 – 1902	4s 6d per day

McKenzie's Mfengu labourers came from the Willowvale and Ketani areas of Transkei. They were apparently "not well off" which presumably explains why they had been obliged to undertake work as coal carriers.[37] They struck on a number of occasions in the mid-1890s. In 1892 the reason for 58 of them doing so was that "whenever they worked during the night they would not work the next day". They were given the option of fourteen days hard labour (probably on construction work at the docks) or a £1 fine.[38] In 1893 some 47 refused to work saying that they had only signed six-month contracts. Although McKenzie denied this and took them to court saying that they had signed for twelve months, the dock workers won their case.[39] Later in the year, 200 of them struck work, successfully, when McKenzie failed to pay them on the right day.[40] In 1896, in another dispute over the length of contract, a group of 45 attempted to leave for Transkei. Arrested, and after another court case, eight were initially sentenced to two months hard labour. But 18 others won their case following corroboration of their argument by a Magistrate in Transkei. Their acquittal presumably cleared all the accused.[41]

There is no record of collective action by dock workers between 1897 and 1901. This may have been due to the fact that the migrant labour system set up by McKenzie, fell into abeyance during these years. Notably, at some stage in 1896 (according to the SANAC evidence) McKenzie went back to paying labourers at the rate of 4s 6d per day. He had presumably done so because his experiment had not been a great success due to the large number of desertions and strikes, themselves made more possible at a time of rising demand for, and wages of, black labour. The end of McKenzie's experiment also meant the temporary end of migrants being semi-compounded in barracks at the docks and thus that their group consciousness was correspondingly diminished.[42] It was only in 1901, in the course and aftermath of their renewed segregation in a location, that dock workers once more became active as a group in defence of their interests. This time it was against their new employers, the Table Bay Harbour Board.

These activities have been described in some detail elsewhere. They included a strike in February 1901 during the plague epidemic. Dock workers feared that they were about to be compounded in the severely restricted Kimberley fashion. Thereafter they refused to work in bad weather and attempted to change the conditions under which they were forced to live in the docks location. From the middle of the year they also became involved in a long running dispute over whether they would have to pay the passage money involved in bringing them to Cape Town from the Eastern Cape.[43]

What was new about the disputes of 1901 was their frequency and the forms, specifically written protests, that some of them took.[44] What was also new was that the dock workers appointed a night school teacher, Alfred Mangena, as their "Senior Secretary" or chief negotiator with the Board. Mangena had been appointed in this capacity during the dispute over passage money. He took up the question of conditions in the docks location and accused the Board of preferential treatment for coloured dock workers. Mangena was saving to study law in Britain. The fact that he was a teacher of African workers in Cape Town and interested in the law explains why he became involved on behalf of dock workers, as he was also to become on behalf of the residents of Uitvlugt.[45]

The position of African dock workers was weakened by the fact that, until at least April 1902, they had to apply for "Plague Passes" to leave the city. Thereafter they were still subject to enforced segregation and the only legal alternative to the dock's location was the one at Uitvlugt, several miles away from their place of employment.[46] Yet African dock workers were not without their successes in the course of 1901, partly because their labour was still very much in demand.[47] The cost of the passage money was eventually borne jointly by the Board and the Cape Government Railways, which also employed African migrant labour.[48] Dock workers managed to resist an attempt by the Board to reduce their wages in November.[49] The military camp provided some with alternative employment.[50] Moreover, the letters from Mangena and dock workers themselves, as well as the presence of banners during an unsuccessful strike over which day of the week they should be paid, show that education and literacy were beginning to be weapons at their disposal.[51] Such weapons were already available to white artisans.

The rise of trade unions: Craft pride and ethnic prejudice

Although it is probable that there were craft unions of carpenters and compositors in Cape Town before the 1890s, it was only in this decade that their activities became visible to the historian. In the absence of their records for this period it is difficult to find the precise dates of their foundation. The first union to make its presence felt was the Amalgamated Society of Carpenters and Joiners. A meeting held under the auspices of this society occurred in March 1890 and attracted an audience of 100. The meeting discussed the questions of shorter hours and overtime.[52] By June 1890, possibly as a result of the March meeting, a Trade Council had been formed, primarily to organise an eight hour movement. Nothing more is heard of the Council until 1897. Represented on the Council in 1890 were plumbers, bricklayers, painters, engineers and plasterers, as well as carpenters.[53] This does not mean that all these trades had formed individual unions by this date, or that unions previously formed were still in existence. For instance a branch of the Amalgamated Society of Engineers was supposedly established in South Africa in the late 1880s. But engineers were described as "unorganised" in Cape Town in 1903.[54] The mobility of these and other unionists, if one of their strengths, may account in part for the stuttering beginnings of trade unionism in Cape Town.

Bricklayers and painters both had false starts, in 1893 and 1897 respectively, before re-establishing unions in 1903 and again in 1905.[55] The reason for their false starts was also connected to the particular insecurities facing unionists in those crafts. Compositors had definitely re-established a typographical society by 1896.[56]

Stonemasons and tailors both formed unions in 1897,[57] plumbers in the same year[58] and plasterers by 1898.[59] But the fact that the latter had already embarked on a strike in 1895 suggests that their union may already have been in existence by that date.[60]

This trade unionism was almost, but not entirely, the prerogative of white artisans, most of whom arrived from Britain or Australia between 1889 and 1902 and who received somewhat higher wages than their coloured counterparts in Cape Town. Often fairly large groups of, say, carpenters or stonemasons, "ordered" by the same employer, would travel to the Cape on the same boats giving them an early chance to gain a sense of mutual identity.[61] These immigrants brought with them the craft unionism they had learnt overseas. Membership entailed paying entrance fees and periodic (often weekly) contributions thereafter. Benefits included payments during unemployment and sickness. Members would normally have served several years of apprenticeship in their trade. With this unionism came the consciousness amongst members of craft pride and the desire to protect privilege.[62] But although members of various unions may have had equal quantities of craft pride, they did not all have the equal ability to protect a privileged position in Cape Town's labour market. After all, they had to compete within their respective trades with local artisans. Protecting privilege thus meant preventing undercutting and, if possible, casualisation.

The chronology we gave above already begins to suggest a differential rate of success amongst immigrant artisans in this respect. The fact that this was the case becomes apparent when comparing the highest rates of pay that unionists, or would-be unionists, were receiving in Cape Town. Plumbers received £5 a week as early as 1895.[63] At the other end of the scale tailors were earning £1 10s in 1897 for the same number of hours per week as the plumbers (forty-eight). Only if they worked about twice as long could they hope to make about £4 a week, the rate that plasterers were receiving by 1899.[64] Printers and painters were struggling to earn £3 a week as late as 1903, by which time carpenters had managed to raise their wages to £4 a week, plasterers to £5 and plumbers to at least £5 10s.[65]

Four factors – skill, sentiment, supply and strategy – could, or did, play a part in determining both the relative success of different white artisans and their generally privileged position vis-à-vis their coloured counterparts. The first of these variables, skill, can be defined as "the capacity to perform technically difficult tasks".[66] It could therefore be argued that, in general, white artisans were more skilled than coloured. Furthermore plumbers and stonemasons were more successful, were able to form unions and receive better pay, because their trade was more difficult than painting or bricklaying. Artisans employed in the latter occupations were only in fact semi-skilled. Stedman Jones says that this was indeed the case for such artisans in London.[67] But Harrison and Zeitlin have argued that, though the possession of skill was undoubtedly important, there was no "simple one to one relationship" between level of skill and the power of the craftsman to extract higher rates of pay. Other, inter-related, factors were important. They included the ability of unionists to understand the extent of demand for their labour and to form alliances with non-unionists within their trade.[68]

A second factor, suggested by Pieter van Duin, is that white employers of labour paid more to white than coloured artisans out of "sentiment" or ethnic solidarity. In pursuing this argument for the early twentieth century, van Duin has said that differences of skill within the building trades were "somewhat artificial". Prejudice on the part of employers for white artisans may have played a role in determining that the latter got higher wages.[69] This argument could explain why some unions, as they did, could opt for white exclusivity in a kind of "bounded" relationship (as Greenberg has put it)[70] with their employers; why painters or bricklayers could eventually form a whites-only union by 1904.[71] But a white bricklayer complained in 1897 that employers preferred, if possible, to use coloured artisans. Moreover, Fred Davies, a white painter, had emphasised the need to organise his coloured counterparts because of the latters' effective competition.[72] In addition, in the brewing industry at least, white and coloured skilled workers could receive the same rate of pay.[73] In addition "sentiment" does not, of course, explain why some white artisans did better than others.

Jon Lewis has suggested that supply and demand might explain why white immigrants initially receive higher wages. They were imported to Southern Africa at times of skilled labour shortages. Their wages had, at least initially, to match in real terms those in their country of origin. Certainly contemporary comment supports the contention that the importation of immigrants from Britain was deemed essential.[74] Moreover, the extent of supply thereafter would have a bearing on whether particular groups of artisans could protect or increase their rates of pay.

The fourth factor, intimately related to the first three, is the question of the strategies employed by different groups of white artisans, once in Cape Town, to protect their privileged position. These strategies could take the form of exclusion, combination or alliance with coloured artisans. Few artisans in the Cape Town of 1891 to 1902 enjoyed a monopoly of skills which, according to Jon Lewis, allowed craft unionism between 1924 and 1955 to be overtly non-racist because effectively protected from black competition.[75] According to Lewis, "racial" exclusivity was one of the two strategies adopted by the un- or semi-skilled. The other was open membership, to gain bargaining strength by force of numbers.[76]

In our period only the engineers, enjoying a monopoly of skills in their state-imposed white exclusivity at the Salt River workshops, would appear to have been in the position of Lewis' craft unionists. As it was, the engineers do not appear to have felt either the need or desire to form (or reform) a union at all before 1903.[77] Of our other artisans, it was those who could most effectively protect their privileged position who chose also to maintain an effectively whites-only union. Yet they did so while talking the language of craft rather than colour exclusivity. Their probable reason for doing so was the awareness of the potential need for alliance or co-operation with coloured artisans, even while in practice the latter were excluded from union membership. Thus by 1901 three of the most highly skilled groups of artisans – the masons, carpenters and plasterers – had unions which were effectively whites-only. But, despite suggestions to the contrary by Simons and Simons, Gavin Lewis and Pieter van Duin, there is no evidence that coloureds were overtly barred from entry. Indeed the Plasterer's Union did have a coloured member in 1899. A representative argued that the Union was not against coloureds per se but because coloureds were "labourers" who "were permitted to do a rough class of work in a style not permitted in any other country where trades were advanced".[78]

What had happened, at least by 1901, was that these three groups of artisans had chosen to define only whites as sufficiently skilled or "competent" to be eligible to join their unions. Their successful adoption of this strategy would appear to have been facilitated more by changes taking place within the building industry in the late nineteenth century than by mere "sentiment" on the part of white employers. Throughout the 1890s and 1900s there are constant references in select committee reports, as well as newspapers, to the difference between "competent" and "rough" work in the building trades.[79] Davison notes similar and genuine distinctions in Melbourne's building industry in this period. They had come about as a result of changes in building techniques.[80] There is considerable evidence to suggest that this is precisely what was happening in Cape Town during the latter's transformation from a Dutch into a Victorian city. As one immigration official put it, in 1902: "the introduction of modern methods ... has created a demand for skilled labour for which the set of workers is insufficient". He went on to say that this had been the reason for the continual rise of wages and the Trades and Labour Council's attempt to prevent the further immigration of this new kind of skilled labour.[81] Other comments testify to the fact that certain skills in late Victorian Cape Town were indeed new and necessitated at least the initial importation of British artisans to perform them.[82]

From what we know of the changes in the building and construction industries in late nineteenth-century Cape Town, these comments were accurate. The introduction of "modern methods" most obviously affected work in the centre of the city, the scene of major infrastructural developments by local and central Government, and by merchants and businessmen. It was the latter, especially during the 1890s, who commissioned architect-designed Victorian edifices which demanded new and exacting standards and expertise from builders and their artisans.[83]

One of the most notable changes was in the growing use of finely cut stone, rather than brick covered with plaster, as both a prestigious and durable building material.[84] The introduction of "modern" drainage produced the need for plumbers who were not just "gasfitters and tinsmiths" as had apparently been the case before this development.[85] Victorian architecture could also require elaborate work from carpenters and plasterers. Thus the *Cape Times* reported that a British carpenter was paid more than other carpenters because of his "expertise with stairs".[86] Plasterers, presumably for similar reasons if perhaps aided by "sentiment", monopolised the quality work required in the construction of the new post office and the luxury Mount Nelson Hotel.[87] Certainly local artisans could be trained in the necessary new "dexterities"; they probably had their own which British artisans were not familiar with. But in the meantime there would appear to have been practical reasons, other than the pure prejudice of the employers, why some unionists took the "cream of the work" during this period and with it the highest pay.[88] Equally there would be good reason thereafter for unionists to protect their position by themselves deciding on who was, or was not, a "competent" workman and thus eligible to join their union.[89] In practice, masons, plasterers and carpenters in our period would appear to have adjudged whiteness a necessary component of such competence. Although painters and bricklayers may have wished to follow suit, their task was made more difficult and their economic position less enviable by the less skilled nature of their tasks and the fact that changes in the building industry worked less to their advantage.

These changes in the building industry both led to the introduction of large numbers of British stonemasons and explains why they were particularly successful unionists.[90] Their expertise with a product newly in demand enabled them to maintain fairly convincingly (unlike other unionists) that there were no coloured masons. The lack of danger from undercutting explains why the operative stonemasons had organised almost all the white masons in Cape Town by 1899, 120 out of 126.[91] It explains why they, like their colleagues in Melbourne, could successfully practice exclusivity.[92] But in Cape Town, as with so many other manifestations of class or status consciousness, this exclusivity took on an ethnic dimension and the union became effectively whites-only. Ethnicity reinforced craft consciousness, thanks to the close correlation between level of skill and colour.

This was also the case with white plasterers when their members refused to work on the same scaffolding as coloured plasterers.[93] In their case, however, the strategy of white exclusivity, made feasible by new demands for their particular dexterities, went hand in hand with an awareness that plastering was more open to undercutting than masonry, if less so than painting or bricklaying. The successful pursuit of their strategy required white plasterers to keep informed of the level of demand for their skills. Thus they chose to go on (a successful) strike in 1903, when the local press was reporting a shortage of skilled labour. Reading the market in this way was obviously facilitated by education, a further skill in the possession of British artisans. As it was, some employers had managed to continue work with "Malay and Indian" plasterers, underlining the relative vulnerability of plasterers compared to masons.[94]

Carpenters, classed by Stedman Jones with bricklayers and painters in their vulnerability to undercutting and casualisation, showed as keen an awareness as the plasterers of the ebbs and flows in demand for their skills. In May 1890 they contemplated a strike, but decided that they were insufficiently prepared, possibly because of the relatively low level of demand in the mini-depression of that year.[95] When they did strike, in 1893, it was during the first phase of the building boom. They won an extra 6d a day.[96] Carpenters were again involved in strikes during the Boer war and shortly afterwards, when the building boom was at its height. Like the Amalgamated Society of Carpenters and Joiners in Melbourne, the Cape Town Society practised an exclusivity that left many white, as well as coloured, carpenters outside the union. They were presumably able to do so successfully partly because of the specific skills they possessed in, say, the production of Victorian staircases. They also adopted the strategy of seeking alliances with non-union, and lower paid, white carpenters in their strike actions of 1893, 1901 and 1903. In the space of these ten years their wages rose accordingly from 9s 6d to 14s per day.[97]

In the absence of State intervention on their behalf, those white artisans most vulnerable to undercutting had to opt for a different strategy to the overlapping craft and colour exclusivity of the masons, carpenters and plasterers. Bricklayers and painters would appear to have benefited less than other artisans from changes in the building industry. Some bricklayers and painters may have attempted to become the elite of their trade simply by refusing to take on "rough" or "plain" work, by defining their own work as particularly skilled and even appealing to sentiment. But their relative poverty compared to, say, plasterers, underlines the difficulty they faced in pursuing exclusivity. One reason may have been the lack of demand for quality work in their trade. Certainly in 1897 a painter talked of the "low standard" of work passed by architects,[98] a bricklayer of the "slop and jerry" work he had come across in the Colony.[99] Four years earlier another bricklayer had complained of the shortage of "better brickwork".[100] But in the case of bricklayers and painters skill would appear to have been more of a "social aspiration" than a genuine capability to perform technically difficult tasks that others would find hard to learn, like stonemasonary.[101] The bricklayer of 1897 could complain of a "set of wasters" working for 3s or 5s a day who "obtain the preference over the whites". Thus the threat was perceived to come from coloured artisans, employers' "sentiment" was obviously insufficient protection.[102]

Both bricklayers and painters struggled and failed to establish their own lasting unions into the mid-1900s. Both may have tried each of the strategies that were open to the un- and semi-skilled, but with little success. At the attempt to organise a bricklayers union in 1893 coloured bricklayers were present and there was no talk of exclusion.[103] Equally, white painters apparently tried in 1897 and again in 1903 to recruit coloureds to their union.[104] The reluctance of coloured painters or bricklayers to join their white counterparts may have been because they feared that, if they held out for the same rate of pay as whites, employers would then prefer the latter as sentiment came into play. As it was, a strategy of white exclusivity, fleetingly adopted overtly by the painters in 1903, had little chance of success.[105] Simons and Simons maintain that there was also a white Bricklayers Society, in 1904. I can find no evidence of its existence which, if it occurred, must have been equally brief.[106] In 1906 both bricklayers and painters became members of a non-racial General Workers Union.[107]

Outside of the building industry, white tailors and compositors were also highly vulnerable to undercutting, which helps explain the strategies of alliance and non-racial recruitment that they attempted. The establishment of a Tailors Union coincided with the gradual move towards workshop production in this trade, away from out-work. The latter continued well into the 1900s, and possibly beyond. The problems facing unionist tailors were compounded by the ethnic divisions of labour within workshops and the fact that Moslems and Yiddish-speaking Jewish tailors were involved in the out-work. Moslems were apparently engaged as trouser hands, white tailors as coat and vest hands. Members of the Tailors Union, in the course of 1897, complained about the "sweating" in their trade, the fact that work was taken home or produced outside a workshop, rather than low standards or differences of skill. They felt threatened by "Malays" who "live cheaper" and Polish Jews who were prepared to work long hours for little money. The Tailors Union, moribund for a few years, was re-established in 1901 to push for higher wages. In the process the Union tried to form an alliance with Malay tailors, who did pledge their support in a meeting organised for this purpose. However, they reneged on their pledge and the strike was confined to "European" tailors. With the Moslems still working within workshops, and the "sweated" trade without, the 200 tailors who did strike only received a derisory seventh of what they had asked for.[108]

In 1897 members of the Typographical Union, seemingly hitherto white, embarked on a strategy not only of alliance with, but also inclusion of, their coloured counterparts. Such a strategy was advisable for artisans whose privilege could be threatened by the employment of semi-skilled women, Africans and boys, due to increased mechanisation in the industry. Coloureds were encouraged to join the Union, although only 20 had done so by 1899. However, in the strike that the Union embarked on in 1897, it received the support of non-union white and coloured printers, as well that of printers brought in to break the strike (the compositors won pay rises of from five per cent to 15 per cent). The timing of the strike, just after a local firm had won the Government printing contract, shows an awareness of the need to read the level of demand for their labour. Successfully persuading the Cape Government, in 1895, to commit itself to keeping these contracts within the Colony shows a similar awareness. It may also have been an early indication of the political power of white workers. Finally, those compositors working on newspapers may have been helped in the 1897 strike by the "perishable" nature of this product. The *Cape Times* immediately settled with its workers for 15 per cent and the *Cape Argus* offered 11 per cent only a day after the strike began. In contrast, those printers working for the firm that handled the Government contract had to settle for five per cent.[109]

The verdict as to whether all, or most, white artisans were racist must be "unproven". Examples exist of inclusion and co-operation of white and coloured artisans. Both resided in large numbers in close proximity in the working class areas and did not always maintain the "social distance" that van Duin argues normally existed between them.[110] A leader in the *South African News* commenting on European artisans in Cape Town, said:

> We have been astonished, and from the standpoint of our social prospects disheartened, to find how surprisingly large is the percentage of such settlers who marry coloured women. Let the Imperial Government take a Census on this point in, say, District Six of Cape Town, and the result will astonish them.[111]

There is no conclusive evidence that white artisans expressed either the pseudo-Darwinist or even evolutionary racism extant amongst bourgeois Capetonians, at least in their relationship with coloured artisans, even if both may have fostered such feelings towards African Capetonians.[112]

On the other hand, defence of craft privilege both could and did go hand-in-hand with white exclusivity for white unionists such as the masons, plasterers or carpenters. In the Cape Town of 1891 to 1902, with its increased segregation, dominant class racism and assertive Englishness, it would have been strange if many white artisans had not displayed ethnic consciousness. After all, it was to a crowd of white artisans and unionists in Cape Town, demonstrating in his favour in 1897, that Rhodes promised "equal rights to all white men".[113] It was white working-class children who would be the chief beneficiaries of segregated education. Yet up to 1902 there was still an absence of racist rhetoric from white unionists in a Cape Town where racism was "respectable", and before the existence of a predominantly white Labour Party which might worry about coloured votes. We can suggest that it was the lack of rigid divisions of labour, specifically in the skilled trades between whites and coloureds, that promoted the need for potential or actual co-operation at the workplace and held such racism in check.[114]

Endnotes

1. V. Bickford-Smith "Commerce, Class and Ethnicity in Cape Town, 1875–1902", (Ph.D., Cambridge University, 1989) – especially chapters 6 to 8 which deal (at some length!) with the period of this paper.
2. R. Hallett, "The Hooligan Riots", *Studies in the History of Cape Town*, 1 (1979), 42–87, (hereafter Studies).
3. I.R. Phimister and C. van Onselen, *Studies in the History of African Mine Labour in Colonial Zimbabwe*, (Gwelo, 1978).
4. Phimister and Van Onselen, *African Mine Labour*, 2.

5. Dubow, citing Goldberg, in Dubow "African Labour at the Cape Town Docks", *Studies* 4 (1981), pp.120–121. See also M. Goldberg "Worker Consciousness: A Formulation and a Critique" (unpublished paper, UCT, 1980).
6. Dubow, "African Labour", 110, 125.
7. A12 – 1890, *Select Committee Report on Labour*, 41.
8. *Cape Argus* 30 March 1893.
9. See e.g.: *Cape Argus* 2 June 1894, 10 April 1897; *Cape Times* 14 December 1896, 8 March 1897. For details of McKenzie's barracks and the food he initially provided see G39 – 1893, *Labour Commission*, 71–2, 79–80: the dockworkers were housed in large sheds where they had to sleep on the ground "in a sack".
10. CA 1/CT 6/226 "Preparatory Examinations", May 1892, case of Nqute, Jack, "Office" and "Rabits Hana".
11. CA CHB 268 "Docks Location", Superintendent to General Manager, Harbour Board, 23 May 1902.
12. G39 – 1893, 80–81, 98–9, 118.
13. C1 – 1891, *Select Committee Report on Colonial Industries*, 24, 25, 46, 57, 65, 90, 91, 95. See also G39 – 1893, 4, 5, 15, 68, 98. A29 – 1899, *Select Committee Report on Employment of Women in the Civil Service*, iii–v, p.1, 44–5. *Cape Times* 21 July 1896 talks of the great extent of "wife labour" in Cape Town; 31.8.1896: women employed in the dairy industry. CPP C4 – 1904, "SCR on Colonial Industries", pp.25, 32, 33, 38, 46, 70, 96, 106. CPP A6 – 1906, "SCR on the Factory Act", pp.4, 5, 8, 55, 56, 74, 80–90, 114, 118, 124–5, 128.
14. See e.g. *Cape Argus* 23 June 1892, 7 November 1894, 9 July 1897; *Cape Times* 29 September 1897.
15. *Cape Times* 12 October 1896, letter from "one who speaks from experience".
16. CA PWD 2/8/20, "Mrs Lancaster's forms of Contract" Agent General of Cape to the Commissioner of Crown Lands and Public Works, 28 November 1889; the servant was required "to receive no visitors without special permission from her Master or Mistress"; "to be within the house every day after sunset except by special permission from her Master or Mistress"; "to inform her Master or Mistress forthwith of any act of drunkenness, theft or immorality on the part of a fellow servant of which she may become aware"; the servant was allowed to attend church only every alternate Sunday and given leave of absence from 2 p.m. to 5 p.m. once every month. See also *Cape Argus* 29 December 1891, 31 December 1891, 4 January 1892.
17. *Cape Times* 1 October 1896; 2 October 1896, letter from "a despairing woman", 21 September 1897; 17 October 1898, the servant who had stolen from her employer claimed that she had done so because she had no clothes; *Cape Argus* 26 September 1892: this time the servant accused of theft had only been receiving 6s a month.
18. *Cape Argus* 31 December 1891, letter from "Paterfamilias".
19. *Cape Argus* 27 November 1845.
20. *Cape Argus* 25 July 1892.
21. CA 1/CT 6/281, June 1896, case of Matthew Mahoney versus Mtetu and eight others.
22. *Cape Times* 5 August 1896.
23. *Cape Argus* 4 April 1899.
24. A18 – 1873 "Masters and Servants Act".

25. *Lantern* 2 April 1881.
26. CA 3/CT 1/1/5/229, "Appendix to Cape Town Council Minutes", January 1890, Skead Cowling and Co. to the Cape Town Council. See below for details of this strike.
27. *Cape Argus* 12 January 1892.
28. CA CHB 262 "Labour Barracks", General Manager of TBHB to Colonel H. Cooper, Main Barracks, Cape Town. See also W. R. Nasson, "Black Society in the Cape Colony and the South African War 1899 – 1902: a social history", (Ph.D., Cambridge University, 1983), ch.2, for detailed information on the competition offered by the British Army to Cape employers.
29. *Cape Times* 17 May 1901. See *Cape Argus* 16 November 1892 and 8 January 1896 for examples of a draper's assistant and domestic servant, respectively, deserting for the same reason.
30. *Cape Times* 5 August 1896, 24 November 1896, 4 February 1897.
31. *Cape Times* 13 October 1896. For a later period see S. O'Sulllivan, "Workers with a Difference: Life and Labour in the Salt River Workshops 1900 – 1935" (B.A. (Hons), University of Cape Town, 1984); S. O'Sullivan "Cameos of Life at the Salt River Works in the 1920s" in *Studies*, 6, (1988), 96–111.
32. *Cape Times* 17 May 1901.
33. *Cowley Evangelist* November 1893, letter from Father Congreve: Songs of Rural Life; 1903, "letter from Father Bull", p.90: "Native acting Songs" described "the ringing of the six o'clock bell calling to work at the 'docksin' [docks location] and ... the hard life of the native in Cape Town, banished from home and comfort, and compelled to eat calves' heads and such poor food. It was quite the Irish style", *South African Native Affairs Commission* 1903 – 1905, 2, p.84: which described African dock workers participating in the "Hloma" dance in the docks location.
34. *Cape Times* 8 January 1889; *Excalibur* 11 January 1889.
35. *Cape Argus* 21 December 1891, 22 December 1891.
36. Based on *South African Native Affairs Commission*, (Transvaal Colony), 1903–5, 5, Annexure 4, pp.10–11; *Cape Times* 8 January 1889 and *Cape Argus* 21 December 1891 show how strikes altered the rates of pay, changes not apparent from the SANAC evidence which is not altogether reliable.
37. C2 – 1892, *Select Committee Report on Labour Supply*, 73–76. The quotation, from the evidence of Johannes Veldtman, Headman and Recruiter, is from p. 76.
38. *Cape Argus* 29 April 1892: the men were on wages of from 30s to 50s a month, but they could earn 6d an hour overtime, i.e. for night work. This presumably explains why night work was preferred to day work.
39. CA 1/CT 6/234, May 1893, case of dock labourers charged under the Masters and Servants Act of 1873; *Cape Argus* 1 May 1893, 2 May 1893.
40. *Cape Argus* 2 August 1893.
41. CA 1/CT 6/281, June 1896, case of Matthew Mahoney versus Mteto and eight others; *Cape Argus* 6 June 1896, 9 June 1896, 25 June 1896; *Cape Times* 10 June 1896, 26 June 1896, 30 June 1896, 21 July 1896.
42. CA CHB 262, Resident Engineer to TBHB, 21 September 1895 and Secretary to Resident Engineer, 25 September 1895 show that the Harbour Board increased its wages at this time because of competition from other employers of labour in Cape Town and further afield such as the Transvaal and Rhodesia; Acting Resident Engineer to Assistant General Manager, 29 May 1902, suggests that the ex-"Kaffir

Barracks" was still leased to McKenzie in 1897. CA NA 457, p.47 and CHB 262 Resident Engineer to Harbour Board, 14 October 1895, 1 November 1895: show that the Harbour Board had explored the possibility of erecting a barracks for McKenzie (and presumably its own) African labourers at the end of 1895, but had met objections to the proposed site from the (White) occupiers of its own cottages.

43. Bickford-Smith, "Black Labour at the Docks at the Beginning of the Twentieth Century", *Studies* 2, (1980), 75–125. Dubow "African Labour" and Budlender "African Labour at the Docks at the Turn of the Century" (unpublished paper, Cape Town, 1980) all focus in some detail on the events of 1901. See also CA CHB 262, for detailed correspondence on the passage money dispute.

44. CA CHB 268, letter from P. Songwevu, S. Sigcume and J. Mbangeni, Headmen, to Secretary TBHB, 10 October 1901 and another, 18 October 1901.

45. See CA CHB 262, correspondence between docks location Superintendent, Secretary TBHB and Father Bull, July to October passim. But see especially Mangena to Secretary, TBHB, 16 October 1901; P. Songwevu and others to Secretary, TBHB, 10 October 1901 and 18 October 1901; Superintendent, docks location to Secretary, TBHB, 15 October 1901 and 19 October 1901; Secretary, TBHB, to P. Songwevu and others, 22 October 1901. See also CA CHB 268, Mangena to Superintendent of docks location, 20 January 1902, complaining about the Board's preferential treatment of Coloured over African Labour. CA CHB 267, Mangena to Docks Superintendent 7 April 1902, complaining that Africans were still facing delays before being given health clearance to return to the Eastern Cape and that there was inadequate transport for them and 15 April 1904, Mangena's acknowledgement of the Superintendent's help. *Cape Times* 21 October 1901, letter Alfred Mangena on passage money dispute. C. Saunders, "The Creation of Ndabeni: Urban Segregation and African Resistance in Cape Town", *Studies*, 1, (1979), 179.

46. See Saunders "Ndabeni" and E.B. van Heyningen, "Cape Town and the Plague of 1901", *Studies*, 4, (1981), 66–107, for detailed accounts of the Bubonic Plague and segregation of Africans in Cape Town in 1901. See also below. See note 45 above re Africans still having to obtain health clearance until April 1902.

47. *Cape Times* 16 May 1901: deputation to the Governor re the need to augment African labour in the city, which included representatives of the Council and other employers of African labour. See also CA CHB 262, Secretary TBHB to Secretary, Chamber of Commerce, 24 August 1901 and attached memo; the board wanted 10 000 African labourers in Cape Town, while the actual number had dropped to below 6 000 according to Saunders, "Ndabeni", 175.

48. Bickford-Smith, "Black Labour", 112–113.

49. CA CHB 262, Superintendent docks location to Engineer-in-Chief, TBHB, 25 November 1901.

50. See note 42 above.

51. *Cape Times* 16 November 1901, 18 November 1901.

52. *Cape Times* 11 March 1890, 16 May 1890, 19 May 1890.

53. *Cape Times* 6 June 1890, 23 June 1890, 18 August 1890, 17 February 1897. D. Ticktin, "The Origins of the South African Labour Party 1880 – 1910" (Ph.D., University of Cape Town, 1973), 46, talks of a trade and labour council being launched in Cape Town in 1894 and re-launched in 1899. But he does not cite contemporary sources for these findings.

54. Ticktin, "Labour Party", 23; *South African News* 7 March 1903.
55. Bricklayers: Cape Argus 27 February 1893, 4 March 1893, 23 March 1897; *South African News* 3 January 1903, 21 February 1903, 4 April 1903, 4 July 1903, 16 September 1905. Painters: *Cape Argus* 1 March 1897, 24 March 1897, 29 March 1897, 31 March 1897, 7 April 1897, 31 March 1897; *Cape Times* 8 March 1897, 11 March 1897; *South African News* 28 March 1903, 4 July 1903, 22 September 1905.
56. *Cape Times* 17 November 1896; A. J. Downes *Printers' Saga*,(Johannesburg, 1952), 2–3, says that there was definitely a typographical association in existence in 1889 because of the fact that a copy of the rules of the association exist for that date. But a revised edition of rules was printed in 1896 when the association may have been revived.
57. *Cape Times* 15 February 1897 and 26 October 1897 respectively. *South African News* 7 July 1899 has more details re stonemasons.
58. *South African News* 20 September 1902.
59. *Cape Times* 16 April 1898, 29 April 1898.
60. *Cape Argus* 28 October 1895.
61. CA PWD 1588, "Lists of Aided Immigrants", gives details of British artisans brought to Cape Town in this way, which ships they travelled on and for whom they were going to work when in Cape Town. G39–1893 gives considerable detail re origins and rates of pay of artisans in Cape Town see pp.25–26, 34–39, 42–3, 82–91.
62. D. Blankenhorn, "'Our Class of Workmen': The Cabinet-makers revisited" in R. Harrison and J. Zeitlin, (eds), *Divisions of Labour* (Brighton, 1985), 24–5. For the existence of these characteristics in the Cape Town unions see: *Cape Times* 6 February 1897, strike pay for printers; *South African News* 8 June 1899, details of Plasterers' Union; 1 July 1899, Typographical Union; 7 July 1899, Operative Union; 1 July 1899, Operative Plumbers. Ticktin, "Labour Party", 15–21.
63. *Cape Argus* 28 October 1895.
64. Tailors: *Cape Times* 27 October 1897, 28 October 1897, 29 October 1897, 3 November 1897. Plasterers: *South African News* 8 June 1899.
65. Printers: *South African News* 23 May 1903. Painters: *South African News* 28 March 1903. Carpenters: *South African News* 7 March 1903, 21 March 1903. Plasterers: *South African News* 7 March 1903.
66. Harrison and Zeitlin, *Divisions of Labour*, 8: this, they say, was the Victorian definition of skill.
67. G. Stedman Jones, *Outcast London* (Harmondsworth, 1976), 59–60.
68. Harrison and Zeitlin, *Divisions of Labour*, 8, 14.
69. P. van Duin, "Skilled Labour, Trade Unionism and Racial Attitudes in Cape Town, 1900–1914", (unpublished paper, Leiden, 1985), pp.10–11.
70. S. Greenberg, *Race and State in Capitalist Development* (Johannesburg, 1980), ch.13.
71. *South African News* 9 May 1903; *Cape Times* 9 May 1903.
72. Bricklayer's complaint: *Cape Argus* 23 March 1897. Painters: *Cape Times* 8 March 1897; *Cape Argus* 8 March 1897, 24 March 1897, 31 March 1892.
73. G39 – 1893, 38.
74. J. Lewis, *Industrialisation and Trade Union Organisation in South Africa, 1924–55: The Rise and Fall of the South African Trades and Labour Council*

(Cambridge, 1984), 14. For comments on the shortage of skilled labour or the need and/or desirability of importing it from Britain see e.g.: *Cape Argus* 27 July 1894, 20 August 1895: *Cape Times* 19 September 1909. G21 – 1907, *Report of Immigration Officer*, Cape Town, 12; A6 – 1908, *Select Committee Report on Imported Contract Labour*, 3, 4.

75. Lewis, *Industrialisation and Trade Union Organisation*, 4.
76. Lewis, *Industrialisation and Trade Union Organisation*, 9.
77. See Bickford-Smith "Commerce", ch.7 for details of this state-imposed exclusivity. See *South African News* 27 June 1903 for the formation of a Branch of the Amalgamated Society of Engineers in Cape Town.
78. J and R Simons, *Class and Colour in South Africa 1850 – 1950*, (London, 1983), 73–4; G Lewis, *Between the Wire and The Wall*, (Cape Town, 1987), 16; P. van Duin, "Trade Unionism and the Relationship between White and Coloured Workers in the Cape Town Building Industry, 1900 – 1930" (unpublished paper, UCT Roots and Realities Conference, 1986), 7–8. Both Lewis and van Duin cite the Simons whose reference is to the *Spectator* 23 March 1901, 20 April 1901. But these editions refer to the fact that the plasterers were de facto whites-only and would not allow their members to work on the same scaffold as coloureds or Malays. *South African News* 8.6.1899: The plasterers did have a coloured member in 1899 and they argued that their admission policy was based on "competence" not colour. There is no evidence produced by any of these authors that the plasterers or masons constitutionally barred coloureds. See *Cape Times* 10.2.1897: "The Malay Mason [so-called]" was not recognised by the legitimate tradesman; *South African News* 7.7.1899, there were no coloured masons. See *South African News* 13.2.1903, 18.4.1903: the plasterers refusal to work with coloured labour led to their disaffiliation from the Trades Council in 1903. *Cape Times* 1.10.1896: the Amalgamated Society of Carpenters and Joiners was theoretically open to "any Africander or any competent man of any nationality"; *South African News* 23.4.1901: at a meeting of the union a coloured carpenter wanted to know if any coloureds could join and the white chairman said his union would help the coloureds form their own, or as a branch of the white union. Although lack of evidence makes it impossible to be sure, it is likely that the plumbers were also effectively whites-only.
79. E.g.: G39 – 1893, 26, 37, 83; *Cape Times* 5 February 1897: "with the present class of labour only one man out of a great many was really a competent man"; 15 January 1903, advertising for "first-class" bench-hand carpenters and "six rough carpenters"; 5 January 1904, "employment of foreigners"; A6 – 1908, 22–30.
80. G. Davison, *The Rise and Fall of Marvellous Melbourne* (Melbourne, 1978), 73–75.
81. Government House (GH) 35/129, "Report on Labour Question, E. Pillans to the Governor", 18 November 1902.
82. See note 186 above. See also Standard Bank Archives, General Manager's Correspondence to London Office, 28 May 1890 re new machinery and new skilled labour.
83. P. Butt, "The Growth and Development of the Master Builders Association in the Cape Peninsula" (M.Sc., Natal University, 1984), 69–94; A.G. Howard, "Progress of Architecture in Cape Town since 1876", *South African Architect, Engineer and Surveyor* (May-September 1907), 139–212; J. Rennie, *The Buildings of Central*

Cape Town, 1, (Cape Town, 1978), 8–15 and 2 (Cape Town, 1878), 195. Compare also J.W. Cell, *The Highest Stage of White Supremacy*, (Cambridge, 1982), 189, which notes that black artisans in the Southern States of America were threatened by "adoption of standardised measurement in building".
84. P.W. Laidler, *The Growth and Government of Cape Town*, (Cape Town, 1939), says that the first building of stone in Cape Town was in 1888. See also Rennie, *Buildings*, 1, 15; 2, 195; Howard, 212.
85. *Cape Argus* 3 August 1892.
86. *Cape Times* 5 January 1904, "Employment of Foreigners".
87. *South African News* 8 June 1899. See also Rennie, *Buildings*, 1, 11.
88. *Cape Times* 13 March 1907, "Transvaal Indigency Commission", reports Mr Cousins, an immigration official, saying that it was the "rawness" of Colonial artisans compared to British ones that allowed the latter to get more pay.
89. A6 – 1908, p.22: the Chairman of the Cape Town and District Trades and Laobur Council, Mr Thomas Maginess, was asked how he "measured" competency as a means to admission of unions. He replied that: "when a member is proposed he must have a proposer and a seconder and men to support him, men who have worked with him and who know his ability, and if that man turns out to be a failure the union fines the men for proposing him". See also pp.27–30. For a similar approach by Australian Craft Unionists see Davison, *Marvellous Melbourne*, 86–88.
90. *South African News* 21 February 1905 and *Cape Times* 10 October 1908 both discuss the relationship bewtween the appearance of stone buildings and the requisite skills supplied by these masons.
91. *South African News* 7 July 1899.
92. Davison, *Marvellous Melbourne* 86.
93. *Spectator* 23 March 1901; *South African News* 8 June 1899, 18 April 1903.
94. Strike: *South African News* 7 March 1903, 14 March 1903; *Cape Times* 9 March 1903. Shortage of skilled labour: *Cape Times* 12 February 1903; *South African News* 14 March 1903, on steady emigration of artisans that had taken place from Cape Town. The quotation is from *South African News* 18 April 1903.
95. *Cape Times* 11 March 1890, 16 May 1890, 19 May 1890.
96. Cape Argus 3 February 1893, 14 February 1893, 15 February 1893, 3 March 1893, 7 March 1893, 9 March 1893, 20 March 1893, 22 March 1893.
97. *South African News* 28 March 1901, 22 April 1901, 23 April 1901, 24 April 1901, 26 April 1901, 6 May 1901, 22 May 1901, 31 January 1903, 7 February 1903, 21 February 1903, 7 March 1903, 14 March 1903, 21 March 1903. *Cape Argus* 3 February 1893, for wages in that year. Davison, *Marvellous Melbourne*, 88. Particularly skillful work was required in cabinet making for which cabinet makers were imported: *Excalibur* 9 August 1889. See also *Cape Times* 5 January 1904, "Employment of Foreigners" and A6 – 1908, 61 comments on the particular skills possessed by British carpenters.
98. *Cape Times* 8 March 1897.
99. *Cape Argus* 23 March 1897.
100. *Cape Argus* 10 April 1893.
101. Harrison and Zeitlin, *Divisions of Labour* 1.
102. *Cape Argus* 23 March 1897.
103. *Cape Argus* 27 February 1893, 4 March 1893.

104. *Cape Argus* 23 March 1897, 24 March 1897. *South African News* 4 July 1903, 6 July 1903; but 11 July 1903 suggests that a large non-racial union was not forthcoming, after an attempted strike ended in "fiasco" in August 1903 (see 29 August 1903), the Painters' Society would appear to have dissolved once more.
105. *South African News* 9 May 1903, 13 June 1903, 27 June 1903.
106. Simons and Simons, *Class and Colour*, 74. van Duin "Trade Unionism", 9, says that a separate Bricklayers Society did not exist until 1910.
107. Bricklayers: *South African News* 29 July 1905, 16 September 1905, 30 September 1905, 17 February 1906, 31 March 1906. Painters: *South African News* 16 September 1905, 22 September 1905, 30 September 1905, 24 February 1906, 17 March 1906, 24 March 1906, 7 April 1906, 12 May 1906. For the origins and principles of the General Workers Union see *South African News* 19 July 1905: "its membership would be open to every wage-earner, male or female, and it would not be cursed by the Colour prejudice which was such a disturbing element in the labour world of South Africa". Established by members of the Social Democratic Federation, the GWU organised workers irrespective of Colour in the course of 1905 and 1906. Nonetheless the GWU had considered the idea of parallel coloured and white unions. See *South African News* 24 July 1905 for the constitution of the GWU. For origins of SDF see *South African News* 11 July 1903: the SDP was formed in 1902.
108. *Cape Times* 26 October 1897, 27 October 1897, 28 October 1897, 29 October 1897, 3 November 1897; *South African News* 3 April 1901, 4 April 1901, 6 April 1901, 24 April 1901.
109. *Cape Times* 17 November 1896, 15 January 1897, 22 January 1897, 2 February 1897, 3 February 1897, 4 February 1897, 6 February 1897, 9 February 1897, 10 February 1897, 18 February 1897, 19 February 1897, 20 February 1897, 22 February 1897, 1 July 1897. Downes *Printers' Saga* 6–7. For a comparison with British compositors and the point about the "perishable" nature of newspapers as a product see J. Zeitlin, "Engineers and Compositors: A Comparison", in Harrison and Zeitlin *Divisions of Labour*, 186–215; nb, 196, that British compositors were careful to proclaim their opposition to underpaid female labour, rather than women *per se*, echoing the emphasis on craft rather than colour exclusivity of Cape Town unionists.
110. Van Duin "Skilled Labour", 6.
111. *South African News* 4 April 1901. See also CA GH 35/40, Governor to Joseph Chamberlain, 23 April 1901, talking of the problems faced by the authorities hoping to deal with the plague in Cape Town. One problem was: "the presence of a mixed population *closely intermingled in their domestic relations*, comprising Europeans, low-class Jews, Malays, coloured persons, Chinese, Indians, and Aboriginal Natives" (my emphasis); *Cape Times* 26 March 1901: talks of the bulk of the population of "Malay quarter" as Malay, but that coloureds and whites also live there. See also R. Hallett, "Violence and Social Life in Cape Town in the 1900s", *Studies*, 2, (1980), 126–176, for occasions of social mixing amongst Cape Town's underclasses.
112. *South African News* 1 July 1899: The Typographical Union, which admitted coloureds and white, was against the employment of African and female labour, though this could again be seen as primarily a matter of protection of craft exclusivity.

113. *Cape Argus* 22 April 1897: the demonstration was at Groote Schuur, Rhodes' Cape Town estate. Workmen present included 800 from the Salt River works, as well as members of the Typographical Union, the Operative Masons, Amalgamated Society of Carpenters and Joiners, Painters and Plumbers Societies and "many others".

114. *South African News* 18 April 1903, had an interesting article noting the disaffiliation of of the white plasterers from the Trades and Labour Council. It began: "The day is approaching too when the united trades of Cape Colony and doubtless the whole of South Africa will have to come to some permanent decision as to the position of coloured labour in relation to white." It went on, "A perfectly organised system of European labour will never tolerate the present anomalous position of the coloured workers. It must absorb them, reject them, or adopt the oft-suggested course of organising coloured labour separate from, but in sympathy with, the white organisation ... whilst the coloured artisans remained unorganised there is always an element of danger to the Trade Unions." *South African News* 23 April 1901: White unionist carpenters have offered to help coloured carpenters establish their own union in 1901. See Ticktin, "Labour Party" for the origins and early history of the Labour Party.

5

"A drink-sodden race of bestial degenerates": perceptions of race and class in the *Educational Journal*, 1915–1940

Mohammed Adhikari

The *Educational Journal*, published from May 1915 onwards, was the official organ of the Teachers' League of South Africa, founded in Cape Town in 1913 as a professional association expressly for coloured teachers.[1] Established at the instigation of the African Political Organisation which dominated coloured politics during the first four decades of the twentieth century, and representing what was by far the largest professional group within the coloured community, the League reflected the social experience and the *Weltanschauung* of the coloured petty bourgeoisie. And, as the mouthpiece of one of the most influential coloured communal organisations of the time, the *Journal* mirrored the values, aspirations and frustrations of the coloured élite.[2]

Despite its rather grandiose name, the TLSA was not a national body. Its membership was confined to the Cape Province and its organisational life was largely centred on Cape Town. By far the greater part of its leadership was drawn from the city and most of the association's annual conferences, executive meetings and social functions were held there.[3] These centripetal tendencies were very much a consequence of the regional concentration of the coloured people. Fully one third of all coloureds were resident in the greater Cape Town area, and about two thirds were located within the Western Cape.[4] Thus, while the Boland branches of the TLSA were able to participate in League activities centred on Cape Town, the more distant ones such as those in Kimberley, Port Elizabeth and the outlying rural areas, tended to be isolated and to lead independent lives.

Although it started off as a relatively small organisation, by the early 1940s the League had grown to the extent that it was able to draw the majority of coloured teachers under its wing.[5] Notwithstanding the dominance of the Cape Town-based leadership, the League was nevertheless fully representative of the coloured teaching profession and, in its social outlook, of the coloured petty bourgeoisie as a whole. Sporting several eminent individuals and leading intellectuals within its ranks, the League and its journal played an instrumental role in the process of coloured self-definition and the construction of coloured identity.

Although conditions of economic exploitation and class domination principally determined the socio-political status of the coloured community, the racial dimensions of its situation were uppermost in the minds of the coloured petty bourgeoisie and, therefore, of League members. They experienced their society primarily as members of a racial category and their consciousness was filtered through the prism of their coloured identity. It was therefore racial oppression rather than class exploitation that informed their political consciousness. Class consciousness within the coloured élite was thus attenuated and largely articulated in terms of their identity as coloured people. This much is evident from the League being a racially exclusive body with the explicit aim of fostering the educational interests of the coloured people.[6]

The most salient features of the coloured people as a group within the broader context of South African society were their marginality and their intermediate status within the social order. They were marginal in the sense that they never formed more than ten percent of the South African population,[7] and that they lacked significant economic or political power. Their marginality also meant that coloureds had little choice in the matter of accepting an inferior social status to whites as well as the second class citizenship imposed upon them by the segregationist white state. Coloureds were, however, successful in holding the middle ground in the South African racial hierarchy between the dominant white and the numerically preponderant African groups by claiming to be culturally more advanced than the latter and being partly descended from the former.[8]

Together, their marginality and intermediate position resulted in ambiguities and unresolved contradictions within coloured identity, and presented coloureds with a series of dilemmas and paradoxes in their day-to-day living. This, in turn, led to inconsistent and equivocal behaviour that was particularly conspicuous within the coloured élite and hence also evident in the *Educational Journal*. These inconsistencies reflected ambivalences over the way in which coloureds perceived themselves as a group and the manner in which they related to other social groups. Coloured identity was therefore fluid and highly sensitive to the immediate context in which it operated. Whereas racial identities are notoriously intractable, being based on highly visible and relatively immutable phenotypical features, especially skin colour and hair texture,[9] coloured identity was by comparison exceptionally versatile. Besides being partly derived from their intermediate status, this fluidity was also a consequence of the coloured people forming a residual category encompassing a wide range of people and social groups. This resulted in the coloured category covering the entire spectrum of racial gradations between the Caucasoid and Negroid somatic norm images. Lacking definitive ethnic or racial indicators or any positive symbols with which to identify, coloured identity was continually in tension between white and African opposites. Indeed, the difficulties of characterising the coloured people with any precision usually resulted in coloureds being defined by a process of exclusion as those people who were neither white nor African. Because of their ambivalent position within society, coloureds were engaged in a process of continually modulating their responses to social situations in order to strike a balance between their assimilationist aspirations, the realities of their exclusion from the dominant society and their fears of being reduced to the status of Africans.[10]

The ambiguities within coloured identity were manifested in a range of inconsistent behaviour within the League and in a disjuncture between the ideals and actions of its leaders. For example, within the coloured community, the League demanded the deference commensurate with its élite social standing, yet often willingly accepted an inferior status to whites. More conspicuously, the *Journal* opposed racial discrimination and rejected race as a principle for ordering human affairs, yet zealously promoted coloured separatism and in this way endorsed the precepts governing the racial hierarchy of South African society. The TLSA, in addition, claimed to stand for a broad South Africanism and strove for the full integration of coloureds into national life. Yet it failed to extend this cherished ideal of assimilation to Africans and did all it could to distance itself from them. Another glaring inconsistency in the make-up of the League was that its leaders had a strong sense of social responsibility towards the coloured labouring poor, and were genuinely concerned about their welfare, but often displayed disdain towards working class coloureds and did little to hide their feelings of class superiority.

Despite coloureds forming a subordinate group, League members displayed a robust disdain towards their working class counterparts. Class prejudice consequently manifested itself in a myriad of ways within the *Journal*.[11]

However, for the quintessential expression of class prejudice towards the coloured labouring poor, one need go no further than Dan Sampson's Presidential Address to the 1916 annual conference in which he attempted a "class analysis" of the coloured community.[12] His speech is important for the coherence and frankness with which it delineated the coloured élite's perception of the social hierarchy within the coloured community. Sampson also exemplified League ideas about the cause of these social problems as well as how they ought to be tackled. Furthermore, Sampson articulated the attitudes and assumptions that underpinned the League's civilising mission towards working class coloureds, which informed its struggle for educational reform throughout this period.

Sampson divided the coloured people into three categories, namely, the sunken, the sinking and the uprising classes. Of the sunken class he commented, "What an accumulation of filth, vice, dissipation and crime! Such a combination seems to defy all the influences of human healing. 'Past social redemption', we exclaim." The sinking class was characterised as containing neither the "openly vicious nor the hardened criminal" but as one that was indifferent to its own advancement and with its faculties susceptible to corruption. Their "indispensable needs are not prison accommodation, reformatories or police officers, but schools and teachers, or in other words, education". The uprising class, predictably, embraced "those who, being concerned about their advancement in life, zealously watch over the moral and intellectual training of their offspring". That the Coloured Commission Report more than two decades later made a similar tri-partite class distinction within the coloured population, indicates that this was a common perception of social stratification within the coloured community.[13]

An important assumption, generally shared by the League, was that hooliganism, crime, immorality and social degradation were largely the result of "ignorance" or "a lack of knowledge". This "ignorance" included not only such tangible concerns as illiteracy, or the lack of economically useful skills, but also such elusive qualities as peoples' insensibility to "virtue" and their indifference to the "noble things in life".[14] In this respect, the religious and professional values of League members converged so that there was an automatic association between ignorance and evil on the one hand and knowledge and virtue on the other. "Ignorance" was seen to breed social degeneracy, while "knowledge" was the basis of progress and civilisation. That the APO, the official organ of the African Political Organisation, contrasted ignorance as "the most soul-withering blight that can afflict mankind" with knowledge as "the wing that flieth to heaven" is an indication of this perception within the coloured élite.[15]

It is therefore not surprising that the *Journal* considered educational improvement to be the most efficient means for recasting the coloured working classes to fit its image of bourgeois respectability. Besides being the most direct agency for exposing them to the superior ways of the dominant culture, education was regarded as the most effective way of instilling the skills necessary for economic success and inculcating the exemplary values of citizenship. These attitudes were evident in the commonly expressed belief within the League that the school formed the "bulwark of civilization".[16]

For this strategy to succeed, it required the cooperation of the state and the dominant society. League leaders recognised that it was only through massive government intervention that sufficient educational facilities and other social services could be provided for the coloured proletariat. But this goodwill was clearly not forthcoming, and the *Journal* therefore blamed the perpetuation of social problems within the coloured community on society's indifference to "the large number of poverty-stricken children who are growing up in an atmosphere of vice and ignorance". The *Journal* considered the corruption of coloured youth to be an ineluctable consequence of prevailing social conditions and society's apathy towards its plight, because:

There are bands of children of tender years roaming the streets who have no homes, there are others who have homes of sorts, but who have to shift for themselves, and there are others, a considerable number, whose parents continue to scrape together sufficient to prolong their school lives to Standard II to enable them at twelve to enter a factory or domestic service. A child at twelve in a factory! What is the future of these children? Let there be no beating about the bush. The girls fall under the suggestive influences of the streets, weaken and take the easiest path, ... The boys become addicted to smoking dagga, drinking, gambling and thieving.[17]

Having drawn attention to the "deplorable condition" of the coloured masses, the natural question for Sampson and the *Journal* was, "Whence are the hooligans who throng our streets and fill our gaols; by whom were they created?" The answer he provided was typical of League reasoning on the matter: "The benevolence of a Creator intended them to be human, but the passivity of the State, with its mistaken economy is largely responsible for their degradation which brings them almost to the level of the brute."[18] The League blamed the state for the social degradation of the coloured masses for refusing to provide them with proper educational facilities. Although not explicitly articulated as such, this argument was also a rejoinder to the all-too-familiar racial explanations that whites commonly tendered to account for the social condition of the coloured community.

Sampson's reference to the "mistaken economy" of the state echoed a favourite refrain in the *Journal*'s periodic call for the reform of coloured education. The League held that it was false economy and socially ruinous for the state to squander an increasing proportion of society's resources on law enforcement, the administration of justice and the other costs of endemic criminality. Instead it advocated the preventative policy of providing all sectors of the population with adequate educational facilities. The League argued that this would in the long run benefit the whole of society by reducing expenditure on the police force, courts, jails, reformatories, hospitals and the like.[19]

It was sometimes hinted that by refusing to improve coloured education, the state was passing up the opportunity of procuring a well-behaved and skilled working class, and that the price for this mistake would be widespread social unrest that might prove to be a "menace to our future peace, happiness and prosperity".[20] In his Presidential Address of 1923, Philip Scholtz warned the authorities: "You may increase your police ... enlarge your reformatories, your palaces of justice, you will need them all and more, if you do not call a halt to this state of affairs."[21] There was, however, not much conviction behind these warnings as League leaders were well aware that neither they nor the state had reason to fear the coloured working classes who were too weak to pose a threat to the social order.

Besides their altruistic motives, there was also an important element of self-interest in the League's incentive to raise the social condition of working class coloureds. The *Journal* recognised that, in the minds of whites, colouredness was intimately associated with a number of negative, racially attributed characteristics. It was extremely conscious of the unfavourable image that most whites had of coloureds – the perception that coloureds were "a backward, lazy, debased people for whom it was better to build strong jails" and that they, for example, "lack sincerity of purpose, are too easy-going, poor in determination and possessing no stamina".[22]

In addition, rowdiness, drunkenness, criminality and the whole gamut of "immoral" and "delinquent" behaviour were sufficiently common amongst the coloured working classes to embarrass "respectable" coloureds acutely. The *Journal*, for instance, was ashamed of the "coloured hooligans and loud vulgar coloured girls who perturb our streets, parks, public gardens, foreshore, trains etc."[23] League leaders accepted that such behaviour provided bigoted whites with ample ammunition to justify racial discrimination. They feared that individual coloureds would not be able to take their rightful place in society so long as they were being discredited by an unruly coloured working class. The coloured élite argued in vain that individuals should be judged on merit, that any community should be evaluated by its upper rather than its lower classes and that the poor could not be held responsible for their predicament.[24]

Denied the option of quietly assimilating into the dominant group because only a tiny proportion of the coloured community had the physical attributes necessary to "pass for white", the coloured élite tended to react to white prejudice by adopting a civilising mission towards the coloured masses. Realising that they would not be able to dissociate themselves from the coloured labouring classes in the minds of whites, League leaders resigned themselves to the task of raising the entire coloured community to a "level of civilisation" where there would be no justification for discrimination against them. The League therefore applied itself to the pragmatic and incrementalist strategy of raising the socio-economic condition of coloureds and patiently demonstrating that there were coloureds worthy of acceptance into the dominant society. Eroding white prejudice gradually in this manner appeared to be the only viable option open to the *Journal*. Although the idea seemed never to have occurred to League members, the repudiation of colouredness could have been little more than an empty gesture.[25]

For the *Journal*, an essential part of the civilising process was the inculcation of traits such as thrift, punctuality, honesty, cleanliness, temperance, moderation, dignity and respect for authority.[26] These values were central to bourgeois perceptions of "civilised behaviour" and opposite to those usually attributed to the coloured stereotype. These were the values taken to separate the "civilised" from the "savage", the "progressive" from the "backward". Discussing the need to instil the habit of providence into the coloured people, "Advance", a regular contributor to the *Journal* asserted, "the savage races of man such as the Bushmen and the Australian Aborigines have no idea of providing for a future supply when food is plentiful" and concluded that "for a race to make progress, it is necessary that thrift habits be inculcated in the young".[27] Because they accepted this reasoning, none of his colleagues contradicted E. C. Roberts when, in his 1937 Presidential Address, he attributed the "backwardness" of the coloured people to "a lack of thrift".[28]

Ernest Moses, a prominent TLSA member and Chairman of the Coloured Welfare Association, neatly summarised the rationale behind the League's civilising mission:

> The progressive development of any nation or people is retarded and its vitality sapped by dire attacks of immorality, drunkenness, hooliganism, gambling and extravagance ... While the Coloured people of South Africa have an aristocracy of their own they also have a large mass of uneducated, undeveloped individuals without ambition, who far outnumber the handful who have been blessed and privileged to develop a taste for the better and higher things of this life ... For many more years to come the coloured people are to be judged according to the number of its weaker members, and that salvation lies only in the general uplift of the masses ... the weaker brothers and sisters should be schooled into virtue, and this can be done by no other method than by educational development.[29]

Thwarted in their attempts to shake off the automatic racial stereotyping of coloureds and to be judged as individuals, League leaders, on occasion, expressed exasperation at both whites and the coloured working classes for their predicament. Thus, E. C. Roberts complained, "It is astonishing to find men, good and sensible, ... who consider hybrid people as possessed of vices only, with no virtues ... [and] relegate the hybrid people to the lowly position of hewers of wood and drawers of water."[30] In his Presidential Address of 1934, Ned Doman vented his frustration at the tendency of whites to "point with scorn and contempt at the lowest type of coloured person he can find ... as an example of the coloured man" when they were in fact responsible for coloured working class degradation.[31] Similarly, an impatient John Abrahamse, despairing of the moral redemption of the coloured people cried out during his Presidential Address of 1938, "We are knee-haltered because a large portion of our people drag us down into a mire of filth."[32]

Within the League, class attitudes were indissolubly bound up with racial perceptions. Like white supremacists, the *Journal* tended to conflate class distinctions with racial differences, but unlike racists, they did not regard these differences as inherent or permanent. Despite its contradictions and vacillations with regard to issues of race, the League ultimately believed that all human beings were potentially equal. It was on this premise that the *Journal* held out hope that coloureds would eventually be fully integrated into a society in which race would be irrelevant to social status. This partly explains why, despite intensifying segregationism throughout this period, the coloured political leadership and the League persisted with its pragmatic incrementalism.[33] However, notwithstanding its egalitarian aspirations, the League in its daily affairs nevertheless had to come to terms with the realities of a racially stratified society and the marginality of the coloured people.

In this regard, League leaders were faced with a moral and political dilemma common to the coloured petty bourgeoisie as a whole. Because their ultimate objective was assimilation on the basis of merit, and because they were the victims of white racism, politicised coloureds embraced the ideal of non-racism as a matter of principle. They therefore rejected race as a basis for ordering society and cosseted the ideal of a meritocratic social system. But coloureds had little practical option but to mobilise politically by appealing to coloured identity. Not only did the coloured political leadership regard colouredness as a given social reality and find the inferior status of coloureds virtually impossible to avoid in practice, they were also aware that there were potential rewards consequent upon their cultivation of coloured separatism. Thus, in contradiction to their cherished ideal of non-racism, virtually all coloured political leaders chose to work within the racial system of South African society.

These ambiguities were clearly evident within the League. It is not surprising that the League did not behave consistently in matters of race and, throughout the period under review, vacillated between accepting and rejecting the inferior status imposed upon coloureds. As a result, the organisation developed an opportunistic attitude towards the racial system and coloured identity. The League realised that it needed to be pragmatic about its organisational objectives. Perceiving no other option but to yield to white power, it deliberately set out to manipulate the racial system to the minimum disadvantage of coloureds. Both within the League and the coloured political organisations of the day, it was generally accepted that more could be gained by adopting a compliant attitude toward white supremacy than by a principled stand on racial equality or a militant assertion of rights. The *Educational Journal* thus tended to object to segregation when it was considered to be detrimental to coloureds but accepted, even applauded, racial discrimination where it was perceived to be to their advantage. Its pragmatism therefore led the *Journal* to a qualified acceptance of white privilege and segregationism and even induced it to try to trade its acceptance of coloured status for concessions from the state.

The *Journal*'s readiness to sanction white privilege was, however, predicated upon the condition that coloureds were not to be denied the opportunity of progressing at an acceptable pace. For example, Israel Oppelt, after pointing to the huge discrepancy between state expenditure on white and coloured education in his 1927 Presidential Address, made it clear that he had "no quarrel with the state at differentiating. But that a difference out of all proportion be made ... is unfair." His explanation that "though we may not succeed in shaking the conscience of the lawmakers so effectively as to obtain half the European child's grant, yet by consistently agitating we shall succeed in getting more than in the past",[34] typified the League's cautious incrementalism.

With the tightening of segregation against coloureds through the 1920s and 1930s, the *Journal* increasingly resigned itself to accepting these racially discriminatory measures. It preferred to try to salvage whatever it could from a deteriorating situation, and to manoeuvre within new constraints, than to assert its rights or to fight the system. This meek acquiescence in their denigration is demonstrated by the League's reaction to the exclusion of coloureds from the Cape Town Technical College in 1925. Quite predictably, initial League objections at coloureds being excluded from the College were ignored.[35] When it became clear that it could not reverse the decision, the League's

Executive tried to negotiate the best deal for coloureds that it could manage. The *Journal* subsequently reported that

> ... interviews with the College Council have been held and the matter discussed calmly and reasonably ... The League has recognised the spirit of the times as manifested in present-day ideals and prejudices and has made no pretentious attempt at trying to force the Council to open the doors to coloured students.[36]

The Editor nevertheless felt that the League could "modestly congratulate itself" for having persuaded the College to allow coloureds to register for segregated classes in a few subjects for which it boasted "the League had been the first to clamour".[37]

The *Journal* was even prepared to accept an inferior professional status for coloured teachers. This was illustrated by the fact that the League did not seem to mind much that white teachers in mission schools received a higher War Bonus[38] than coloured teachers. It did, however, object to coloured teachers who had managed to pass for white, qualifying for the higher bonus. It would appear that it was especially female teachers who, "with the adventitious aids of rouge and powder – lots of it", were able to claim the higher bonus paid to whites. This was an emotive issue within the profession for, as a correspondent to the APO explained, it was unfair that distinctions be made between "European-Coloured" and "Coloured-Coloured" teachers.[39]

The League's readiness to accept an inferior professional status was, however, nowhere more apparent than when it endorsed the Watermeyer Commission's finding that coloured teachers had no claim to equal remuneration with white teachers.[40] The *Journal* conceded that "The European teacher will have the best pay ... No one will cavil at this." But, the corollary to this acquiescence was that the League expected the Education Department to implement the recommendation that coloured teachers be paid between sixty and seventy-two per cent of the equivalent white teachers' salaries. The League was prepared to countenance Watermeyer's proposals because it would have led to a substantial improvement of existing salaries.[41]

In cases such as this, the League accepted discriminatory measures as a way of highlighting the shortcomings of existing conditions by the standards that whites themselves set for coloureds. To the leadership of the League, any improvement in prevailing circumstances counted as progress. And no matter how small a step it was or how distasteful its implications might have been, what mattered was that it brought them a step closer to their ultimate goal. Their "progressionism" led League representatives to believe that such incremental improvements would eventually result in the attainment of their longer term ideal of assimilation.

League leaders were prepared to compromise their non-racial ideals not only because it appeared futile to make demands for full equality, but also because they considered it to be counter-productive to anger the authorities, to alienate possible allies and to forego opportunities for advancing their cause. A *Journal* editorial explained that with

> ... the intrusion of the element of Colour in a discussion of any of our ordinary human relations ... immediately a lofty wall is erected, barring all possibility of progress ... so convinced have most people become of the futility of getting any further along the road towards solving this vexed question that the little difficulties are shelved and the whole matter relegated to a temporary and convenient oblivion.[42]

Another reason that the *Journal* did not want to complain too loudly about discrimination was that they did not wish coloureds to stand out too conspicuously as a group. Wanting nothing more than for coloureds who had acquired the necessary social skills to filter quietly into the dominant society, making too great a fuss about discrimination would have compromised their assimilationist aspirations.

However, the strains of adopting non-racism in principle but accepting the racial system in practice, emerged from time to time. They surfaced most forcefully in the organisation's ambivalent response to the government's announcement in 1938 of its intention of implementing residential segregation for coloureds. J. G. Beukes in his Presidential Message to the League proffered the well-worn response of the *Journal* to the inexorable advance of segregation. He urged coloured teachers to strive for the upliftment of their community and tried to communicate a message of racial tolerance to the wider society by pointing to the interdependence between the various racial groups:

> Let us remember that we who educate are also "race- builders". Let us instill racial pride into our pupils, make them love the members of their group. There need be no clash with other groups – no antagonism, as all the different groups in South Africa must be taught to be tolerant towards each other, with mutual understanding for the common good of the whole nation. As the five fingers make the one hand, so the different groups must needs comprise a happy and prosperous South African nation.[43]

But the extreme urgency with which politicised coloureds viewed the issue of residential segregation was sufficient for the Editor of the *Educational Journal*, Fred Hendricks, to depart from League custom and to hit out at segregationists. He rejected the argument that the cultivation of coloured separatism was beneficial to the coloured community in that it stimulated the supposedly "enviable quality of race pride". This he held to be an absurd argument for coloureds to make:

> For to be proud of one's race is to be proud of one's language, ancestors, customs and achievements. And the language of the coloured man is the language of the European; his forebears are Europeans; his mode of living is that of the European and what he has achieved thus far has been in collaboration with the European. Only idle fancy of a warped imagination can visualise for the coloured people of South Africa a set of qualities or ideals entirely distinct from those of the European.[44]

The *Journal*'s rejection of race as a valid measure of human worth on the one hand, and its propagation of coloured separatism on the other, were contradictory but were not necessarily mutually exclusive. These contradictory ideas could be held simultaneously because they reflected different levels of consciousness amongst members and because they applied to different spheres of the organisation's existence. The non-racism belonged to the ethereal realm of the ideal and of abstract morality that formed part of the ultimate goal of their striving, while the accommodation with racism was necessary for them to come to terms with the realities of everyday living. Although the League had utterly compromised its ideal of non-racism, assumptions about the theoretical equality of humankind continued to inform its thought and discourse. These contradictory values continued to exist side by side within the organisation and to inform the thought and actions of its members.

In keeping with its non-racial ideal, the *Journal* intermittently denied the inherent inferiority of blacks. This, for instance, was the spirit in which the *Journal* commented on such issues as the segregation of public transport and the discourtesy of white shop assistants toward coloured customers.[45] A *Journal* correspondent echoed League sentiment in this respect when he appealed for "social and economic standards and not colour" to determine access to rights and privileges within society.[46] The League nevertheless recognised that there were substantive disparities in the objective abilities of different "races" – that some were indeed superior to others. This apparent contradiction needs to be understood in terms of the world-view of the League, in the way it comprehended its society.

The League regarded humanity as consisting of distinct population groups or "races", although the actual concept of race – as with all popular ideas – remained vague and fluid. The *Journal*, for example, described the British Empire as consisting of "... many races from the bronzed races of the East to the fur-clad tribes of North-West Canada".[47] It was accepted that some races or peoples were "advanced" and others "backward", with the basic division between the two being that of colour. The League interpreted the undisputed global domination of the Western powers and their overwhelming technological lead as proof of the "superiority of the white man". Also, in comparing whites and blacks in their daily experience, the former appeared unambiguously superior in all respects. Faced with what appeared to be incontrovertible evidence of white superiority, the League numbered the coloured people amongst the "backward" races of the world. Assumptions of coloured inferiority were also implicit in such oft-articulated fears and self-deprecating statements that the coloured people were "rapidly sinking to a level far below that of a civilised race", that coloureds were becoming a "drink-sodden race of bestial degenerates" or that coloureds were "at last emerging from the Dark Ages".[48]

The acceptance of coloured inferiority did not necessarily contradict the League's egalitarian principles because the superiority of whites was assumed to be due to historically and environmentally favourable conditions which allowed them to outpace the rest of humanity. The implication was that any of the "backward" peoples would, under the same circumstances have developed at a similar rate and to an equivalent level.[49] The *Journal* advanced this thesis on the occasion it broached the question of why the "White race is so much more intelligent than the Black". It explained that "... this greater or higher mentality is second nature, due to favourable circumstances" and rhetorically asked:

> If the black Negro were to be placed in similar favourable circumstances and remain free from all mixture with lighter-skinned races would he steadily become more intelligent and ultimately reach the level of the white race in mentality, while remaining black-skinned?[50]

The assumption that coloured inferiority was temporary and not due to innate racial disabilities, was critically important to the self-perception of the coloured élite because it allowed them to square their acceptance of coloured subordination with their non-racial ideal. Thus, while the *Journal* conceded that "We know the problem of the coloured population is a difficult one", it argued that "there are forces and potentialities in it that are perhaps undreamt of at present".[51] The League firmly believed that coloured "backwardness" would in time be overcome through improved education and exposure to the proper social and cultural environment. Eventual parity between white and black was seen to be the inevitable outcome as the level of education of disadvantaged communities improved and as Western culture and technology spread across the globe. A *Journal* editorial therefore rejected the "pathetic belief in the utter immutability of primitive nature".[52] And John Abrahamse in his 1938 Presidential Address explained, "There is truth in the advantages of birth bringing with it inherited qualities, but the claims of a race being inherently superior denies the evidence of education and opportunity being able to transform a backward people into a society of the highest culture."[53]

The League pointed to the rapid advances made by blacks worldwide as proof that coloureds not only had the potential to match whites, but also that its prediction of future racial equality was becoming a reality. Like other publications aimed at a coloured readership, the *Journal* thus drew attention to the achievements of black people, painting an exaggerated and romanticised picture of the progress being made by American Negroes, West Indians, Africans and Asians.[54]

In this respect, the coloured élite held special admiration for the Japanese who had transformed their society from an insular, tradition-bound people into a world power within a few decades. Coloureds were particularly enamoured of the Japanese because they perceived them to be a "brown race" like themselves. And in their visits to Cape Town, the predominant manifestation of the Japanese presence was that inimitable symbol of power and technological development, the warship. There is no more revealing expression of coloured petty bourgeois attitudes toward the Japanese during this period than J. R. Strydom's observations when a Japanese warship visited Cape Town harbour in 1922. Strydom, a regular contributor to the *Journal*, drew hope for the future of coloureds from those "little yellow men", the Japanese. "Commend me to the silent Japanese" he enthused:

> The wonderful little Japs ... those little, narrow-eyed, high-cheekboned and determined-looking sons of the Land of the Rising Sun [who have] ... rapidly risen to one of the most exalted and powerful positions in the civilised

world ... We saw them associating with our most distinguished and autocratic citizens on a footing of exact equality, and I believe it did our hearts good to see it all. Hopes were refreshed and revived ... Some saw our future in a different light and new possibilities appeared on the horizon, for here we saw the members of a race not quite dissimilar from ours in variegation of origin and the circumstances that attended their progress ... in the civilised world.[55]

That Strydom attributed the success of the Japanese to their "ever moving, ever Westernising" tendencies is an indication of the belief within the coloured élite that Western bourgeois culture represented the apogée of human achievement. The coloured élite therefore aspired to the acquisition of the social attributes and practices of white middle-class society because they genuinely believed Western culture to be inherently superior to other forms of human culture. Anxious to make the point that it was "culture" and "civilisation" and not colour that mattered, the *Journal* endorsed Sir John Carruthers Beattie's opinion that: "It was not merely by having a white skin that we should maintain a white aristocracy but by being white in mind and spirit and achievement."[56]

To many petty bourgeois coloureds one of the most important aspects of the "white achievement" referred to by Beattie was artistic and cultural in nature. They thus felt that an effective way of proving themselves was to demonstrate their proficiency in these activities of élite culture. The emphasis placed on aspects of Western élite culture, especially literature and music, was partly motivated by belief that these "refined" practices constituted a critical distinction between "civilised" and "barbarous" peoples. In addition, the white supremacist assumption that the inability of "inferior races" to perform esoteric "arts" was proof of their inferiority, further spurred the coloured élite to show off their talents in this regard. It was with this consideration in mind that the *Journal* wryly commented, "in this land of racial prejudice it is a relief to know that our voices do not depend upon our colour".[57] By indulging in appropriate forms of musical and literary activity, members of the coloured élite hoped to dispel suppositions about coloured inferiority and to assert their claims for acceptance into the dominant society.

It was in this context that Mr C. Dantu complimented the Music Society of the Spes Bona Club, "if the Musical Society were able to present one of their programmes in the North, it would certainly do away with much of the prejudice now prevalent in that Province".[58] Although Dantu, a former APO stalwart who had lived in the Transvaal, presumably did not really believe this to be the case, his suggestion does reveal the common hope within the coloured élite that racists would change their views if confronted with sufficient evidence of their error.

There was also an implicit belief within the coloured élite that people, if exposed to high-minded cultural influences, would be infused by the ideals and values embodied in the particular activity or work of art. Thus, for example, J. R. Strydom, one-time editor of the *Educational Journal*, described the effect of "great music" on the individual in the following terms:

> He becomes conscious of a deeper purity and nobility of mind, and all that is ideal and refined in him is lifted to a lofty standard ... Yet surely, though imperceptibly, in the lives of those who frequently listen to the best of music there is a steady change taking place all the time. Gradually the finer feelings and nobler nature of the musician and listener are being strengthened and developed and raised to a more elevated position.[59]

Similar profound processes were deemed to be at work by the *Journal* articles which described "collective singing" as having a "civilising" influence on the participants and which equated the playing of the piano with "nobility of mind and character".[60]

"Cultivating the arts" was but one way in which the League tried to manipulate South African racial ideology to the advantage of coloured people. The League's opportunistic attitude towards race was also apparent in the way it sought to establish a status of relative privilege for coloureds vis-à-vis Africans on the grounds of their higher "civilisation", and their blood ties to the white community.[61]

The political strategy that arose naturally from this situation was for coloured communal organisations such as the League to try to secure the intermediate status of coloureds, and to use this position of relative privilege to agitate for further concessions and reforms. The result, as a 1939 *Journal* editorial put it, was that "the Coloured people have quietly and steadily segregated themselves either voluntarily or under pressure of circumstances".[62] Calling on the League to capitalise on the increasingly rigid segregationist distinctions being made between coloureds and Africans, David van der Ross in his Presidential Address of 1922 urged his colleagues to use their coloured identity in more creative and affirmative ways to benefit their "race". He argued that "The classification of the races of this country under three distinct heads has come to stay, and is being more rigidly observed each day. It is expected of us now, as a people, to assert our individuality and to take the initiative in devising means for our advance."[63]

This racial ordering was recognised by the state and was built into government policy. It found expression in education policy through the ever more rigorous separation of schooling into the three racial categories of white, coloured and African. After the 1905 School Board Act achieved the state's primary aim of segregating white from black and of providing whites with compulsory public schooling, the Education Department progressively separated coloureds from Africans in the ensuing decades.[64] Indeed, a relatively thorough segregation between coloured and African schooling had developed as a matter of course, because by far the greater proportion of coloureds lived in the Western half of the Cape Province and relatively few Africans resided in this area. Also, where coloured and African people lived together, both the Education Department and the churches had, wherever feasible, implemented a rough and ready classification to allocate educational resources along racial lines.[65]

The League was encouraged in its separatism by both church and state which legitimated the racial order and implemented segregation ever more rigorously within the education system during this period. The *Journal*, therefore, claimed early in its life to find the segregatory policies of the Education Department a "welcome sign" that it was making "a genuine attempt to place coloured education on a definite basis, apart from that of the Native and the European".[66] Clearly, the *Journal* also displayed mixed feelings towards Africans. On the one hand, there was genuine empathy towards Africans within the League and a recognition that they were fellow citizens who suffered even more severely from racial oppression than coloureds. But at the same time, there was also a strong feeling that coloureds were superior to Africans because of their closer assimilation to Western culture and because they were partly descended from Europeans.[67]

The coloured élite recognised that for whites the primary racial distinction was between white and black, and because of this they often felt threatened that coloureds would lose their position of relative privilege and be relegated to the status of Africans.[68] These feelings of insecurity put the moderate coloured political leadership at pains to underscore an expressed affinity between coloureds and whites and to stress their differences with Africans. It was with the aforementioned considerations of colour and class in mind that the League Executive passed a motion thanking Canon Sydney Lavis for his evidence before the Provincial Finances Commission:

It is a mistake to judge of the educational ability of coloured children as a whole by the lower class only and one which happens to approximate more nearly to the Aboriginal. Colour is not one thing, but many, and in dealing with children who are perhaps 70 percent European in blood, it should not be surprising to find that they have intellectual ability equal to that of European children, and expressing itself on European lines.[69]

The League therefore often responded to segregatory measures by arguing that coloureds and whites shared a symbiotic relationship and that by discriminating against coloureds, whites would ultimately also harm themselves.[70] This sentiment was evident when the *Journal* highlighted a quotation from the local press that "the coloured population was now interbred throughout our whole social life and the well-being of the white depended on the well-being of the coloured".[71] This was also the premise that lay behind Dr Abdurahman's warning to whites in the *Journal* that, "The coloured man is going to drag you down if you don't educate him."[72]

Although the League did not initially include explicit racial bars in its constitution, in practice it restricted its membership to coloured teachers. Whereas earlier versions of the Rules and Bye-laws did not place racial restrictions on membership to the League, it later stipulated that "membership shall be open to all Coloured teachers" but made the vague provision that "others" who were "interested in the advancement of coloured education, may join as associate members".[73] In practice, this meant that the League did allow those few white mission school teachers who sought membership to join the association, but that it excluded African teachers. The *Journal* responded icily to a suggestion in the APO that African teachers be allowed to join the League. It replied emphatically that "The view held by the League has always been that our body stands for the coloured teacher as distinct from the European and Native." Soon after this, when a group of African teachers volunteered to affiliate to the League as a separate branch, they were spurned.[74] It was only in 1934 that the TLSA was prepared to accept African teachers as full members and this privilege was extended only to the handful of Africans teaching in coloured schools.[75] And the necessary amendments to the League's constitution were made against the sustained opposition of a minority group within the organisation.[76]

The *Journal* justified its racial exclusiveness by arguing that coloured separatism was necessary for coloureds to attain their fulfilment as a people and that this would in itself help to make for more harmonious intergroup relations. The *Journal* therefore tried to reassure others that,

"We are not of those that preach antipathy toward any race in this land. Our profession is one that makes for harmony amongst the various peoples and communities."[77] In spite of its separatist rhetoric, there was a tacit understanding within the League that the white, middle-class sector of the population was the role model that they were trying to emulate.[78] David van der Ross intimated as much when he informed the inaugural meeting of the Caledon Branch that "... the Teachers' League was not established to work in opposition to the Europeans but to make them their friends and in such a way improve their own race".[79]

The problem of Africans being disadvantaged by coloured exclusivity was very seldom directly addressed by the *Journal*. Unlike the preoccupying question of the social injustice which coloureds suffered at the hands of whites, League leaders rarely confronted the moral problem of their exclusion of Africans from the association. The League's attitude, that Africans were a group apart which needed to attend to their own interests, was settled at the founding conference. This much was clear from the absence of African teachers from the inaugural gathering and the unanimous acceptance of the motion requesting that the Education Department separate statistics on black education into coloured and African categories.[80] On one occasion, however, Philip Scholtz berated the coloured teaching profession for being too conscious of class distinctions within its own community and of racial differences in general: "We blame the European for making distinctions; and we do the same, in some cases with more severity." He quoted a couplet from Kipling to drive his point home:

> On our own heads on our own hands
> The sin, and the saving lie.[81]

It is clear that the men and women who formulated League policy and produced the *Educational Journal* were sensitive, compassionate individuals motivated by strongly humanitarian ideals. The moral dilemmas of exploiting the racial system to the advantage of coloureds did not escape them. Neither were they oblivious to the implications that their acceptance of a second-class citizenship held for their dignity. But League members did not accept the inferiority of coloured status, as evidenced by their assertions of a theoretical equality between human beings and their ideal of assimilation. Their acceptance of the racial hierarchy and their willingness to work for coloured advancement within that framework was a direct result of coloured marginality. The

League leadership and the coloured petty bourgeoisie as a whole faced the age-old predicament of marginal or colonised élite groups. This was having to weigh up the merits of resistance as opposed to cooperation with an oppressive ruling power. The ideological inconsistencies and the contradictions within the pages of the *Journal* should therefore not simply be seen as hypocrisy, glib casuistry, or the result of self-serving justification for personal advancement and opportunism, as latter day "radical" critics tend to do. The position of the coloured petty bourgeoisie within South African society was ambiguous and this was reflected in its ideology and behaviour. Coloured subordination and intermediate status together engendered ambivalent responses to white domination and the predicament of marginality. In the words of Shula Marks, "Ambiguity has been the price of survival in a contradictory world."[82]

Endnotes

1. *Cape Times*, 24 June 1913; *APO*, 28 June 1913; *Educational Journal* (hereafter *EJ*), May 1915.
2. M. Adhikari, *"Let us Live for our Children": The Teachers' League of South Africa, 1913–1940* (Cape Town, 1993), esp. Introduction and chp 3.
3. Adhikari, *"Let us Live for our Children"*, Appendix III, chapter 3.
4. *Union of South Africa Census*, 1911, (UG 32–1912), 2–3; *Union of South Africa Census*, 1946, (UG 51–1949), 4–5. Nearly 90 percent of all coloureds were in the Cape Province.
5. *APO*, 28 June 1913; *Cape Standard*, 7 June 1938; 28 June 1938; *EJ*, August 1940; August 1943.
6. *Rules and Bye-laws of the Teachers' League of South Africa*, (Cape Town, 1913), 1; Rules and Bye-laws, (Cape Town, 1916), 1; See *EJ*, June 1931; June 1933; February 1936 for updated versions of the Rules and Bye-Laws.
7. Compare the population statistics in *Union Census*, 1911, 2–3 with those in *Sixth Census of the Population of the Union of South Africa*, 1936, vol. I, (UG 21–1938), 4–5.
8. G. Lewis, *Between the Wire and the Wall: A History of South African "Coloured" Politics* (Cape Town, 1987), 2–4, 24–6, 121.
9. M. G. Smith, "Pluralism, race and ethnicity in selected African countries" in J. Rex and D. Mason, eds, *Theories of Race and Ethnic Relations* (Cambridge, 1986), 191; S. Wallman, "Ethnicity and the boundary process in context" in Rex and Mason, 229; M. Banton, *Racial and Ethnic Competition* (Cambridge, 1983), 10.
10. R. van der Ross, *The Rise and Decline of Apartheid: A Study of Political Movements among the Coloured People of South Africa, 1880–1985* (Cape Town, 1986), 71 ff.; I. Goldin, *Making Race: The Politics and Economics of Coloured*

Identity in South Africa (Cape Town, 1987), 29 ff.; Lewis, *Between the Wire and the Wall*, 2–4, 60.
11. See *EJ*, May 1915; June 1917; May 1922; October 1932; August 1937 for some examples. See also M. Friedling, "The Jeanes Plan and its Application to Coloured Education" (B.Ed. thesis, University of Cape Town, 1940), 71, 84; F. Joshua, "An Analysis of the Social, Economic and Educational Background of Coloured School Children in the Cape Peninsula", (B.Ed. thesis, University of Cape Town, 1943), 111, 117–8.
12. Sampson's speech was serialised over three editions of the *Educational Journal*, namely, August 1916, September 1916, and October 1916.
13. *Report of the Commission of Enquiry Regarding the Cape Coloured Population of the Union*, 1937 (UG 54–1937), 13–16.
14. *EJ*, January 1917; January 1931; January 1933; October 1936; Sun, 27 June 1941.
15. *APO*, 28 January 1922.
16. *EJ*, October 1916. See also for example the January 1923 and March 1929 issues.
17. *EJ*, October 1917; See also the *EJ*, August 1915 and January–June, 1927 issues.
18. *EJ*, August 1916. For other examples see the May 1923 and January 1931 issues.
19. *EJ*, August 1915; July 1917; March 1922; July 1923; January–March 1925; October 1931; *APO*, 15 July 1912. *EJ*, October 1917.
20. *EJ*, May 1915; January 1917; March 1921; July 1923; January–March 1925; January–June 1927; J. H. Rhoda, "A Contribution toward the Study of Education among the Cape Coloured People," (B.Ed. thesis, University of Cape Town, 1929), 51, 72.
21. *EJ*, July 1923.
22. *EJ*, June 1916; August 1932; February 1936; August 1937.
23. *EJ*, September 1921.
24. *EJ*, March 1929; Rhoda, "A Study of Education", 44; Evidence of a coloured deputation from Beaufort West before the Cape Coloured Commission, 13 May 1936, Abdurahman Family Papers, University of Chicago.
25. See R. van der Ross, *Myths and Attitudes: An Inside Look at the Coloured People*, (Cape Town, 1979), 26–29 for commentary on this issue.
26. *EJ*, April 1917; March 1922; July–September 1926; September 1928; August 1934; February 1938.
27. *EJ*, August 1932.
28. *EJ*, August 1937.
29. *EJ*, March 1929.
30. *EJ*, August 1937.
31. *EJ*, August 1934.
32. *Cape Standard*, 5 July 1938.
33. Lewis, *Between the Wire and the Wall*, 119 ff.; Goldin, *Making Race*, 33–40; *Cape Standard*, 27 June 1939.
34. *EJ*, July–December 1927.
35. *EJ*, April 1923.
36. *EJ*, April–June 1925.
37. *EJ*, April–June 1925; July–September 1926.
38. The War Bonus was a temporary salary supplement paid to teachers between 1916 and 1921 to compensate them for the erosion of the purchasing power of their salaries as a result of war-time inflation.

39. *APO*, 30 October 1920; *EJ*, November 1920; December 1920.
40. C. E. Z. Watermeyer, "Report on Coloured Education", 15 March 1920, *SGE Report*, 1919.
41. *EJ*, September 1920; October 1920; April 1922.
42. *EJ*, February 1921.
43. *EJ*, April 1939. For another example see the April and May issues of 1922.
44. *EJ*, April 1939. See also *Cape Argus*, 29 June 1938.
45. *EJ*, April 1917; June 1918; July 1921; January 1922; April 1922; July–December 1927; November 1928; August 1938.
46. *EJ*, April 1939.
47. *EJ*, April 1916.
48. *EJ*, June 1916; March 1917; November 1920; June 1922; June 1929; August 1932; May, 1934; May, 1935; August 1938.
49. *EJ*, June 1918; August 1938.
50. *EJ*, June 1918.
51. *EJ*, October 1920.
52. *EJ*, January 1921.
53. *EJ*, August 1938.
54. See for example *South African Spectator*, 18 May 1901, 15 June 1901; *APO*, 26 March 1910, 1 June 1912; *EJ*, August 1916; January 1917; November 1917; June 1918; March 1922.
55. *EJ*, March 1922.
56. *EJ*, December 1917. Beattie was about to become the first principal of the University of Cape Town.
57. *EJ*, January 1934.
58. *EJ*, September 1918.
59. *EJ*, January 1925.
60. *EJ*, November 1916; March 1923.
61. A similar veneration of Western bourgeois culture and denigration of indigenous culture has been noted amongst assimilated black élites in other parts of the world. See C. Degler, *Neither Black nor White: Slavery and race relations in Brazil and the United States* (New York, 1971), 110; F. Fanon, *Black Skin, White Masks* (New York, 1967), 18; A. Memmi, *The Coloniser and the Colonised* (Boston, 1967), 120–23; L. Spitzer, *Lives in Between: Assimilation and marginality in Australia, Brazil, and West Africa, 1780–1945* (Cambridge, 1989), 66–67, 139–40, 159–60.
62. *EJ*, April 1939.
63. *EJ*, August 1922; September 1922.
64. See for example, *SGE Report*, 1918, 15; Cape Archives Depot, Cape Town, (hereafter CAD) PAE, Vol. 250, SF/A2/6, S.G.E. to Administrator of the Cape, 21 January 1920; PAE, Vol. 1882, EM/372, correspondence spanning 2 September 1919 – 10 February 1920; *Education Gazette*, 17 November 1938; 27 July 1939; 10 August 1939; Maurice, (1966), 384–85.
65. CAD, 1/ECO, Vol. N2/3/3/106, correspondence spanning 17 October 1932 – 4 May 1933; *SGE Report*, 1932 – 1933, 50; *SGE Report*, 1938, 18–19; *EJ*, July–December 1927.
66. *EJ*, July 1917.
67. *EJ*, May 1915, April 1916, March 1917, April 1921, June, 1923; *Cape Coloured Commission*, 14–15; Maurice, 328.

68. *Cape Coloured Commission*, 14–15.
69. *EJ*, September 1923, December 1923.
70. *EJ*, July, 1921, July–September, 1926, August 1932, August 1939, August 1943; *Cape Times*, 11 April 1923; *Sun*, 5 May 1933.
71. *EJ*, July–September 1926.
72. *EJ*, July–September 1926. See also for example, CAD, PAE, Vol. 1862, EM/62, General Secretary of the Cape Malay Association to the Administrator of the Cape, 23 November 1928.
73. Whereas the 1913 and 1916 versions of the Rules and Bye-laws did not contain explicit racial bars, the 1931 version did. Although it is not clear when the change was introduced my guess is that the amendment was probably made in 1920 – 1921 when the League was confronted with the question of whether or not it should admit Africans and decided against it.
74. *APO*, 30 October 1920; *Sun*, 24 March 1933, 10 March 1935; *EJ*, December, 1920; David van der Ross interviewed 29 June 1981.
75. See the statistical indices on the racial designation of teachers at schools in the Cape Province in the *SGE Reports*, 1934 – 1940.
76. *Sun*, 29 June 1934, 6 July 1934, 13 July 1934.
77. *EJ*, November 1920.
78. *Report on the Commission on Coloured Education*, 1925 – 1926 (CP 1–1927), 6; *Education Gazette*, 3 September 1931, 9 August 1934; *Cape Standard*, 11 June 1940; *Sun*, 9 August 1940; Maurice, 338.
79. *EJ*, May 1922; See also Rhoda, "A Study of Education", 54–5.
80. *Cape Times*, 25 June 1913; *Cape Argus*, 25 June 1913.
81. *EJ*, July 1923.
82. S. Marks, *The Ambiguities of Dependence in South Africa: Class, Nationalism and State in Twentieth Century Natal*, (Johannesburg, 1986), 14.

6

The struggle for survival: The municipalisation of business enterprise in Langa township and the African response 1927–1948

Muchaparara Musemwa

When Langa Township was opened to African occupation in 1927, the Cape Town City Council was averse to the idea of encouraging African trade there. Langa residents were compelled to purchase their personal requirements from the city and the profits were pocketed by European proprietors instead of circulating among the African community. There was, thus, an unwritten covenant between the city local authority and white business capital that the denial of trading rights to emergent African entrepreneurs would create a large pool of customers for the businesses in the city. Although the policy of territorial segregation ostensibly meant the paramountcy of European interests in European areas and African interests in African areas, the municipality spread its tentacles into what was "exclusively" the African's domain. The outcome was a municipal monopoly over what had been the petty African trader's sole means of eking out a living. This provoked incessant struggles between the rulers and the ruled over the latter's only and indispensable means of subsistence.

The municipalisation of trading activities in Langa was embarked upon by the City Council from the late 1930s to 1948 under a thinly veiled paternalistic justification – the welfare of the Langa populace. For instance, in 1938 the Council argued for the virtues of a municipal beerhall to cater for the drinking requirements of the "bachelor" class which could not brew its own beer in terms of Location Regulations. Again, under the guise of combating malnutrition amongst the bachelors in the Main Barracks, it expropriated the eating-house from the African traders who operated their businesses there. What is characteristic of the council's trading activities in Langa is that it closed almost all the existing avenues through which such enterprises could find an outlet.

Contrary to the Council's apparently benevolent pronouncements that its monopolistic ventures were non-profit-making, intended to benefit the African in Langa, there is abundant evidence suggesting municipal profiteering. This chapter, while seeking to unravel the Council's ulterior motives, focuses on the opposition that its encroachment upon African enterprise engendered from the various affected parties in Langa, the traders, consumers, churches and civic organisations.

The municipalisation of trading activities in Langa was largely based on a reworking of the institutions already established by the Africans, such as the domestic brewing of traditional beer, which the City Council sought to transform into the beerhall system based on the Durban model. The chapter will also investigate how the people tried to preserve their culture, vis-à-vis the threat by the Council to undermine it. Symbolically the drinking of traditional beer and the act of brewing provided a continuity between the town and the countryside, in spite of an increase in its commercialisation in response to harsh economic conditions in the location. The significance of this cultural expression will be evaluated.

Attention will be paid particularly to the role played by the women of Langa as they, poignantly and quite distinctly, came to the fore in resisting the Council's encroachment upon an area they regarded as their exclusive spheres of influence: the manufacturing and selling of beer and trading in foodstuffs. This will provide us with an opportunity to view women not simply as passive, silent and as mere functionaries in the making of history but also as equally active participants as men, in the arena of popular resistance.

Crucial to our understanding of these developments is the premise upon which Council policy proceeded. It was meticulously designed to frustrate the mushrooming of a potentially strong and competitive African business class in Langa. It was also intended to ensure that both the African trader and consumer did not entrench himself in Cape Town, as this would naturally subvert the migrant labour system upon which, and for which, Langa African Township had been established.

The chapter is divided into three parts. The first deals with the way in which the total prohibition of beer brewing engendered an intense feeling of resentment among the Langa residents and how they reacted to police searches for liquor and arrests. It also considers how the failure of this policy gradually paved the way for the hated beerhall system.

The second part will concentrate on attempts by the City Council to establish a beerhall in Langa, something it failed to do on three occasions. This failure is unusual in the history of the liquor question in South Africa. In other urban centres such as Bloemfontein, Durban and Johannesburg, beerhalls were established first and riots against the institutions came later. Therefore, the unusual developments in Langa will help us to analyse the changing nature of popular but passive resistance compared with other centres. The surfacing of African political organisations in the 1940s and their involvement in the beerhall question adds a new twist to the evolving history of popular resistance in Langa.

The third and last section deals with the actual establishment of a monopoly by the Council in trading activities in Langa and the way in which it unceremoniously pushed the African traders out of business. Of interest, in this section, will be the protest by women against municipal trading, informed by an analysis of their living conditions.

Part one: Langa – A township of teetotallers?

"The question of liquor in general and 'Kaffir beer' in particular runs threadlike through the history of the African working class in South Africa".[1]

Nowhere else in southern Africa has the beerhall institution been so violently opposed and assumed such political overtones as in South Africa. The origins of the beerhall system in Durban form the major part of Paul la Hausse's seminal work.

A commission appointed in 1906 to enquire into matters connected, inter alia, with the illicit sale of liquor to Africans and the restriction of beer drinking, recommended that the manufacture and sale of beer in the urban areas should be regulated and placed entirely under municipal control. This recommendation became the foundation upon which the Natal Native Beer Act of 1908 was passed. It provided for the licensing, by municipalities, of individual Africans to sell beer. Alternatively, the municipalities could establish a monopoly in their areas.[2] For obvious reasons, the latter was preferred. In terms of the Act profits from the municipal beerhalls were channelled into the Native Administration Fund (which became the Native Revenue Account in 1924). The Fund was supposed to meet the expenses incurred in the administration of the Act for the "welfare" of the African population residing in the locations, but in practice it never did so.[3] Thus the Durban system became the model of African administration which was not only applied in South Africa but was also exported to Zimbabwe, Zambia and East Africa.[4]

But Paul la Hausse is by no means the only historian to work on the beerhall system and the subsequent riots in Durban in 1929. Helen Bradford plugged a glaring lacuna in her illuminating article which showed that the women were at the helm of the struggle against the Durban System. Her main concern was to bring to the fore the hitherto subsumed role of women in the 1929 riots in Natal. They were fighting against two oppressive systems, the tendency of patriarchal society to subordinate them to second-class status; and the racist oppressive state that instituted discriminatory policies against them.[5] For example, the 1908 Act made the drinking of beer in the municipal beerhalls a privilege exclusive to men, and also made it illegal to brew in their homes for commercial purposes. This robbed women of their sole lucrative source of income as their potential male customers gravitated towards the municipal "drinking cage".[6] Bradford transmitted "history" into "herstory" thus ascribing a significant role to women which previously had been ignored by radical feminists.[7]

Although riots against the beerhall system were a frequent occurrence in South Africa's rural and urban centres, they were not the only manifestation of African discontent. The riots in the 1920s were not merely against municipal beerhalls. There were no beerhalls in Bloemfontein but there was an equally bloody riot in April 1925 staged by women against the series of political raids and arrests for domestic beer brewing as Baruch Hirson has graphically shown.[8]

Purporting to have the welfare of its subjects at heart, the City Council of Cape Town decided to inaugurate the new African township of Langa in 1927 with the total prohibition of liquor including *utshwala*, commonly but disparagingly referred to as "Kaffir beer". Relying on its experience in Ndabeni – the location which preceded Langa, where a permit system was in operation – the Council argued that permits were open to abuse and "detrimental to the morale of the native in that it creates a sort of monopoly, only a certain number being able to get a permit to brew". Permits were issued to married householders for domestic brewing only, and they were not issued to the more than 3 500 single men who formed the largest part of Ndabeni's and Langa's population.[9] The municipality maintained that this permit system created a temptation both to these single men and to the permit holders who were tempted to sell to them illegally.[10]

Evangelical organisations in Cape Town such as the Wesleyan Methodist Church of South Africa, the Cape Town Diocesan Synod of the Province of Southern Africa, and the South African Temperance Alliance, including the Ndabeni African ministers of Independent Churches, were alone in congratulating the Council on this unrealistic policy. Their moral and Christian view-point was blended with their apparently racist fears that, "the native, once he has acquired the alcohol habit, *is physically much less capable of moderation than a European*".[11]

From the beginning, the regulation on total prohibition was a dead-letter since people had not been consulted. It was bound to be transgressed as long as Langa remained a dry island, and as long as alternative forms of entertainment and recreation continued to be virtually absent. Beer drinkers in Langa soon asked why they were the only ones not allowed to brew their own beer. Why Langa was governed by regulations totally different to Ndabeni remained a mystery to them.[12] This denial of what they considered to be a privilege, if not a right, was to bring together the beer brewers, the consumers, and in some cases teetotallers, against the municipality in a struggle over the liquor traffic. There is nothing new about this. Ndabeni residents had built a reputation for defending what they considered to be their inalienable rights.[13] What tended to bring together the beer brewers and their consumers was the symbiotic relationship between them:

> In fact that was one of the most prosperous businesses you could run then, because people had nothing to do from work – coming back just to prepare their food, the next thing... drinks [beer].[14]

As with women elsewhere in Africa, the migrant labour system, with its "rigid sexual and racial division of labour ... [which] excluded

African women from jobs in the formal, industrial sector" meant that the women of Langa depended on beer brewing, the smuggling and selling of whiteman's liquor, and petty trading, for survival.[15]

The women of Langa reworked the tradition of beer brewing and adapted it to a survival strategy by commercialising *utshwala* which traditionally had been used for ceremonial functions only. In the words of P. A. McAllister:

> People do not generally preserve old habits of customs for their own sake, but adapt these or introduce new ones, as the need arises. New institutions emerge from the old; established customs may be reinterpreted or given new meaning.[16]

In the light of the above considerations, in 1930, three years after the opening of Langa, the Superintendent of Langa, Mr G. P. Cook, was to report that it had become "practically impossible to stop illicit brewing of kaffir beer, and to control the introduction of bottled liquor",[17] in spite of frequent police patrols. In the previous month, December 1929, sixty-nine bottles of liquor were confiscated at Langa and £97.10s in fines imposed, one thousand gallons of *utshwala* confiscated and £297.15s in fines imposed.[18]

That total prohibition was an unwelcome regulation among the concerned Langa residents was made overtly clear by a resolution they made at a meeting with the Superintendent on 22 January 1930 in connection with beer permits. They called upon the Native Affairs Committee of the City Council to

> consider the *urgent necessity* of granting permits for the domestic brewing of Kaffir beer on the same conditions appertaining to Ndabeni Location, as many of our people are getting into trouble through the drink question.[19]

The Superintendent's readiness to endorse the demand vindicated the point that the situation had become untenable. The Council rescinded its resolution and removed the anomaly by regulating the brewing of *utshwala* in Langa on the same terms as in Ndabeni by permits.[20]

The municipality hoped that, armed with this regulation, it could still effectively control the liquor trade. After all, the Liquor Act No. 30 of 1928 was in place and could be invoked any time to check the smuggling of liquor. It provided for the denial to Africans of brandy and bread-yeast. There were also restrictions on methylated spirits, used mostly by the "well-to-do" Africans,[21] for the lighting of primus stoves, for fear of their being used as intoxicating gases.[22]

Even so, Africans often managed to obtain liquor by hook or by crook. White or "coloured" shebeen operators purchased liquor at retail outlets and clandestinely sold it to them. Alternatively, Africans could send "coloureds" to buy it for them,[23] although this alternative could be unreliable.[24]

Under the Natives Urban Areas Act No. 21 "intoxicating liquor" could also be obtained "for bonafide sacramental purposes".[25] This was not as easy as it might sound. The ordeal one had to go through was described by Rev. C. N. Citashe of the Ethiopian Church of South Africa:

> The Native Clergyman must apply to the Magistrate who refers the matter to the liquor branch of the C.I.D. whether the applicant is called and interrogated and the final approval obtained and the Clergyman is permitted to buy his Sacramental wine by the production of his PASS which must be endorsed by the storekeeper everytime he buys. He must frequent the Bottle Store as the permit does not allow another to deputise for him.[26]

If the process of obtaining wines for sacramental purposes was cumbersome, that for obtaining permission to brew beer for traditional ceremonies such as the Fingo and Moshoeshoe celebrations was equally tedious and people considered themselves very fortunate to have beer until the end of the ceremony. Mr F. Galo testified:

> when there was what we call "Umcimbi" maybe circumcision then we would see there's some beer there, or maybe it was through the "mercy" of the officials if they come there and they decide that they can allow this, if they decide to spill everything they just kick that bucket [of beer].[27]

Clearly, the liquor laws were a threat to the religious and cultural beliefs of the Africans in Langa as the successful completion of any ceremony, Christian or traditional, was at the mercy of those in the corridors of power.

Although the Langa residents had clamoured for the introduction of the permit system, they soon discovered it was open to abuse. The Superintendent of Langa used the system to extort rent from defaulters. The forced removal to Langa from 1927 had been characterised by resistance to the higher rents compared with Ndabeni. Very few of those who took up residence at Langa paid rent regularly. Now the Superintendent issued permits allowing four gallons per day for every married resident who was not in rent arrears.[28] That the Superintendent was using his discretion, independent of the municipality, is clear from his admission: "Whether l am, by law, allowed to refuse a permit if the applicant is in arrears with rent, is a moot point."[29] To a local authority which by 1930 had an accumulated deficit of £42 500 on Langa,[30] its "loyal and obedient servant" was being administratively efficient and deserved a pat on the back.

Ironically, however, those householders who were refused permits depended on the sale of *utshwala* to raise the money for their rents. Failure to do so usually led to summary ejection from the township. Caught in this dilemma, the tendency by the affected women was to continue brewing and risk being raided, arrested and imprisoned.[31] The sentences ranged from fines to imprisonment with hard labour. Cases in point are those of Kopolo Siyaya of No. 274 Married Quarters who was sentenced to one month, suspended for one year, for being in possession of ten gallons of *utshwala*, together with a fine of £10 or three months in jail.[32] Maria Mashoba, of No. 442 Married Quarters, was sentenced to three months with hard labour for being in possession of two flasks of brandy and six bottles of wine. Again, Emily Labule was sentenced to three months with hard labour for possessing brandy.[33] The list is endless, but these severe sentences were not a deterrent at all for the liquor traffic continued unabated.

For the shebeen operators the most unsavoury part of the raids was the high-handed approach of the Superintendent who conducted the raids himself. There were numerous cases where he met with a severe reprimand from his victims and one incident on 9 April 1939 will illustrate this. On this fateful day, the Superintendent went into the Langa Location in the early morning around 6.30am to raid for liquor. At about 7.00am he got to No. 457 Married Quarters where he asked for admission to the house, which was refused. After being delayed for twenty minutes, the Superintendent forced his way into the house and, according to him, found fourteen gallons of beer – ten gallons in excess of the permitted quantity. While the beer was being measured about sixty women took part in a "hostile demonstration" outside the house and the two African Wardsmen accompanying the Superintendent were assaulted. The woman of the house also assaulted the Superintendent.[34] Realising the threatening mood of the women, the Superintendent sent for the police, who apprehended the two ring leaders but again, two European policemen were assaulted. When the prisoners were taken to the police station, the rest of the women followed and "created a disturbance in the streets and became very rowdy outside the police station, shouting for the release of the two accused and demanding admittance to the Charge Office".[35]

The two ring leaders were charged with assault on 26 April before the Magistrate at Wynberg. The first accused was fined £10 or two months' imprisonment with hard labour, and the second, £5 or one month with hard labour. Moreover, the registered occupier of the house, No. 457 Married Quarters, was fined £3 or three weeks with hard labour for obstructing the Superintendent "by failing or refusing to open the door of his house in the execution of my duty" and fined £5 or five weeks for being in possession of ten gallons excess quantity of *utshwala*.

A few observations can be made about the women's conduct. Initially, they were protesting against the Superintendent's raiding for beer as they considered that he was doing a police duty. They accused the Superintendent of taking an active part in order to bring the system of domestic brewing into disrepute to justify the Council's proposals for the establishment of a municipal brewery.[36] At the heart of these allegations was a rejection of the Superintendent's interference with their way of life. While they did not necessarily approve of shebeens, the Superintendent's actions were a naked challenge to an institution which was not only traditionally and culturally significant but which was economically indispensable. For others, it was an opportunity to vent their anger against the harsh treatment meted out to them by the registration office when they entered the location.

In this incident one can also observe some incipient tendencies towards female assertiveness over male authority. It was unusual, if not unheard of, in predominantly patriarchal societies, the Xhosa-speaking one included, for a woman to beat up a man. But in this case, the women of Langa, without much ado, assaulted everyone from the Superintendent and the Wardsmen, to the *European Policemen* – collectively a symbol of oppression.

Most remarkable, though, was the extent to which the women of Langa rallied behind a fellow woman to the point of physically defending her. The mass hysteria that can seize a mob of this nature cannot be ruled out but, whatever reason made them act in the manner they did, it was their ability to fight single-handedly (without men) against a system that threatened their very existence that is so striking.

In September 1939 there was a general attack on the beer regulations by the Langa Advisory Board. The arrests for the possession of unfermented beer, the heavy fines imposed for the possession of even a small excess of beer over the prescribed quantity, and the fact that tired workers, as householders, had to queue for hours every week for permits, were all intensely disliked. As there was also much talk about establishing municipal beerhalls nation-wide in 1938, the Advisory Board attributed these difficulties to the municipality's "campaign against home-brewing to make way for the 'beerhall mania' of the politically-motivated Native Administration".[37]

The Langa Advisory Board was not alone in voicing its discontent. The Langa branch of the National Liberation League (NLL), a political organisation which claimed to fight for "Equality and Freedom", petitioned D. B. Molteno, the parliamentary representative of Africans in the Western Cape, on 2 November 1939. Firstly, the Langa branch sought clarity on who exactly was responsible for conducting searches in houses for beer.[38] Of late the Superintendent had increasingly assumed the role of the police in conducting raids, which the Langa residents felt were "manifestly undesirable", since "the Superintendent of Natives (Mr S. A. Rogers) who is head of the Native Administrative Branch of the Council and source of appeal by residents in matters affecting the location, should be placed in the position of having to discharge duties of a police nature".[39] As the women's assault indicated, the Superintendent was no longer to be trusted by the residents.

The second grievance was the right of a pick-up van to stop anywhere in the location and search people for liquor.[40] Amongst the numerous cases reported was that of D. Mahloane, Vice-chairman of the Langa Vigilance Association. Mahloane was stopped by an African constable on 25 October 1941 who demanded to search his attache case on the street. Mahloane refused to be searched publicly and asked to go to the police station. The African constable complied. Little did Mahloane know how his request would be interpreted. Although no liquor was found Mahloane was charged with obstructing the policeman in the course of his duty. He was refused bail and a fine of £1 was demanded from him which he refused to pay. Afterwards a senior policeman allowed bail of £2.[41]

The secretariat of the Langa Vigilance Committee was later to condemn the treatment given to Mahloane in the strongest terms:

> We wish to protest against the rough and bullying treatment meted out, and the bad and obscene language used by responsible officials at Langa Police Station, to people arrested and detained there. (Mahloane's case furnishes an

excellent example of these). Instead of achieving its purpose, such undignified behaviour casts a very bad reflection on both the victims and officials responsible for them.[42]

Their voice of protest was also echoed by the Episcopal Synod of the Province of South Africa.[43]

Finally, the Langa Branch of the NLL queried the conduct and right of the African police to search passengers alighting from the train at Langa for liquor. People resented being pitched into the pick-up van which was always parked nearby, when they objected. An informant vividly recalled how an African policeman nicknamed *Ndiyakukrokrela* (I suspect you), would stand at a strategic position at the railway station and "as people were coming home from the sub-way, he would look at them and say *Ndiyakukrokrela*! then you must just go to him".[44] The interviewee also confirmed that if one refused to be searched or was found with liquor, one was thrown into a pick-up van.[45] Nothing indicates more strongly the people's deep-seated hatred of the system than the fact that a certain *Ndiyakukrokrela* was stabbed to death as a protest against these searches.[46]

The struggles between the Langa residents, the police and the City Council, through its administrative branch in the location, were characterised by fear, mistrust, and animosity. The Langa residents were not cowed into subservience when they witnessed their rights being trampled. The brewers' resolute stand against the Superintendent's frequent raids for beer, the failure of the high fines and severe sentences with hard labour to act as deterrents, the refusal of the general Langa residents to kowtow to police searchings all demonstrate the nature of their implacable resistance.

Part two: The City Council and the "beerhall mania" of the late 1930S and 1940S

The total prohibition of domestic beer-brewing and the permit system were ineffective in checking an illicit liquor traffic which was a product of economic pressures. As a result, the Native Laws Amendment Act No. 46 of 1937 reversed this policy and provided for the operation of three methods of manufacture and sale of traditional beer viz:

- *Municipal Monopoly* – this system, if adopted, would automatically exclude both the following methods;
- *The Licensed African Brewer* – under this system, one or more African brewers could be allowed to operate under licenses issued by the local authority or regulations made by the responsible Minister;
- *Domestic Brewing and Possession of Traditional Beer.*[47]

The effect of this Act was tremendous as local authorities in the main cities of the Union implemented it forthwith. From January 1950 when the Act became officially operative, ten local authorities in the Transvaal and one in the Cape Province implemented the first system. These numbers subsequently increased to seven in the Cape, fifteen in Natal, eighteen in the Transvaal and six in the Orange Free State.[48] The Cape Town Council was not to be outdone in the marathon to establish beerhalls, but, although it had the will to do so, it lacked the requisite power because of the concerted opposition to municipal trading by a wide spectrum of the Cape Town community.

Following visits to urban centres with beerhall establishments in the Union and Zimbabwe, Colonel W. H. Quirk, Chairman of the Native Affairs Sub-Committee of the City Council, and Mr S. A. Rogers, the Assistant Superintendent of Langa Location, recommended that the Municipality assume the exclusive right to manufacture, sell and supply beer within the urban area of the City of Cape Town.[49] The merits of a beerhall were three-fold: firstly, it would cater for the requirements of the bachelor population of Langa who "have no legal method of obtaining their customary beverage except through friends or relatives living in the Married Quarters".[50] Secondly, it would reduce the consumption of liquor and thirdly, it would torpedo the illicit liquor traffic.

The sub-committee believed that domestic brewing was so profitable that men from the Transkei sent for their wives and started breweries. There were also instances of "loose" men and women who claimed married quarters in Langa on the grounds that they were married according to African custom, proliferating the breweries.[51] The third justification for the municipal monopoly was that it would bring an end to the "disgustingly filthy conditions" under which the beer was often brewed – a specious concern about the health of the bachelors, whose overcrowded conditions were ignored.

The financial position of the Council may perhaps throw some light on the local authority's real motives. The Native Revenue Account suffered from a perennial annual deficit almost every year from 1927. For the years 1937, 1938 and 1939 they were £6 041, £7 031 and £9, 624 respectively. For a local authority which did not want to burden the white taxpayer by subsidising the Native Revenue Account, which was supposed to be self-balancing, these amounts were quite large. Moreover, the base for the Native Revenue Account was very limited. Funds from the Langa residents came from fines, pass and contract registration fees and rents.[52] Given the historically erratic payment of rents, the deficit continually increased. As most of the Langa residents were migrant labourers and received very low wages, and there was no large scale business sector in the township, there was no reliable tax base.[53] If the policy of African self-reproduction was to work, Africans had to fund their own administration out of beer consumption profits.

Developments in other urban centres show beyond reasonable doubt that Cape Town's proposal was economic. Two examples demonstrate this. Since the beginning of 1938, the Johannesburg Municipality had made handsome financial returns from its beerhall centres. In 1938, the profit was £7 092, in 1939, £32 768 and in 1940, it spiralled to £63 752.[54] The profits for Durban were £38 775 in 1940. For the Cape Town Municipality to say that the financial aspect was purely fortuitous[55] in its desire to establish a beerhall, was to hide behind a transparent veil.

It is partly this exploitative profit-raising aspect of the Council's proposal which was objectionable in Langa. In June 1938 the Council's offices were inundated with protests from individuals, church, civic and political organisations.

The African traders viewed the competition of municipal enterprise with intense dislike. A municipal monopoly was also to the detriment of the consumer. The Bantu Commercial Union, an organisation of African traders, as well as the Langa Vigilance Committee argued that the brewing was better done by private enterprise.[56] The municipal scheme would throw the majority of African traders out of business as most of their trade was made of items required in the manufacture of beer.[57] Moreover, it was not in accord with the Native (Urban Areas) Act of 1923 which provided for the restricted promotion of African business or trading.[58]

Municipal intentions were made abundantly clear by the deliberations at a conference of municipalities on 28 and 29 September 1938 to discuss the provisions of the Native Laws Amendment Act of

1937. The system of licensing African brewers was rejected as undesirable.[59] Essentially the Councils wanted to limit African economic competition and control the traders tightly. The municipalities pointed out that it was not necessary at all to *"concentrate so lucrative a business in the hands of one native, however high his repute might be"*.[60] The implication of their rationalisations was indicative of the extent to which the municipalities viewed the African as a "temporary sojourner" to the city who should never join the ranks of big businesses.[61]

The beerhall proposal was also disturbing to the Christian fraternity. The Methodist Church of South Africa, Women's Auxilliary, the Western Association of Congregational Churches and the Western District Congregational Women's Association of South Africa all protested at the detrimental effects of a municipal beerhall on the welfare of the Langa residents. They vehemently argued that the municipal beerhall militated against the spiritual, social and moral upliftment of the Africans at Langa.[62]

The Christian churches considered it ungodly to sell beer on Sunday under the proposed system. They contended that it was biblically unethical and blasphemous to do so. They feared that if beer was sold on Sundays, very few people would attend church services.[63] The churches called for the diversion of funds earmarked for the beerhall scheme to the provision of educational facilities which were badly needed in Langa, given that municipal participation in the provision of education in Langa was virtually nil.[64] There were no proper classrooms and church vestries had to be used.

The Langa residents also resented the European "overstaffing" and the monopoly of jobs in the Langa Administrative Offices, whilst blacks were relegated to menial ones.[65] They regarded this as an "unfair and unreasonable practice of grabbing the African people's rights". In 1938, they were witnessing yet another attempt by the Council to create employment opportunities for Europeans in the form of a beerhall. The Langa residents complained through the Cape Peninsula Joint Council of Europeans and Africans that: "The reason for the ever mounting 'bureaucratic incubus' appears, in large measure, to be the creation of more and more posts for European administrators."[66]

The beerhall proposal also threatened to regiment the Langa residents' social, traditional and cultural practices.[67] Beer-drinking was part of an indigenous system of hospitality which meant that one consumed one's beer with one's friends and relations and important social and political issues would be discussed.[68] Some of these customs were still being observed in Langa although there is a strong possibility that they were changing in form under the influences of urbanisation. The beerhall system threatened to alter this much prized custom of limited social consumption. The conservative traditionalists argued that the white conception of the "public house" was completely alien to them.[69] The beerhall system was akin to "drinking in a cage",[70] where all and sundry would congregate, making it difficult for them to drink only with their chosen friends and guests.

Traditional norms dictated that only senior men and their immediate juniors, who were established heads of households, could drink beer. It was taboo for boys, let alone girls, even as teenagers or in their early twenties.[71] Although this was changing, parents and elders in Langa could still exert their control over the young people. But with the coming of the beerhall the older generations feared that the lever of control would slip out of their hands:

> The younger boys, who would not be allowed to partake in home drinking by reason of their age, acquire the habit of drinking in the open public bars. No one is responsible for another and each one drinks his fill in a rowdy atmosphere. Under such conditions the social custom of drinking together is degraded into drunkenness resulting in violence and crime.[72]

Langa elders also lamented the fact that juvenile delinquency would increase. Home-brewing was an institution whose decorum checked drunkenness and rowdiness, particularly among the young generation.[73] They were vindicated in this belief as the levels of drunkenness, gauged by the number of convictions, were quite low according to the Office of the District Commandant of the Police, compared with that of Bellville and Cape Town.[74] Prosecutions for traditional beer offences were, in fact, much lower than those for the possession of hard liquor.[75] This record, according to the Langa Advisory Board and Vigilance Committee, was one that a township of 4 000 inhabitants need not be ashamed of.[76]

There was support for this view that home-brewing was socially useful from the Native Economic Commission of 1932, set up to enquire into beer brewing. It recommended that home-brewing and other institutions and customs of the Africans should not be broken down. The Commissioners stated that "this can only be granted if a case is made out for it, but that it should only be refused if a strong enough case can be made against it".[77] Invoking this recommendation, the Advisory Board and Vigilance Committee challenged the municipality to allow home-brewing to continue undisturbed.

The strength of the collective arguments persuaded the City Council to shelve its proposal in 1940[78] and later it postponed consideration of the Native Affairs Sub-Committee report on 28 July 1938 and only revived the matter twelve months later.[79] But in spite of the stinging criticism it had received, the Council decided to put the proposal to a second test. Again it met with resistance.

The suspension of the beerhall proposal in 1939 was by no means the end of opposition to the system. The Native Affairs Commission of 1941 presented a much wider platform for the articulation of protest. The evidence given to the Commission by the All African Convention Committee (Western Province), the South African Communist Party (S.A.C.P.) and the African National Congress (A.N.C.) was significant for its radical departure from the mundane issues that had previously been highlighted. Their contributions were based on an in-depth analysis of the economic conditions which obtained in the Langa township.

The approach of these organisations, particularly the S.A.C.P. and the A.N.C., can only be understood within the context of the political developments of the 1940s. Unlike the decade prior to 1940, during which political activity was dormant, the 1940s were quite fervent politically. It was an era in which political movements started coming to grips with the new challenges and opportunities wrought by the wartime industrial expansion which in turn produced an increase in numbers of the African proletariat.[80]

At the outbreak of the Second World War there rose a sharp demand for labour and Africans moved to the major cities and towns from the countryside. Movement was encouraged by the relaxation of influx and labour controls by the State up until 1948. This in no way symbolised a change of heart on the part of the State but was a strategy of appeasing the Africans so as to avoid political confrontation at a time when its efforts were directed towards the war and also when black labour was needed badly. Wages too were relatively higher than before the war. However, because of widespread poverty both in cities and the countryside, and shortage of labour in the post-war period, the wages were undermined tremendously. At the same time there was a sharp rise in commodity prices of staple food and fuel, not to mention shelter and clothing.[81] This bleak situation saw an increase in the adoption of survival strategies that the cities could offer to the unemployed, such as hawking, beer-brewing and prostitution.

To the working class there were so many grievances to be addressed that, with the non-recognition of African trade unions by the State, strikes ensued. It is against this background that the S.A.C.P. and the A.N.C. began to champion the cause of the African urban proletariat.

One of the many issues that political organisations tried to address was domestic brewing. The All African Convention (A.A.C.) Committee (Western Cape) took issue with the "undue prominence" that the City Council of Cape Town gave to the plight of the more than 3 500 bachelors who were not provided with their own beer. Giving evidence to the Native Affairs Commission, the A.A.C. attacked the paternalistic attitude of the Council.[82] Most of the bachelors were migrant labourers whose object was to earn and save money to support their families in the rural areas. The beerhall system, unlike domestic beer drinking, encouraged wasteful expenditure which was undesirable socially and economically.[83] The Cape District Committee of the South African Communist Party and the President-General of the A.N.C., Dr A. B. Xuma urged that what needed to be radically addressed was the economic position of the Africans in Langa and elsewhere.[84] The root cause of the commercialisation of domestic brewing was the low economic status of the Africans which no magic wand or a beerhall could exorcise.

The S.A.C.P. and the A.N.C. argued that it was not enough just to improve wages to salvage the people from their economic plight. The solution lay much deeper. They attributed the African's miserable economic position to the denial of basic human rights and personal liberties. The freedom of the African had to be restored first by the total removal of the Pass Laws, Native Service Contract, Masters and Servants Act and the Native Laws Amendments. This discriminatory legislation placed severe restrictions on the free movement of the Africans as they could not sell their labour where they deemed fit. Their bargaining power was limited or stripped altogether. Thus they became potential victims of any unscrupulous employer. The City Council's proposal to municipalise beer brewing tended to create an erroneous impression that African rights in urban areas were dependent on their right to brew and sell beer and not on their political freedom, economic prosperity and social advancement. With the churches, the two organisations proposed that instead of spending money on a beerhall, more schools and playgrounds should be built.

Lobbying against the Council's proposal by church, civic, commercial and political organisations and above all the Langa residents, demonstrated the effectiveness of passive resistance. There was nothing really revolutionary about it. Although the solutions proposed by the S.A.C.P. and A.N.C. were radical, they were not calling for revolutionary overthrow of the state but for reforms. Understandably, the political organisations' approach was also a way of seeking a political base in the cities by addressing the African urban dwellers' problems at a time when there were few effective means of articulating grievances.

The tradition of resistance explains why the municipality failed to establish a beerhall on three occasions before 1948. Even though the Council succeeded in opening a beerhall in Langa sometime between late 1965 and early 1966, this was a transient victory.[85] The Student Uprisings of 1976 saw the destruction of 250 bottle stores and beerhalls across the country including the Langa beerhall.[86] This was a veritable manifestation of the extent to which the beerhall had become not only a political target but also a symbol of exploitation and oppression.

Part three: Muncipal trading in Langa

If the municipality of Cape Town failed to establish a beerhall as part of a new system of controlling trade and business on the Durban model, it did succeed in eliminating private African enterprise. In achieving this, the time-honoured pretext of improving the health conditions of the Africans in Langa was invoked by the Council.[87] In 1938 it was the condemnation of the "disgusting filthy conditions", under which domestic beer-brewing was practised in Langa that led to the Council proposal for the beerhall system.[88] In 1943, it was ostensibly the malnutrition of the bachelor class and the unhygienic conditions of the eating-houses at the Main Barracks operated by African traders, which caused the municipality to take over the business. In the same year, the Council resorted to health regulations to terminate the trading activities of the women in Langa when, in reality, it wanted to do away with the threat they posed to the eating-house business.

Ironically, when taking over the eating-house from the four African traders on 1 June 1943, the municipality described its monopoly scheme as a measure against the "prevalence and pernicious advance of nutrition amongst Natives, particularly those residing under bachelor conditions";[89] conditions for which they themselves were responsible. Their actions occurred against the background of an inquiry by the Union Inter-Departmental Committee on the Social, Health and Economic Conditions of Urban Natives (1941–2) which found an appalling amount of malnutrition amongst urban Africans.[90] The Committee recommended municipal distribution of protective food-stuffs. The nature of this involvement was left to the discretion of the municipalities and the Cape Town Council decided to administer a dining hall that would provide: "good, wholesome meals, giving a properly balanced diet, at cheap rates in the interests of the health and well-being of Natives in the Barracks and quarters at Langa".[91]

But malnutrition was not the only problem affecting the bachelors in Langa. The same Committee also noted the inadequacy of general health care.[92] Residential conditions in the locations were appalling, contributing to chronic disease. Instead of attacking these problems the City Council chose to concentrate on a cost-effective project – the eating-house.

The municipal trading scheme gave rise to considerable opposition from vested African interests. They perceived it as an incursion into their natural domain:

> If White and Black are divided into separate camps, it is manifestly fair and in accordance with the basic conception of segregation that the black man should be permitted to serve his own people in his own camp.[93]

What also exasperated them was the Council's back-tracking from a principle it had "wholly" committed itself to, namely that only Africans would carry on the trade in Langa location.[94] It was this betrayal that was disturbing to the traders, particularly those directly affected by the take-over of the eating-house.

Since 1927, municipal policy had been a "progressive" one. It had hired out the eating-house premises at the Main Barracks, which was comprised of four sections, to four African tenants, to sell food to the bachelors. The policy worked quite well as the bachelors were not allowed to cook their own food in the barracks.[95] However, the premises suffered from lack of maintenance. When the Committee visited the eating-house in Langa in November 1941, they described the condition as a nightmare.[96] This became the excuse for removing the four lessees as the Council blamed the bad conditions on "the incompetence and indifference of the lessees who, lacking energy and enterprise, rested on their somewhat monopolistic position to maintain their livelihood".[97]

But the up-keep of the premises was the responsibility of the local authority. In protest against the eviction orders the four tenants, Messrs Plaatje Petu, Henry Cuba, Julius Malangabi and Harry Siyaya, put it to the Mayor that for a number of years they had operated their businesses under practically impossible conditions because of the Council's total neglect in repairing the premises. Almost every year the Council had been reminded about the near derelict conditions.[98] Each section of the eating-house consisted of one bare room in which both cooking and serving were done. Now the wooden window frames had rotted and the window panes had fallen out. The tenants had to cover these apertures with sacks. The worn-out stoves installed by the Council were broken, so that the smoke, instead of escaping through the chimney, passed into the eating-house, depositing soot and grime everywhere.[99]

Repeated complaints were also made by the customers through the Langa Advisory Board. The Board wrote to the Council in 1940:

> The Eating Houses from which the men obtain their food are in a very bad condition, through no fault of the Proprietors. The Ovens smoke, there is not adequate room for storing flour and meat and everything gets covered in soot and dirt. The Eating Houses should be reconstructed.[100]

The limited variety of foodstuffs provided, along with bread and "vetkoekies" did not justify the Council's take-over of the eating-house. The Council restricted the tenants to cooking certain foods and to supplying specific commodities only. In spite of the fact that the lessees paid the same licence fees they were not allowed to trade in an assortment of goods like other General Dealers in the city.[101] These restrictive conditions militated against the growth of a strong African business class in Langa. Thus Council policy can be described as one of ensuring the submergence and not emergence of an entrepreneurial African class.

The municipalisation of the eating-house shook the pillar of the African tenants' survival. It generated a feeling of disgust against the Council which was determined to "rob us of our means of livelihood built up after years of effort, without even consulting us first and giving us an opportunity of discussing the matter with the Native Affairs Committee and making representations. We feel this is harsh and unjust." The trauma suffered by these men is evident as the three of them, Petu, Cuba, Malangabi wondered how they would fend for their families of eight, three and four children respectively, some of whom were at colleges and required school fees.[102]

As an alternative the Council offered to erect two bakeries at the Main Barracks and two at the North Barracks. If the tenants objected to the offer, and it was obvious that they would, bread would have to be bought outside the location. The rent for the bakeries was prohibitive. Firstly, they faced an increase of rent from £2.10s to £10 a month. Secondly, they would find it impossible to subsist out of these bakeries, as they were restricted to selling bread and "roosterkoek" only, unlike the bakeries in town which made most of their profits out of the sale of cakes. Unlike the eating-house business, they stood to lose the profitable trade in boiled meat, beans, mealies, "vetkoek", *amarewu* and *amasi*.[103]

These restrictions were further compounded by yet another set of regulations for the bakeries. As licensed bakers they had to operate under the general regulations that fixed bread prices and wages at certain standards which they could not afford, given the nature of their market. For example, they used to sell bread in the eating-house at $2\,^1/_4$d per lb loaf, compared with the 3d charged outside the location.[104]

While pretending to be considerate, the municipality made the offer and set regulations in the full knowledge that the tenants would find it difficult to comply with them. As the municipality expected, the four tenants could not accept the bakery business. The Council put itself effectively in control of the business without competition.

The municipality demonstrated its creeping monopolistic tendencies by arbitrarily terminating the licences of the tenants. At two meetings, held on 24 October and 2 November 1941, resolutions were passed, largely by the bachelors, rejecting the municipal scheme.[105] This was symptomatic of the strong communal spirit among the residents of the barracks and the tenants, as well as women traders, as will be seen later. The eating-house was important to the bachelors in that they could get food on credit, and could get loans and aid when they were not working.[106] They could not, therefore, support the take-over by Council of their reliable form of "social security".

The Langa Advisory Board and the Vigilance Committee urged the Council, instead of establishing a municipal eating-house in the location, to emulate what had been done in other cities. For example, in Durban the municipality opened eating cafes near places of work in the town itself. Such a cafe was desperately needed in Cape Town as well as at the Dock area, where most workers bought from Greek shops at exorbitant prices. They argued that in Langa the eating-house should be renovated and the tenants supported.[107]

Without giving the Langa residents and other organisations a platform to state their case as they had done before, the Council unilaterally decided to take over the eating-house. Its disregard of the voice of the official African body – the Advisory Board – suggests that both the Council and the residents viewed it as a "sham democracy".

Contrary to its pronouncements that it was not interested in profiteering, the Council recorded some handsome financial returns on the eating-house. Takings at the kitchen rose from £397 in June 1943 to an average of approximately £1 200 per month, with the revenue fluctuating broadly between £1 100 and £1 400.[108] It suggests that, by eliminating competition, the people had no alternative but to buy at the municipal eating-house.

The proceeds earned from the eating-house made the Council more ambitious as it set about introducing new profit-generating projects in Langa. It also approved the distribution by the municipality at cost of milk, vegetables, fruit and fuel,[109] and the City Council took over the selling of these items in April 1944 "for the benefit of the residents of the Location".[110] In order for the fruit, vegetable and coal depot to be self-supporting, the Manager of Native Administration, Mr S.A. Rogers, developed a garden next to the Main Barracks. He did so, although no land had been made available to the residents for such a purpose, despite the 1942 Union Inter-Departmental Committee recommendation that:

> The production of vegetables and fruit in the locations themselves by *the private efforts of their occupants* is potentially a very useful method of supplementing dietaries otherwise deficient in these protective foodstuffs.[111]

The Committee went on to suggest the inhabitants be offered free seeds or seedlings (from a municipal nursery) and prizes for well-kept domestic vegetable gardens. The Johannesburg Municipality tried the scheme and it proved a success,[112] but the Cape Town Council chose instead to own and monopolise the vegetable gardens. By July 1945, Mr Rogers was able to report that he had made a profit of £18 on the fruit, vegetable and coal depot and a profit of £256.6s on the vegetable garden for the five months ending 31 May 1945.[113]

What was perhaps resented most about the Council's unpopular trading practices was the way in which they nibbled at the means of survival of the women of Langa. It has been pointed out elsewhere in this chapter that the 1940s was generally a politically turbulent decade. Poverty, the rising cost of living and food shortages became the order of the day in the Union. Prices of staple foods rose sharply by 91 per cent between 1939 and 1944 with the result that both the cost of living allowances and wages were far outstripped.[114] This had been further compounded by dislocations in the supply system during the Second World War, which led to a shortage of basic food-stuffs in shops.[115] This scenario had a direct impact on African mothers in that:

> Price rises and food shortages directly threatened the health and stability of their families and infringed on their daily lives in such a way as to force them to look outside the home to the wider political and economic context in which they were located.[116]

It is precisely within this context that women in Langa reacted with bitterness to the Council's interference with their mainstay.

For the women of Langa, petty trading was nothing new. In Ndabeni they had successfully supplied foodstuffs such as cakes, bread, fruit, vegetables, ginger and hop beer to the bachelors. Before 1943, they used to operate "freely" despite the existence of the Health Regulations. But the women's small-scale trade was a direct challenge to the municipal eating-house business and the Council was determined to see it eliminated because it was "... losing hundreds of pounds as food at the Eating House was left over".[117] It was in this situation that the Council invoked sanitary considerations. Dr T. S. Higgins, the Medical Officer of Health, reported:

> When the central eating-house in the township was taken over by the municipality the practice [of selling cakes and bread] grew considerably and children and others are seen hawking the cakes in the bachelor's quarters under undesirable conditions and also selling ginger beer and hop beer.[118]

The Council's crackdown policies against the women becomes clear when it is observed that this type of trade had been going on for years and no action had been taken against them before. Not surprisingly the women questioned the Council's sincerity in enforcing the Health Regulations. They protested:

> Dr Shaddick Higgins condemned the Barracks at Langa only a couple of years

ago and yet these are still not improved, in fact they are worse. Further, when the eating houses were run by private African individuals the Council neither cleaned nor renovated them – the condition of these deteriorated and became unsafe for health.[119]

What is striking about the women is their perception of their petty trade as a survival strategy and not a hobby. The selling of refreshments, home-made cakes, minerals, sheep heads and sheep "feet" and other foods showed the resourcefulness and innovativeness of the hard-working and economically active women who could not penetrate regular wage employment. For those doing "piece-jobs",[120] petty trading was a way of supplementing their meagre incomes or their husband's. Their husbands received low wages ranging from £5 to £10 per month. But it was not every husband in Langa who worked and it was also not every woman who had a husband to fend for the family – some were widows.[121] It was such a background that forced the women to devise strategies for surviving. Accordingly, the Women's Council Section of the Western Province Joint Vigilance Association (W.P.J.V.A.) titled its statement of protest to the Mayor in 1943, "Necessity is the Mother of Invention".[122]

Theirs was not a business of such gigantic dimensions as to warrant any trading licences, or one that could subvert the Council's monopolies. It was

> a sort of reciprocal supplementing of earning power, an agreement is made whereby a house-wife agrees to help a certain number of friends with these commodities that appeal to them. The friends, in turn agree to repay the housewife, in cash, for her humane services.[123]

The women felt that their system was one that was not only geared towards the generation of profit but was also characterised by magnanimity – it was a kind of social service based on mutuality, as payment was made by friendly agreement on the convenience of the "debtors". They unreservedly condemned Council actions:

> We are totally against any form of trading at Langa by the Municipality. Africans are not allowed to trade anywhere else except in the locations, so therefore, instead of taking away this only right of ours, we feel that the Council should rather extend suitable facilities for our trading e.g. building premises and letting these to Africans.[124]

It is no wonder that the African women of Langa joined the Women's

Food Committee, an organisation that was formed in response to the unbearable pressures brought to bear upon them by the rising costs and uncertain supplies of food. The so-called "food crisis" forced the Government to bow to pressures from the Food Committee to ensure a systematic rationing of basic foodstuffs. In response the Government introduced mobile food vans. The vans sold groceries that were scarce in townships and suburbs at regular prices. It was out of the queues of women that formed to wait for the vans that the Women's Food Committees grew. It was to become the recruiting ground of both the Communist and the National Liberation League in Cape Town.[125]

Conclusion

What emerges from the discussion is the centrality of the economic conditions among Africans to their struggle, not only to keep the municipal monopoly system at bay, but also to survive. The success of this enterprise could only be realised if the social, political and economic conditions of the people were radically improved. Municipal beerhalls serve as part of a whole range of recreation and entertainment provisions where people could go freely to "steam off the mind" after a hard day's work. Its success depended on competition, as this ensured maximum efficiency and provision of the best quality of goods. None of these indispensable ingredients existed in the Cape Town municipal proposals for a beerhall and therefore it could not appeal to would-be patrons.

The problem of malnutrition was one that could not be solved at branch level by the establishment of an eating-house. The root of malnutrition was the ridiculously low purchasing power of the urban Africans. Malnutrition could only be overcome by a general rise in wage levels, and a non-paternalistic promotion by both Government and local authorities in the promotion of socio-economic community projects that raised people's living standards. This could be realised by the extension of legislation, such as that which operated for the benefit of European women and children, like the Children's Act, to include all the races, particularly Africans. This could only materialise in circumstances in which Africans were not denied their political rights.

The municipalisation of trading activities in Langa and the Council's attempts at social control, form a distinct area of urban conflict. Moreover, the residents' handling of this conflict sharpened their political awareness and strengthened their resilience. This also prepared them for their reception of the political programmes of the C.P.S.A. and the A.N.C. in the 1940s. Not only do they strike at the centre of African urban existence but they also lay bare the contradiction between official versus popular perceptions about life in the city.

Endnotes

1. P. La Hausse, "Alcohol, the Ematsheni and Popular Struggle in Durban: The Origins of the Beer Hall in South Africa 1902 – 1908", Africa Seminar, Centre for African Studies, U.C.T. 1983,
2. *Report of the Native Affairs Commission 1941* (UG 42–1941). Also la Hausse, "Alcohol, the Ematsheni and Popular Struggle in Durban", 15.
3. UG 42–1941.
4. H.F. Wolcott, *The African Beer Gardens of Bulawayo* (New Jersey, 1974), 24; E. Colson and T. Scudder, *For Prayer and Profit: The Ritual, Economic, and Social Importance of Beer in Gwembe District, Zambia 1950 – 1982* (California, 1988), 55.
5. H. Bradford, "'We are now the men': Women's Beer Protests in the Natal Countryside, 1929", in B. Bozzoli, ed, *Class, Community and Conflict*, (Johannesburg, 1987).
6. Africans regarded the beerhall as being synonymous with a cage in which they would not drink freely as they would do at their homes as they would be under the watchful eye of the beerhall policemen.
7. Bradford, "We are now the men", 316–317. Bradford makes the point that radical feminists promote "a tendency in patriarchal society for 'her story' to be transcribed into 'history'" by which she meant the role of women in history is almost always made to be overshadowed by that of men.
8. B. Hirson, *"The Bloemfontein Riots, 1925: A Study in Community Culture and Class Consciousness"*, Collected Seminar Papers, 13(13), University of London, Institute of Commonwealth Studies, 1984.
9. Cape Archives (hereafter CA), 3/CT 4/1/5/1262.
10. CA, 3/CT 4/1/5/1262.
11. CA, 3/CT 4/1/5/1262, Memorandum to the Mayor of Cape Town from Archbishop of Cape Town, Charles Savage et al., July 1924. The emphasis is mine.
12. CA, 3/CT 4/1/5/1262.
13. C. Saunders, "The Creation of Ndabeni; Urban Segregation and African Resistance in Cape Town", *Studies in the History of Cape Town* (hereafter *Studies*), 1, (1984), 176–184.
14. Interview, Mr F. Galo, Langa, 24 August 1991.
15. C. Walker, ed, *Women and Gender in Southern Africa to 1945* (Cape Town, 1990) 190.
16. P.A. Mc Allister, "Beer and the Unity of Study: Notes on the History of Xhosa Beer Drinking and on Combining Cultural Analysis and 'Political Economy'

Approaches in Anthropology", Rhodes University Conference, 1987, 1.
17. CA, 3/CT 4/1/5/1262, Superintendent's Report on 29 January 1930.
18. CA, 3/CT 4/1/5/1262.
19. CA, 3/CT 4/1/5/1262.
20. CA, 3/CT 4/1/5/1262.
21. Liquor Act No. 30 of 1928.
22. Manuscripts and Archives, University of Cape Town, Molteno Papers (hereafter MP), BC579 D1.9.
23. W. Schärf, "The Impact of Liquor on the Working Class (with particular focus on the Western Cape). The Implications of the Structure of the Liquor Industry and the Role of the State in this Regard", (M.Soc.Sci. thesis, University of Cape Town, 1984) 78.
24. Interview, Mr Galo, Langa, 24 August 1991.
25. Natives (Urban Areas) Act No. 21 of 1923, Section 19 (1).
26. MP, BC 579. D.1.9.
27. Interview, Mr Galo, Langa, 24 August 1991.
28. CA, 3/CT 4/1/5/1266, Report from the Native Affairs Committee.
29. CA, 3/CT 1/4/10/1/1/8, Superintendent's Report, 6 Nov. 1935.
30. *Cape Times*, 1 October 1930.
31. CA, 3/CT 1/4/6/6/4/1/2.
32. CA, 3/CT 1/4/10/1/1/10, Superintendent's Report, 10 Feb. 1942.
33. CA, 3/CT 1/4/10/1/1/10.
34. CA, 3/CT 1/4/6/6/6/4/1/2, Superintendent's Report, 8 May 1939.
35. CA, 3/CT 1/4/6/6/6/4/1/2.
36. CA, 3/CT 1/4/6/6/6/4/1/2, Superintendent's Report, 8 May 1939.
37. CA, 3/CT 1/4/6/6/6/4/1/2, Mins of the Langa Advisory Board meeting, 12/9/1939.
38. MP, BC 579 A24.55 NLL – Memorandum to Molteno, 2 November 1939.
39. CA, 3/CT 1/4/6/6/6/4/1/1 – Memorandum from the Langa Advisory Board to the Town Clerk, 1 July 1939.
40. MP, BC 579 A24.55.
41. MP, BC 59 A24,431.
42. MP, BC 59 A24,431.
43. MP, BC 59 A24,431.
44. Interview, Mr Zandi S. Ntshuntshe of 61 Special Quarters, Langa, 31 August 1991.
45. Interview, Mr Zandi S. Ntshuntshe of 61 Special Quarters, Langa, 31 August 1991.
46. Interview, Mr Zandi S. Ntshuntshe of 61 Special Quarters, Langa, 31 August 1991.
47. The Native Laws Amendment Act No. 46 of 1937.
48. Report of the Native Affairs Commission 1941.
49. MP, BC 579 B.25 Report of the Native Affairs Sub-Committee, May 1938.
50. MP, BC 579 B.25. See also CA, 3/Ct 1/4/10/1/1/12 Reference by Council 10 March 1947.
51. MP, BC 579 B.25.9.
52. W. Schärf, "The Impact of Liquor on the Working Class", 49.
53. W. Schärf, "The Impact of Liquor on the Working Class", 49.
54. *Race Relations News*, 3(8).
55. CA, 3/CT 1/4/6/6/4/12, Report of the Native Affairs Sub-Committee, July 1939. The Sub-Committee was set up by the Native Affairs Committee of the Cape Town City Council.

56. CA, 3/CT 1/4/6/6/4/1/2, Statement of views of the Bantu Commercial Union June 1938.
57. CA, 3/CT 1/4/6/6/4/12, Report of the Native Affairs Sub-Committee July 1939.
58. Natives (Urban Areas) Act No. 21 of 1923.
59. CA, 2/CT 1/4/6/6/4/1/1, Memorandum to Town Clerk on Conference of Municipalities, 22–29 September 1938.
60. CA, 3/CT 1/4/6/6/4/1/1. The emphasis is mine.
61. CA 3/CT 1/4/6/6/4/1/2.
62. CA, 3/CT 1/4/6/6/4/1/2.
63. CA, 3/CT 1/4/6/6/4/1/2.
64. M. Wilson and A. Mafeje, *Langa: A Study of Social Groups in an African Township*, (Cape Town 1963), 103.
65. CA, 3/CT 4/2/1/1/617, Native Affairs Committee Ordinary Minute 1947.
66. MP, BC 579 B25.64, Memorandum on Beer Supply at Langa March 1947. CA, 3/CT 1/4/6/6/4/1/2, The Cape Peninsula Church Council – memo to the Town Clerk, 18 July 1938.
67. MP, BC 579 B25.64.
68. MP, BC 579 B25.11.
69. MP, BC 579 B25.11.
70. MP, BC 579 B25.9.
71. *The South African Outlook*, 71, (November 1941), 219.
72. MP, BC 579 B25.24.
73. MP, BC 579 B25.24.
74. 33, 27 and 22 convictions for 1938, 1939 and 1940, compared with 3501, 3577 and 3711 in Cape Town. MP, BC 579 B25.32 Figures from the Office of the District Commandant Aug. 1941. UG 33–1945, *Report of the Cape Coloured Liquor Commission of Inquiry 1945*, 23.
75. CA, 3/CT/1/4/6/6/4/1/2, Superintendent's Report, 9 June 1939.
76. CA, 3/CT 1/4/6/6/4/12, Report of the Native Affairs Sub-Committee, July 1939.
77. UG 22–1932, *Report of the Native Economic Commission 1932*, para. 762.
78. CA, 3/CT 1/4/6/6/1/2.
79. CA, 3/CT 1/4/6/6/1/2; CA, 3/CT 1/4/6/6/4/12, Report of the Native Affairs Sub-Committee July 1939.
80. T. Lodge, *Black Politics in South Africa since 1945*, (Johannesburg, 1990), 11.
81. Lodge, *Black Politics in South Africa*, 12.
82. MP, BC 579 B25.24 A.A.C. evidence to the Native Affairs Commission on the Beer Question, 1941.
83. Wilson and Mafeje, *Langa*, 147.
84. *Inkokeli ya Bantu*, (October 1941), Dr A.B. Xuma's Evidence given before the Native Affairs commission. (1941). See also: MP, BC 579 B25.41 Cape District Commission of the S.A.C.P. Evidence given before the Commission, Oct. 1941.
85. *Cape Times* 23 November 1965.
86. W. Schärf, "Liquor, the State and Urban blacks" in D. Davis and M. Slabbert, eds, *Crime and Power in South Africa: Studies in Criminology* (Cape Town, 1985), 56.
87. For details see M.W. Swanson, "The Sanitation Syndrome: Bubonic Plague and Urban Native Policy in the Cape Colony 1900–1909", *Journal of African History*, XVIII, (1977).

88. MP, BC 579 B25.24.
89. CA, 3/CT 1/4/6/1/1/10, History of Main Barracks Eating House, Langa Township, June 1943.
90. UG 7–1942, *Report of the Inter-Departmental Committee on the Social, Health, and Economic Conditions of Urban Natives (1941–2)* (Chairman Mr D. Smit), 5.
91. CA, 3/CT 1/4/6/1/1/10, History of Main Barracks.
92. UG 7–1942.
93. MP, BC 579 B11.40, African Traders' memo to the Mayor, 30 October 1941.
94. MP, BC 579 B11.40.
95. CA, 3/CT 1/4/6/1/1/10.
96. *The South African Outlook*, (December 1941).
97. CA, 3/CT 1/4/6/1/1/10.
98. MP, BC 579 B11.40.
99. MP, BC 579 B11.40.
100. MP, BC 579 B11.40.
101. MP, BC 579 B11.40.
102. MP, BC 579 B11.40.
103. CA, 3/CT 1/4/10/1/1/9, Minutes of the Langa Advisory Board, 10 September 1940.
104. CA, 3/CT 1/4/10/1/1/9.
105. MP, BC 579 B11.45 Statement by the Cape Peninsula Joint Council of European and Africans, 7 November 1941.
106. CA, 3/CT 1/4/10/1/1/9, Minutes of the Langa Advisory Board, 10 September 1940.
107. CA, 3/CT 1/4/10/1/1/9, Minutes of the Langa Advisory Board, 10 September 1940.
108. CA, 3/CT 1/4/6/1/1/10.
109. UG 7–1942.
110. CA, 3/CT 1/4/6/1/1/10.
111. UG 7–1942, para. 71. The emphasis is mine.
112. UG 7–1942, para. 71.
113. CA, 3/CT 1/4/10/1/1/10, Manager of Native Administrator's Report, 10 July 1945.
114. P. Walshe, *The Rise of African Nationalism: the African National Congress, 1912 – 1952*, (London, 1970), 302.
115. C. Walker, "'We fight for food': Women and the 'Food Crisis' of the 1940s", *Work in Progress*, 3, (1978), 18.
116. Walker, "We fight for food", 20.
117. MP, BC 579 A24.403, Statement on the Case of African Women's Protest.
118. MP, BC 579 A24.438, Medical Officer of Health Report on Making and Sale of foodstuffs by housewives at Langa Location.
119. MP, BC 579 A24.403.
120. "Piece jobs" are different types of jobs a person can do in a week or more to supplement his/her little income.
121. MP, BC 579 A24.403.
122. MP, BC 579 A24.403.
123. MP, BC 579 A24.403.
124. MP, BC 579 A24.403.
125. Walker, "We fight for food", 19.

7

The planned destruction of District Six in 1940

Naomi Barnett

Cape Town's District Six was dealt its deathblow on 11 February 1966, when it was declared white under the Group Areas Act. In little more than a decade it was bulldozed to the ground, its people scattered over the Cape Flats. Only a handful of churches and mosques remained amidst the rubble and weeds to bear witness to the existence of what had undoubtedly been Cape Town's most lively and exotic quarter. Apartheid had ended its existence. Yet, the end of District Six had been planned over a quarter of a century earlier, on the drawing boards of town planners, architects and engineers employed on the planning and designing of what was to be named the "City of Cape Town – Provisional Town Planning Scheme of that portion of the municipality extending from Bakoven to Woodstock/Trafalgar Park".

In 1934, a Town Planning Ordinance was introduced which stipulated that the Cape Town Council produce a plan for the city within three years. The same year saw the passing of the Slums Act which, it was hoped, would help to eliminate slums comprehensively. The two pieces of legislation precipitated a proposal for the destruction of District Six which preceded the better-known removal by about 30 years. By the 1930s slum clearance had been continuing sporadically in the city for nearly 20 years. But town planning was a relatively new art. The City Engineer's department tackled the inner city first, since it was obviously the area where the need for zoning, street layout, slum clearance and rehousing was most urgent. The development of the new foreshore with land reclaimed from the sea was also imminent. These three aspects of the city's advance all had bearing upon one another and needed master-minding into a harmonious whole. That, no doubt, is what the Cape Town City Engineer's department hoped to achieve.

The Cape Provincial Ordinance No. 33 of 1934, with similar town planning ordinances in the other three provinces, was to lead to planned "urban renewal" in Cape Town, Johannesburg, Durban, Port Elizabeth and other larger towns. In practice, this meant the clearing out of the inhabitants of those densely populated areas within city centres which were in closest proximity to commerce and industry. In Cape Town, working class people had congregated in District Six in increasing numbers after World War I in search of shelter and a means of livelihood. Its location was attractive. District Six was within walking distance, or a short bus ride away, of places of employment for most of the local bread-winners. One of the oldest inhabited suburbs of the city, it was also well provided with schools, churches, synagogues, mosques, bioscopes, shops, fish and other markets, butcheries, hotels, cafes, restaurants, pubs, bottle stores, garages, workshops, industrial buildings and other amenities. In the 1930s, it was to acquire a well-run cultural centre and library, the Liberman Institute. It was the birthplace of leading writers, musicians, actors, politicians, teachers, lawyers, doctors, and academics. Its overcrowded slums were also home to the unemployed, to gangs, and to criminals of various kinds. But the bulk of its inhabitants were law-abiding citizens with deeply-rooted family and community ties.[1]

When the major cities of South Africa started planning urban renewal in the 1930s they were influenced less by British models of town planning, which had evolved from an ideology of social reform and the garden suburb, than by the United States. American planners laid greater influence on the rational arrangement of urban space through zoning in order to expedite efficient economic production.[2] In South Africa, where class and race were interlinked, urban planning, economic zoning and policies for urban renewal became closely associated with those of segregation.

When the Provisional Town Planning scheme was displayed for public viewing in the Drill Hall in the early months of 1940, it was immediately apparent that its main focus was concentrated on District

Six and that it constituted a very real threat to the continued existence of the area. The *Cape Argus* quickly got the message, broadcasting it in banner headlines: END OF DISTRICT SIX PLANNED ... £1 MILLION TO WIPE OUT DISTRICT SIX![3] It is not surprising that part of the provisional town planning scheme evoked the most interest, called forth protest and, as a corollary, justification.

Shortly before the scheme was put on public display the City Engineer, W. H. Lunn,[4] had issued a special memorandum[5] asking the Council "to define a line of policy taking into consideration every aspect of the probable growth of the city and the facts that might have an influence on the future development of this area", including the unhealthy slum conditions, overcrowding, dilapidated structures, and extremely bad layout. He reiterated that the new developments on the foreshore "demanding a continuity of the existing city, affect any improvement scheme for the area, and that there existed a demand for industrial development within the area but that, nonetheless, some accommodation must be reserved for residential purposes".

Only a replanning scheme on "drastic lines and on such a scale as to practically wipe out the existing layout", could create substantial improvement and remove slum conditions. Schools, churches and industrial buildings that could be retained would be absorbed in the replanning. The slum area of District Six covered approximately two hundred acres with 3 325 affected buildings, of which 2 985 were residential – mainly single one-storey dwellings. Working from the most recent census returns, Lunn reported that there were 1 738 Europeans, 932 "natives", 973 Indians and other Asiatics, and 23 952 other coloured persons, making a total of 27 595, ie about one quarter of the 108 000 people living in the whole area covered by the Provisional Town Planning Scheme.[6] A strip along and including Hanover Street[7] was excluded from the slum clearance area because "most of the highly-valued properties in District Six abut Hanover Street".[8] The buildings were mostly commercial and not in slum condition.

One of the most drastic aspects of the scheme was a proposed new road system, since Hanover Street was too narrow to serve as a main artery and the cost of widening prohibitive. This system was outlined in greater detail in a later report.[9] In District Six, Hanover Street was to remain undisturbed but a new 100 ft wide street was to extend from Darling Street and run roughly parallel to it. This new road would "form part of an arterial road from the City serving not only the District Six area, but extending through to Woodstock". It was sited within the demarcated slum clearance area and was at present "almost entirely covered by slum dwellings". Listed as another "important improvement" was the proposed widening of Constitution Street and Upper Constitution Street to 90 feet. This would form part of the scheme extending Wale Street to Buitenkant Street and hence to De Waal Drive.

The planners were also seeking to provide an entrance to the new foreshore area from De Waal Drive without traffic having to traverse the city. For this purpose, there would be a large vehicular bridge over the railway track system from Stuckeris Street in District Six to link up to the new Marine Drive and the south-east end of the new dock basin. Stuckeris Street would be connected with De Waal Drive by a wide road which would go almost entirely through the slum clearance area. Widening and improving Tennant Street (on the outskirts of District Six) would enable traffic from the Gardens and Oranjezicht areas to approach the new foreshore area and the roads leading to the north, without the necessity of passing through the city. Tennant Street, extended to a width of 90 feet, would link up with the new extended Strand Street near the early morning market, go right across District Six to Mackenzie Street (on the opposite outskirts of District Six) and join up with the ring road that extended Jutland Avenue (lower Vredehoek area) to Camp Street and Tamboerskloof – opening the way to Camps Bay. Thus:

> In the scheme of replanning District Six a complete redevelopment plan has been devised on the assumption that all the buildings, except those that are of sufficient value to preserve will be demolished as part of the slum clearance scheme and the land acquired under the Slums Act, so that the existing street system to a great extent has been entirely ignored and the desirable street system devised as though a new area were being dealt with.[10]

The City Engineer considered it was unnecessary to provide for the redevelopment of the slum areas "at this juncture". Indeed, his report stated:

> The clearance of such large areas would obviously take a number of years and while in progress and even as an interim measure to prevent waste and fruitless effort, it is recommended that ... all development within the slum areas be prohibited, unless new structures are contemplated which will conform to the proposed provisions of the scheme for the redevelopment of these areas.

This delay arose from the perception that the District Six renewal was intimately connected with proposals for the Foreshore development. Until the layout of the latter was complete and accepted, the necessary links with District Six could not be implemented. Lunn's report did not have a smooth passage, meeting opposition from the press and public, and internally from the Housing and Slum Clearance Committee, and the Medical Officer of Health, Dr T. Shadick Higgins.[11]

Initially, Lunn had endeavoured to prove that the changes planned for District Six could be achieved at "little or no cost" to the Council. Apart from emphasising the "cheapest money available" proposition, he also advised the Council to reimburse itself by pointing to the advantages of selling the newly-zoned land. The commercial zone, where "industries, warehousing, shopping and residential buildings would be permitted under proper restrictions", had a land saleable value of £619 218, he reported.[12] That of the proposed residential zone he estimated at £269 474. This could be sold and developed under private enterprise or be utilised by the Council for housing schemes. He anticipated that not more than half the present population of between 27 000 and 28 000 could be accommodated in the area. Moreover, he considered that the value of the land (in District Six) would make a sub-economic housing scheme impracticable. The £1 million he estimated it would cost to acquire the properties in the slum clearance area could, he was sure, be "gradually recovered"[13] and, indeed, would ultimately enrich the city.

The City Engineer emphasised that there could be no half measures in solving "this problem" (ie the redevelopment of District Six) – local improvements would only be a waste of energy and money. "Unless this sore can be entirely obliterated, it will recur and break out in other parts."[14]

Lunn's report was adopted at a special meeting of the City Plans and Development Committee on 26 February 1940 without any recorded discussion and submitted to the full Council for consideration at the end of the month.[15] Meanwhile, the required procedure was set in motion: the scheme was advertised in English and Afrikaans once a week for three weeks in the *Provincial Gazette*, in local newspapers and by public posters. Associations and the public were given six weeks to make representations and objections.

Thus, at the February Council meeting the Plans Committee, stressing that the Council would not in any way be committed by the adoption of the Provisional Town Planning Scheme, "which is merely a basis upon which the final Town Planning Scheme will be built", asked Council to adopt it "with the sole object of placing it before the public" so that the views of ratepayers, architects, surveyors and technical bodies might be ascertained.[16] With such assurances, the scheme had an easy passage through Council, though some councillors, sensitive to the public criticism which descended on their heads when the scheme was exhibited in the Drill Hall, later claimed that they had been "tricked" into voting for it. Even before this the scheme evoked considerable internal wrangling within the City Council committees and departments.

The Housing and Slum Clearance Committee had decided to do some investigation of its own. A specially appointed subcommittee including Councillors M. J. Adams and A. Z. Berman, asked Higgins for his views on the proposed plans, particularly as it affected two delimited slum zones in the central city area. The MOH noted that in the larger of the two slum zones (District Six), the City Engineer proposed that only 71 of the 200 acres be used for residential purposes and be retained for a housing scheme. Forty acres zoned for commercial development and destined for ultimate resale were situated in the very heart of Cape Town's residential slumland, Higgins pointed out.[17] In the same way that Lunn shrugged off responsibility for rehousing, so the MOH refused to take town planning into account. Town planning was not their concern, he told the Housing and Slum Clearance Committee: they had to look at the matter from the aspect of solving the "formidable housing problem" which faced the Council.[18] The Council had already acquired a considerable amount of slum property in this neighbourhood with a view to ultimate demolition and replacement by new housing. The new Canterbury Square (formerly Wells Square) and the Bloemhof Flats adjoining the delimited area, were nearing completion. Within the delimited area itself, 177 houses occupied by 2 248 persons, had been acquired in Stone, William and Caledon Streets. Their redevelopment would have to await the implementation of the town planning scheme.[19]

The MOH alone was authorised to initiate proceedings under the Slums Act. He had to inspect properties and recommend their acquisition by the Council, which could not act without his authority. This he had been doing assiduously since the promulgation of the Slums Act in 1934, but in 1937 he had stopped this practice, since rehousing was not keeping up with slum demolition. The question now was whether the policy of slum acquisition leading to ultimate demolition should be resumed on the great scale contemplated in the City

Engineer's proposals. For Higgins, the solution to the housing and slum problems in Cape Town could only be found in the building of sufficient new houses to overtake the shortage, and render unnecessary sub-letting and overcrowding. Without this, the abolition of slums in one place would be followed by their creation in another. Higgins estimated the black population of Cape Town to be increasing by about four thousand per annum. He, therefore, advocated a vigorous prosecution of the Council's programme of sub-economic housing and "native" housing. New estates on open land without any large-scale demolition of existing houses would contribute more effectively than slum clearance schemes to the solution of the problem. "For the time being the prevailing policy should be to press on with additional housing until there shall be sufficient accommodation available to justify a programme of demolition."[20]

The MOH's objections to the Provisional Town Planning Scheme, it is clear, were more a matter of degree than of principle. He wished to rehouse in the area as large a number of the present inhabitants of District Six as he felt was possible. But, as the records make clear, he had no objections to the segregated "Coloureds only" housing schemes on the Cape Flats. In fact, he urged the Council to grant priority to such schemes to meet the housing shortage. Thus, both the MOH and the City Engineer believed that a proportion of the District Six residents would have to move to the Cape Flats. The difference lay in their priorities. Higgins, less ruled by a concern for economic considerations, never posited the destruction of District Six. He believed that 20 per cent of the residents would have to find accommodation outside the District. Lunn was convinced that at least 50 per cent would have to be moved. He more than once used the phrases "starting from scratch" and "the elimination of District Six".[21]

There was "considerable debate" when the Housing and Slum Clearance Committee met on 15 May 1940 to discuss the report by the MOH and the City Engineer. Endorsing Higgins's views, the Housing Committee emphasised the need for housing to be provided in the City itself and recommended that those portions zoned "general commercial" should become entirely residential and used for rehousing purposes. The Committee also wanted the new street system for Districts Six and Seven to "be revised in the light of the requirements of a residential area". Some of the suggested new streets should be eliminated, the width of others reduced, and the proposed new arterial road be made "considerably narrower". The Jerry Street area (the docks area) should be sold for industrial purposes.[22]

The Housing Committee's proposals, broadly endorsing Higgins's view, were subsequently embodied in a memorandum of 25 May 1940 which also questioned Lunn's optimistic costing. Experience had shown that in previous slum clearance purchases the Council had paid, on an average, 1 1379 times the municipal valuation, and there was no reason to believe that the same would not apply to the present proposals.[23]

The City Engineer was forced to admit that under the Slums Act, the opinion of the Housing and Slum Clearance Committee carried considerable weight and reluctantly agreed that the whole delimited area be utilised for housing and that the "general commercial zone" be scrapped. This amendment was incorporated in the new Provisional Town Planning Scheme which the Council adopted on 29 May 1941. But he would not be moved on the street system. The main streets formed an integral part of the city plan as a whole and the proposed width of 100 ft for the arterial road was no more than adequate.[24]

The Housing and Slum Clearance Committee may have been influenced in its arguments by public protests which were gathering pace by this time. Early in April 1940 the Drill Hall opened its doors to display the plans. A columnist in the *Cape Argus* reported that the City's Town Planning Officer, J. G. Collings, was holding the Council's first exhibition of surrealist art.

> This is the impression that his great charts of the new town plan ... gives to those who visit the plans. The maps are coloured in every shade imaginable ... After exhausting the paint box he had to fall back on different designs – blue triangles, black spots – to show his intentions.[25]

The public were unimpressed by the surrealist planning laid before them. Public protest over the scheme took place against a background of considerable ferment in Cape Town, particularly on the question of the War: should Coloured people go to war? At least one protest meeting was banned – a public meeting called by the NEUF for the evening of 14 May 1940. The meeting was to have discussed segregation on the beaches, the colour bar at the Claremont public library and the District Six town planning scheme. A police official told the *Cape Argus* that it was considered that the agenda of the meeting was not purely confined to civic matters, and that the time was inopportune for meetings of this nature.[26] After the scheme was thrown open to public scrutiny, it did not take long for objections to reach the Council.

The first were received from the Chemical and Allied Workers' Union, the Sweet Workers' Union and the Tin Workers' Union, protesting particularly against the effects of the scheme "on the Non-European community who live and trade in Wards Six and Seven".[27] Others followed from the National Liberation League of South Africa, the General Workers' Union, the Domestic Workers' Union and the Office Cleaners' Union. The Non-European United Front (NEUF)[28] was soon leading the protest movement under the leadership of Mrs Z. (Cissie) Gool, herself a city councillor.

Protest against the scheme hinged on what the workers' organisations regarded as the threat of segregation – or, as they labelled it, "segregation in disguise". In his report, Lunn chose not to convey this message directly to the Plans Committee, but only acknowledged that the charge had been made in his denial of it. The City Engineer's response was predictable. He denied that no provision had been made for rehousing Non-Europeans but repeated that rehousing was not a town planning responsibility. Above all, he rejected the claims that the real purpose of the scheme was to segregate the District Six inhabitants.

The whole object of the scheme was to "effect an improvement" not only on the city as a whole, but also to benefit those living in the area. The slum clearance area contained such "awful slum conditions due to congestion of buildings and overcrowding, the structure of the buildings as a whole was so bad and the area so ill-planned, that there can be no effective remedy other than to completely obliterate what exists today and to derive a new layout that will give healthier conditions ...".

Lunn was "at a loss to understand" the reason why the objectors had "erroneously assumed" that the scheme contemplated, or opened up the possibility, of segregating the Non-European inhabitants.

> Such an idea has never been thought of and indeed would not be entertained for one minute ... It is recognised that in this area there is essentially a Non-European community and any improvements suggested are meant for those inhabitants.[29]

It was a fallacy to think that the general commercial use zone, which extended from Hanover Street to Sir Lowry Road, would preclude occupation by blacks in that area. It was in reality a mixed zone, "where people may live as they do today, but where building of a business, shopping or industrial nature will also be encouraged". The area above

Hanover Street had been zoned for general residential purposes and "is intended solely for the rehousing, as far as possible" of those now living within the area. Nevertheless, while in the report Lunn ridiculed fears of segregation, he also had this to say:

> While there is no intention to attempt segregation it is a fact ... however intense the form of redevelopment may be, it is impossible within the area to rehouse under healthy conditions, the same number of people ... Probably one-half the existing population would have to be found accommodation elsewhere ... this fact ... has no connection whatever with segregating Non-Europeans.[30]

The City Engineer's department was governed by thinking which took little account of popular feeling. One was the recognition, shared by the MOH, that the inner city could no longer accommodate the growing population. The dilemma was real enough but handled with a brutal insensitivity which may have sprung from underlying assumptions about the desirability of segregation. Certainly, popular suspicion was reawakened.

Equally insensitive was the desire for a "clean sweep", so common amongst town planners of the day. Here reference may be made to the expert town planner, Monsieur E. E. Beaudouin, whom the Council imported from France to advise on the new foreshore development. Supporting the City Engineer, Beaudouin named District Six specifically as one of the areas to be affected by the new foreshore scheme. It was he who suggested that De Waal Drive be extended in a straight line from Groote Schuur Hospital to become a "Park Avenue" to line up with the Monumental Esplanade on the foreshore.[31] Thus was foreshadowed Boulevard East which was to lay waste a huge slice of District Six and provide a foretaste of the more drastic bulldozing some two decades later. Of the 578 items on the schedule of properties to be acquired for the construction of the Grand Boulevard East in the early sixties, over 350 were situated in District Six. These included some 307 dwellings, fifteen flats, twenty-seven shops and stores, sixteen factories, four schools, two halls, two churches, three hotels, two bioscopes and seven stables, sheds, workshops and garages.[32]

The establishment press was initially enthusiastic about the scheme. Banner headlines in the *Cape Argus* on 8 April 1940 declared: END OF DISTRICT SIX PLANNED ... CITY'S GREAT SLUM QUARTER TO BE INDUSTRIAL AREA. The plans were arousing the "keenest interest" among visitors to the Drill Hall, said the *Cape Argus*. It pinpointed the "remodelling of District Six" as the biggest scheme in the whole plan and the "biggest single blow aimed at the city's slum areas". Three thousand buildings were to be demolished and 29 595 people evacuated – with the exception of Hanover Street, every road in the area would disappear. Ten days later the same newspaper, under the heading £1 MILLION TO WIPE OUT DISTRICT SIX – CITY'S WORST SLUM ON A HEALTHY AND VALUABLE SITE – quoted at length the City Engineer's report that District Six was capable of being the finest suburb in the city and that "the sore must be obliterated entirely".[33]

The *Guardian* was one of the earliest non-establishment newspapers to hold aloft the banner of the NEUF. "What is wanted is a rebuilding scheme which will supply the workers of Cape Town with good housing conditions and low rent in District Six, their traditional home." The workers' organisations certainly agreed with the elimination of the unsightly slums of District Six, but they were totally against this "new move to segregate the Non-Europeans".[34]

"Strong opposition" was first reported by the *Cape Times* under the headlines, DISTRICT SIX PROTESTS – £1,000,000 SCHEME OBJECTED TO – RUINATION FOR MANY SHOPS – HARSH PLANNING SCHEME LAID ON NON-EUROPEANS – STRONG OPPOSITION.[35] The *Cape Times* quoted the manager of a large business in Hanover Street who said that merchants and shopkeepers in the area appeared to be unanimous in their objection to the scheme. "We will fight it tooth and nail." Hanover Street would be "left in the cold" and would deteriorate. At least half the population would have to be moved to other suburbs altogether; businesses in District Six, half of which were in the hands of Europeans, would lose half their customers.

The same *Cape Times* report carried news of a deputation from the NEUF, led by Mrs Gool, to the Select Committee for Lands. The deputation objected to what they described as "segregation in disguise". They maintained that since the land available for redevelopment in District Six was highly valued, sub-economic schemes for blacks would be found to be impracticable. Lunn had suggested as much in his report. They foresaw that the entire present population of the area, close to 28 000, would be forced out. District Six had for a hundred years been a black area. It was especially convenient because of its central position and proximity to the place of employment of most of the people living there. It would be an "unbearable hardship" to move the poor to a distant suburb where they would be faced with bus or train fares which they could not afford. The deputation agreed that it was necessary to abolish the terrible slums but maintained that it would be possible to replace them with well-designed residential and shopping areas, including playing fields, and capable of housing a large black population under healthy conditions.

A few days later, two thousand people at a public meeting in the City Hall called by the NEUF, reiterated their fear that the plan for District Six was nothing but "disguised segregation". As a result of the new harbour development, District Six was becoming a valuable site, said Mrs Gool.[36]

Some months later *The Sun*'s regular education columnist queried the motives underlying the plans for District Six.[37] "Is the term "town planning" as used in Cape Town just a little bit of camouflage to hide the ambitions of big businessmen?" he asked.

> Like the people who built the new harbour, they have been preparing against the day when – with the closing of the Mediterranean – Cape Town becomes a premier port. Thus since Big Industry likes to be as conveniently situated as possible in relation to the Docks, they set about doing a little bit of town planning to get the sites they need ...[38]

Opposition to the scheme was also fanned by revelations about conditions on the Cape Flats. In mid June 1940 there were once again banner headlines in the *Cape Argus*: MIGRATION TO THE CAPE FLATS OPPOSED ... DISTRICT SIX FOR THE NON-EUROPEANS IS THE CRY OF THE NEUF. The report drew attention to the dissatisfaction of residents in Athlone at the conditions in which they were living: unmade roads which turned into quagmires in winter; plagues of flies and mosquitoes; and the vile smell "frequently odious and unbearable" which emanated from the sewage disposal works. "We cannot help concluding from all the surrounding circumstances and from the statements made by municipal officials that the object of the town planning scheme is to effect the wholesale removal of an unnecessarily large section of the Non-European people in District Six to the Cape Flats area, in order to effect the segregation of the Non-Europeans", said the NEUF.[39]

The People's Club (a recreational and literary club open to all) and the Cape District branches of the Communist Party of South Africa were among other organisations to protest, the latter calling the scheme an "unjustifiable interference with the inalienable right of all citizens in a civilised country to live where they please".[40]

Public protests continued elsewhere: The *Cape Standard* added its voice to condemn the "cunning segregation scheme". In an editorial, the paper said:

> ... it is quite apparent that the proposed changes will not solve the problem of slums but will merely drive out the present residents and force them to seek accommodation in other parts of the city ... The present scheme as applied to Ward Seven indicated the removal of practically every resident without providing suitable accommodation elsewhere within the confines of the city, though vague promises are made with reference to beautiful cottages in the Cape Flats.[41]

Objections came to a head with a meeting which took place on the evening of 25 July 1940, when the Liberman Hall in District Six was packed to the doors. Many people were unable to gain admission, and the proceedings were "extremely lively at times". Newspapers the following day revealed a new angle to the protest: CITY COUNCILLORS "TRICKED" reported the *Cape Times*, and the *Cape Argus*: SEGREGATION "TRICK" DEPLORED.[42]

A number of leading councillors, generally very much part of the establishment, had joined the protesters. Councillor A. Bloomberg presided at the meeting. He advised all the people living in the affected area to protest against the scheme without delay. Councillor Louis Gradner said councillors had not protested at the time because they had been "tricked" into thinking the scheme was a provisional one. "What the Council is proposing to do under the guise of slum clearance is to disperse 27 000 ratepayers who were born and brought up in the district. They will erect beautiful houses for fourteen thousand of you, but you will never be able to occupy them because the rents will be more than you can afford." The Council, he said, was bent on "wholesale eviction". There was not a single man or woman, European or Coloured, who was in favour of the scheme, said Mrs Gool.

A resolution moved by Councillor Adams, urging the Council to discard the present scheme and to discuss a new scheme with the people in the wards, was carried unanimously. So was another, put forward by Councillor Mrs Gool, protesting that the scheme was calculated to bring about the segregation of the blacks. When it was noticed that Councillor Adams had refrained from voting on the second motion, there were cries of "vote", "vote". Amidst a burst of applause, Adams signified that he was in favour of the resolution condemning segregation.[43] After the meeting, Adams explained to a representative of the *Cape Argus* why he had voted for Mrs Gool's resolution:

> It must not be assumed that I have changed my views on segregation. On the contrary I am more convinced than ever that if we are to prevent civil war between Europeans and Non-Europeans it will be by means of segregation. But it does not mean that you must trick Coloured people into segregation through a town planning scheme. The question is far too serious for such tactics.[44]

The Liberman meeting led to fresh discussion in the Council chamber. The chairman of the Plans Committee, Councillor F. Bakker, did not think it necessary to review and rescind the scheme which represented the work of thirty-two men over three years. If advisable, it could be amended. Only seven of 54 objections received referred to segregation, which had never been their concern. People who attended the meeting at the Liberman Institute had been misinformed – the scheme was not designed for the purpose of segregation. Moreover, the scheme met with the approval of the current consultants on the foreshore scheme. The councillors who had been present at the Liberman Institute reiterated their views. Above all, they felt the plans were too sweeping and ambitious while commercial competition from the new street would destroy Hanover Street.

The Council's acceptance of an amendment to the District Six scheme which now reserved the general commercial area for purely residential purposes, was conveyed in a letter in September from the Acting Town Clerk to the NEUF. It denied any intention to segregate, recognising that in the area there was an "essentially Non-European community". However, the present unhealthy conditions of the District were primarily due to overcrowding, and "it may prove impossible to rehouse under healthy conditions the same number of people".[45] The people were not entirely convinced. On 26 November 1940, the NEUF made another attempt to interview the Plans Committee but their request was refused – it was inadvisable to discuss the scheme with "any outside organisation".[46] This showed an arrogant and patronising disregard of the feelings of the residents.

Discussion continued in the City Plans Committee itself. Lunn reassured the dissenting councillors that only certain parts of the scheme would be put into operation at a time, allowing normal development and building operations to take place in the rest of the City.[47]

The City Engineer had already pointed out that some time would elapse before the final scheme could be put into operation. After adoption by the Council, it would have to be submitted to the Administrator who would refer it to the Townships Board, and every owner of immovable property would be able to inspect the scheme anew, and object once more. A public investigation of all the objections would then be held by the Townships Board, and the Council would have the opportunity of making further amendments if this were considered necessary. The scheme would then again have to be submitted to the Administrator under the title "Approved Preliminary Scheme", and only after the Administrator had approved this, would the final scheme be drawn up. As Lunn emphasised, the scheme must always be regarded as "flexible and subject to frequent review".[48]

After a number of adjournments, on 29 May 1941, full Council finally approved the Amended Town Planning Scheme. Councillor H. F. Gearing seemed to have the final say before voting: "It will cost the city millions to implement ... it is far too ambitious and most of it is unnecessary."[49] Twenty-two councillors, upon a show of hands, voted in favour and three against. A division was demanded and the voting then was twenty-five for, five against. Fifteen absent councillors were noted. One of the chief opponents of the scheme, Gradner, voted in favour. Councillors I. Albow, C. Barnett, Mrs Z. Gool, Martin Hammerschlag and Mark Jones voted against. Notable absentees were A. Z. Berman, A. Bloomberg and A. Ismail.[50]

Now the whole matter lost its urgency, and comparative quiet descended on the town planning scene. From September 1940 to January 1945 there was no specific housing committee in the City Council to deal with housing and slum clearance. These matters fell to the new Public Health Committee. The Housing Committee was reconstituted only in January 1945.

In 1944, the newly appointed Post-War Reconstruction Committee of the Cape Town City Council recommended that the central government be approached for £14 500 000 for "extra-normal" development, which was of top priority if the City wished to overcome the stultifying effects of the war. Of this sum, £2 500 000 was to go towards the replanning of District Six, including the acquisition of necessary properties, but excluding housing. Funding was also requested to provide services for the foreshore reclamation scheme (£1,25 million); for the establishment of industrial areas on the Cape Flats (£3,25 million); a further £3 million for the Cape Flats reclamation scheme and £0,75 million for the initial development and acquisition of properties in Windermere (at this stage a huge squatter settlement on the perimeter of the city).[51] At the end of the war, the reconstruction and building of houses in Windermere and neighbouring Factreton went ahead; industrialists were allocated sites at Ndabeni from late 1944. In 1949 it was reported that the industrial township of Epping was rapidly taking shape. "Rising from virgin soil," it was bigger than Ndabeni.[52] But nothing was done about District Six.

When the controversy about the town plan for District Six was at its height, *The Sun*'s columnist B. J. U. captured popular feeling about District Six in an article under the heading "Alas Poor District Six". It is reproduced practically in full to illustrate that District Six was a legend already in its lifetime.

> Alas, poor District Six! They are planning your downfall. They wish to make an end of the live, throbbing, pulsating ward that always adds to the joys and terrors of candidates for municipal and political honours and that, incidentally, sends (as a rule) such troublesome representatives up. They are making Darling Street a dagger pointed straight at your heart.

What is to become? asked B. J. U. and speculated:

> Would it be a 100 ft. wide Darling Street opening up a glorious vista of Devil's Peak, with sleek cars rolling up and down, flanked by select private flats, like those of De Waal Drive today, and with white residences spreading outwards, interspersed with an imposing commercial house or a mansion-like factory, but with on the fringes the most exclusive of the ultra-respectable Coloured, the ones who get on the white voters' roll and to their dismay are called up to serve in the defence force? Will the municipal wash-house become a sub-station, the Liberman Institute a highly exclusive lecture room, and the new swimming bath, duly disinfected, a white resort till such time as it turns black again for all time?

And if he should ask a wayfarer what had become of all the Coloured people "who are as truly a part of Cape Town as old Table Mountain", would the columnist be told:

> "Oh they? Take a Mowbray tram. Wait if it rains in the Non-European shelter for the Gleemoor bus." Should I then see them all, still earning the same semi-civilised wages, as befits a people who have reached the "fringe of civilisation", still living in Council houses, still indulging in the same old pleasures, going in Non-European conveyances to 4th Beach or Strandfontein where they have voluntarily segregated themselves, and returning in the dusk to their Council houses, where they are unseen by Cape Town, no longer a

source of shame to South African whites before overseas visitors, but abiding there unhonoured and unsung but by no means unhated?

At present, the writer continued, a large part of Cape Town was occupied by whites

> ... of every kind of descent ... but there are parts where the Coloured man has obtained a hold and has lived for generations. District Six has been a workers' district and it is a matter for shame that parts have been allowed to acquire notoriety ... The Coloured man must cling to his place in Cape Town ... It is pleasing to see that there is at least one organisation having ... the guts ... to make vocal public opinion ... touching this vital issue.[53]

The City Council never implemented that part of the provisional town planning scheme which referred to District Six, except for Boulevard East. Towards the end of 1940 it was announced that owing to the war and financial stringency, any redevelopment of District Six was to be temporarily stopped. The Council did not abandon its District Six scheme, however. From the mid-1940s it was once more planning to acquire properties in District Six, including some thirty buildings in the Horsburg Lane and Hanover, Clifton and Caledon Street areas which had not been declared slum, but which were required "to form an area of convenient shape and dimensions" for redevelopment or housing. Only the Hanover Street business and shopping area was to escape the "clean sweep".[54]

In January 1948, Lunn estimated that 4 150 dwellings (for 4 150 families) could be accommodated in the 166 acres reserved for residential purposes in the replanned District Six, and that 1 660 families would have to be moved out of the District.[55]

It has to be borne in mind that no final decisions on District Six could be implemented without an agreed foreshore plan. The foreshore scheme was adopted in June 1947, giving little time for the Council to decide what to do with District Six before the Nationalist government took power in 1948.

The solution of the "problem" of District Six as accepted in 1941 was surely not the only one open to the City Council and its town planners. With a little more imagination and some consideration for the needs and feelings of the people and for the historic heritage symbolised by District Six, and with less emphasis on a purely mercenary exploitation of a "valuable site", an historic part of Victorian Cape Town could have been preserved. Nor was it necessary to consign the "surplus" peoples of District Six so unquestioningly and unhesitatingly to the segregated hinterland available on the Cape Flats. Ironically, the Cape Town City Council in 1938/39 with only the dissenting voice of Councillor Adams, rejected the Cape Provincial Council's move towards the legal enforcement of residential segregation. Yet this was not because they were opposed to segregation *per se* as their own segregated housing policy demonstrated, but because they were arrogantly confident that such segregation would come about "naturally". The Council's housing policy from the earliest days had more in common with Nationalist Party ideology than councillors then and in the future would care to acknowledge. Its "liberal tradition" notwithstanding, the Cape Town Council shared with Nationalists the common assumptions about the desirability of residential segregation and the need for social engineering to maintain white supremacy. The Cape Town Council, as also the United Party, however, still had regard for the political voice of the Coloured people, limited though it was, whereas the Nationalists were waiting impatiently to remove that voice. No matter which government took office in 1948, District Six was doomed.

It is nevertheless tempting to speculate on the fate of District Six had the Nationalists not won the elections. With District Six in the eye of the City Engineer and others, "a very valuable site" commanding a view of Table Bay and the proposed "monumental approach" to the city; with industries moving to the Cape Flats where lay the Council"s "Non-Europeans only" cottages; with the Council having made the maximum use of the Slums Act to acquire areas "of convenient shape and dimensions", would the Cape Town City Council have kept its word that the District Six renewal was not "segregation in disguise"? Or would it, having lifted its eyes to the north, to Johannesburg and Durban and taken cognisance of what was happening there, have decided otherwise?

In Johannesburg, the Slums Act was used to provide segregated urban areas for poor whites.[56] The removal of Sophiatown – a "mixed" area similar to District Six – and neighbouring Martindale and Newclare was first mooted as a major scheme in the 1940s and formed an integral part of the Johannesburg City Council's post-war reconstruction plans. Owing to a shortage of funds the plan was not implemented nor was it officially rescinded. It was adopted in its entirety after Verwoerd became head of the Native Affairs Department in the 1950s.[57] In Durban, "the English dominated municipality was so enthusiastic for racial segregation in the 1930s and 1940s that it actually produced a comprehensive race zoning plan for the city in 1943 – a plan almost precisely affecting the final outcome of Group Areas policy which became applicable to Durban in the 1980s".[58]

There was plenty of evidence that segregation was on the rise well before the Nationalist Party victory of 1948. State-sanctioned residential segregation had already edged its way into the debating chambers of the legislature, and its initial defeat in the Cape Provincial Council in 1939 was only a temporary setback.[59] The ruling United Party and its press were also on the segregationist bandwagon. The Nationalist Party was actively propagating incipient apartheid. *Die Burger* was eloquent about the "evil" of *saamwonery* (living together of white and coloured) and chastised the "Smuts party" for voting against the draft segregation ordinance in the Provincial Council.[60]

The Group Areas Act saw the light of day in 1950. By now, it was clearly out of the hands of the Cape Town City Council to do as it wished with District Six. Government intentions were kept well hidden. When the axe fell on 11 February 1966,[61] the whites-only announcement was a devastating surprise. Echoes of Cape Town's shocked reaction still lingered on some twenty years later, as the barren wastes of District Six, dotted with five or six churches, incongruous outposts, bore witness.

Yet, the Nationalist Government has had relatively little satisfaction from its conquest of District Six, and very little chance to realise the potential of this "valuable piece of land". In 1971, Government plans for a multi-million rand luxury suburb for whites had to be abandoned because of massive public protest. At least two large oil companies had to abandon plans to open service stations in the District. By the mid-1980s only houses for policemen's families and other civil servants had been erected in District Six and an initially "whites-only" technicon was sprawling over huge areas of the man-created wasteland by the early 1990s, when small developers managed to start some housing schemes in the area. Big business, notably BP, from time to time unfolded plans for an "open" District Six, meeting with little enthusiasm from the public.

By the time the Group Areas Act was scrapped in the early 1990s, too little remained of the original District Six to be resurrected, nor was there a popular demand for this to be attempted. To the many thousands who had lived there and were so cruelly removed, and to their offspring, it is sacred ground – a place of pilgrimage to which parents and grandparents bring their children to feel and touch this "salted earth".

Endnotes

1. S. Jeppie and C. Soudien, eds, *The Struggle for District Six: Past and Present* (Cape Town, 1990).
2. G. E. Cherry, *Cities and plans. The shaping of urban Britain in the nineteenth and twentieth centuries* (London, 1988), ch.4; J. J. McCarthy and D. P. Smit, *South African city: theory in analysis and planning* (Cape Town, 1984), 7.
3. *Cape Argus*, 8 and 18 April 1940.
4. Walter Stanley Lunn became City Engineer in 1936 after working for some years in the department. He was largely responsible for town planning in Cape Town from the 1930s to his retirement in 1950. He attributed his concern for good town planning to his childhood in revolutionary Russia saying: "The revolution had its origins in those people who were too poor to live happily and decently, and eventually rose up to wipe out people like ourselves." *Cape Standard*, 8 August 1939.
5. Cape Archives (hereafter CA) 3/CT 1/4/9/2/1/3, Housing and Slum Clearance Committee, City Engineer's report "Proposed redevelopment of Slum Areas District VI and VII", 22 February 1940 (hereafter Proposed redevelopment Feb. 1940). It would have been more correct to speak of Wards VI and VII – there was no "District VII", and District Six fell within both Wards VI and VII.
6. Proposed redevelopment Feb. 1940, pp. 1–5. The racial classification here is taken directly from the City Engineer's report.
7. Hanover Street was the main thoroughfare of District Six. It could be said to have been synonymous with the hustle and bustle of life in District Six. Now renamed Keisergracht, it is a skeleton of its former self, denuded of human life and buildings with indigenous scrub struggling to survive amidst builders' rubble and mountain rock.
8. Proposed redevelopment Feb. 1940, p. 6.
9. Cape Town City Engineer's Department, *Report on Amended Provisional Town Planning Scheme of the Portion of the Municipality extending from Bakoven to Trafalgar Park* (Cape Town, 1941).
10. City Engineer's Department, *Report on Amended Provisional Town Planning Scheme*, passim, particularly 44–8, 57 and 178.
11. Dr T. Shadick Higgins was Cape Town MOH from 1923 to 1944, with previous experience in Britain.
12. Proposed redevelopment Feb. 1940, 8.
13. Proposed redevelopment Feb. 1940, 9.
14. Proposed redevelopment Feb. 1940, p. 10.
15. CA, 3/CT 1/4/13/1/1/5, City Plans and Development Committee minutes, 26 February 1940
16. CA, 3/CT 1/1/1/94, Proceedings of Council, 29 February 1940, 745–750.
17. CA, 3/CT 1/4/9/2/1/3, Housing and Slum Clearance Committee minutes, 22 April and 30 April 1940. Also MOH report on proposed redevelopment of District VI and VII, 30 April 1940 (hereafter, MOH report 1940).
18. MOH report 1940, 2.
19. MOH report 1940, 3. At this stage the Council owned 605 slum dwellings in the city. *Cape Times*, 21 April 1940.

20. MOH report 1940, 3–5.
21. CA, 3/CT 1/5/19/1/1, Minutes of Proceedings of Foreshore Development Investigation Committee (hereafter Szlumper Commission), Cape Town, January-February 1945, 10.
22. CA, 3/CT 1/4/9/2/1/3, Housing and Slum Clearance Committee minutes, 15 May 1940.
23. CA, 3/CT 1/4/9/2/1/3, Housing and Slum Clearance Committee, "Memorandum on proposed redevelopment of slum areas in Districts VI and VII", 25 May 1940, 8. Originally dated 10 May 1940, this memorandum was amended over the following fortnight (hereafter Housing Committee memo May 1940).
24. CA, 3/CT 1/4/13/1/1/6, City Plans and Development Committee, City Engineer's report, 20 July 1940. Proposed redevelopment of slum areas District VI and VII and at Loader Street and Jarvis Street, Cape Town, 20 July 1940.
25. *Cape Argus*, "Surrealist Art", 8 April 1940.
26. *Cape Argus*, 14 and 16 May 1940.
27. CA, 3/CT 1/4/13/1/1/6, City Plans Committee, memorandum "Objections to provisions of town planning scheme, slum clearance area, Districts VI and VII", 20 April 1940, 5 (hereafter Objections to provisions April 1940).
28. The Non-European United Front was established in April 1938 at a conference organised by the National Liberation League and attended by 45 organisations, amongst them the ANC, the CPSA and the Trades and Labour Council. At the time of its protest against the Provisional Town Planning Scheme as it affected District Six, the NEUF represented eighty-three affiliated organisations, with a membership of 32 000.
29. Objections to provisions April 1940, 11–13.
30. Objections to provisions April 1940, 11–13.
31. E. E. Beaudouin, "Outline of scheme (foreshore) for Cape Town, South Africa", Cape Town, 13 June 1940, 5 and 26. See also D. H. Pinnock, "State control and street gangs in Cape Town" (M.A. thesis, University of Cape Town, 1982); D. H. Pinnock, *The Brotherhoods* (Cape Town, 1984).
32. Cape Town City Council Archives, Railway and Foreshore Special Committee, Volume 1. December 1948–August 1949.
33. *Cape Argus*, 8 and 18 April 1940.
34. *Guardian*, 12 April 1940.
35. *Cape Times*, 20 April 1940.
36. *Cape Times* and *Cape Argus*, 23 April 1940; *Guardian*, 26 April 1940; *The Sun*, 26 April 1940.
37. A weekly paper, started on 23 September 1932, *The Sun* was subtitled "South Africa's Non-European newspaper", catered mainly for the educated coloured élite, taking a strong stand against segregation.
38. *The Sun*, 2 August 1940.
39. *Cape Argus*, 22 June 1940; *Guardian*, 21 June 1940. See also City Plans Committee minutes, March – August 1940.
40. *Guardian*, 3 May 1940.
41. *Cape Standard*, 16 April 1940. See also 30 April, 21 May, 25 June and particularly 30 July 1940.
42. *Cape Times* and *Cape Argus*, 26 July 1940.
43. *Cape Times*, 26 July 1940.

44. *Cape Argus*, 26 July 1940. Adams was always a controversial figure in the Cape Town City Council. His death at the age of 71 was reported in the *Cape Times* and *Cape Argus* on 24 January 1941. Starting life as a carpenter's apprentice he became a master builder. He had been a city councillor since 1931. In 1939 he was the only member of Council to support the pro-segregation proposals of the Cape Provincial Council. In 1940 he was described by B. Hertzberg as an "apostle of segregation and as the advocate of the theory that the various races should develop along their own lines, of course in locations". *Cape Times*, 10 April 1940. In his obituaries the newspapers described him as a champion of housing for the poor, a power behind the Citizens' Housing League, and deeply interested in the poor white problem. An editorial in the *Cape Times* on 24 January 1941 noted that towards the end of his life he became convinced that segregation of the Europeans and Coloureds would be in the interests of both.
45. *Guardian*, 26 September 1940; *Cape Standard*, 1 October 1940.
46. CA, 3/CT 1/4/13/2/1/1, Plans Committee minutes, 20 December 1940.
47. CA, 3/CT 1/4/13/2/1/1, Plans Committee minutes, 18 March 1941.
48. CA, 3/CT 1/4/13/2/1/1, Plans Committee minutes. Letter from City Engineer to Plans Committee, 8 March 1941. See also 3/CT 1/1/1/95 Proceedings of Council, 29 April 1941, 768–9.
49. *Cape Times*, 30 May 1941.
50. CA, 3/CT 1/1/1/94, Proceedings of Council, 29 May 1941, pp. 829–830.
51. CA, 3/CT 1/1/9/8, Council-in-committee minutes, Memorandum: City Treasurer's department to Finance and General Purposes Committee, 27 April 1944.
52. *Cape Times*, 9 March 1949. Ndabeni and Epping are on the edge of the Cape Flats.
53. *The Sun*, 27 April 1940; see also 30 May, 21 June and 26 June 1940.
54. Cape Town City Council Archives, Housing Committee Minutes, 19 September 1947.
55. Cape Town City Council Archives, Housing Committee Minutes, City Engineer's report, 15 January 1948, marked "Confidential – not for Publication". The figures are suspect. The City Engineer was still using the MOH's 1932 social survey of the poorer parts of Wards II–VII as the basis of his calculations.
56. S. M. Parnell, "Council housing provision for whites in Johannesburg, 1920–1955" (M.A., University of the Witwatersrand, 1984); S. M. Parnell, "Public housing as a device for white residential segregation in Johannesburg, 1934–1953", *Urban Geography*, 9,6, 9 Nov/Dec 1988).
57. D. P. van Tonder, "Sophiatown: removals and protest, 1940–1955" (M.A., University of South Africa, 1990), 9–11, 23, 24, 31, 32, 71 and 203.
58. McCarthy and Smith, *The South African City*, 59.
59. A. Mabin, *"Doom at one stroke of the pen*: planning and Group Areas, c. 1935–1955", University of the Witwatersrand, History Workshop, 1990.
60. *Die Burger*, 24 and 26 July 1940.
61. *Government Gazette*, 1370, 11 February 1966.

8

"No place in the world to go to" – control by permit: The first phase of the Group Areas Act in Cape Town in the 1950s

Uma Shashikant Mesthrie

In early 1991, the Group Areas Project was launched in the Sociology Department at the University of Cape Town.[1] The project has a fairly ambitious and wide scope. It aims, firstly, to uncover the history of the Group Areas Act (GAA), particularly its origins, its machinery and its implementation – largely from the perspective of the state's intentions. The second objective is to examine the process of removals and resettlement and the responses of the communities affected. Finally, the erosion of the Act in the 1980s, and the effect of its demise in 1991 on residential patterns will be investigated. Within this broader outline of the project, which will assume a national focus, at least in terms of state intentions, it is hoped to illuminate as a case study – the unfolding of the GAA in Cape Town, with special emphasis on the way the lives of ordinary people were affected and how they responded.

The project was motivated by the realisation that a systematic study of this Act, which has so profoundly affected the lives of thousands of families (mainly black), is lacking in the available literature. The recent appearance of two edited collections on the South African city by Anthony Lemon and Mark Swilling *et al.* respectively,[2] simply underscores the need to understand the process by which the allocation of urban space has been (and will be) contested and determined.

In terms of Cape Town specifically, it is not surprising that most of the available literature focuses on the impact of the GAA. In this regard, John Western's work,[3] published ten years ago, towers above all. His special skills as a social geographer served to elucidate, in a highly readable account, the relationship between the space that individuals occupy and the construction of identity. His conclusions were based on 100 interviews with families removed from Mowbray to the bleakness of the Cape Flats.

The Centre for Intergroup Studies produced a short superficial overview of the application of the Act to Cape Town[4] and case studies of the consequences of the Act have been undertaken by Rosemary Anne Hill and Don Pinnock.[5] Jayne Garside's work focuses on a different aspect, the grey or open areas of Woodstock and Lansdowne.[6] Julia Knight speculates on how the repeal of the GAA may change Cape Town.[7]

The publication of a series of essays on District Six,[8] which is aimed at both a popular and academic audience, makes a valuable contribution at least in terms of understanding life in an area prior to the invidious Act and the responses of residents to their subsequent removal.

Two publications by the South African Institute of Race Relations in the 1950s are of considerable value as they represent contemporary surveys of people in places, before apartheid restructured the city.[9] In terms of understanding the unfolding of the Act in Cape Town, Western's chapter on "Putting the Plan into Practise: Cape Town since 1950" is perhaps one of the weakest in his book, largely because of the limited information available to him at the time of writing. As archival material and manuscript collections become available, it is possible to consider the feasibility of constructing a history of the process of separating people into different group areas.

This chapter, based on very preliminary research, forms a tiny portion of the whole picture. It aims to examine the very first way in which the GAA touched the lives of ordinary people in Cape Town, long before group areas were declared and individuals became "disqualified persons" and were forced to leave neighbourhoods that had been theirs for generations. It was by the permit system, under the Act, that individuals first began to feel the heavy hand of the state as their right to buy property and occupy the premises of their choice was seriously curtailed.

The background to the Group Areas Act

In May 1950, just before Dr Donges introduced the second reading of the Group Areas Bill in parliament, the principal of the Wolraad Woltemade School in Woodstock, Mr L. Pienaar, sat down to write a letter to the minister.[10] He complained about the "indringing van kleurlinge" (the penetration of coloureds) in areas such as Woodstock, Salt River and great parts of Observatory. He was particularly concerned about keeping the areas around white schools and churches white and wanted whites to reclaim, what he alleged, the coloureds had taken away.

He visualised a very simple method of how the situation could be rectified. The first step, he advised Dr Donges, would be to define areas for whites, coloureds, Africans and Indians. Of course it would be foolish, he argued, to reason that areas – where coloureds constituted a majority – should be declared coloured. The next step would be the "uitruiling van huise" (the exchange of houses). He explained by way of an example:

> 'n Blanke gesin woon moontlik in 'n buurt wat as kleurling buurt verklaar word. So 'n gesin trek oor na 'n buurt wat as Blank verklaar word en 'n kleurling gesin vul die huis waaruit die Blanke getrek het. Op die wyse kan baie gedoen word sonder enige onkoste vir die Staat.[11]

Similarly, in District Six, Africans should move out and coloureds should take their place.

The GAA piloted through parliament by Donges was not in any way as simple as the "uitruiling van huise". A complicated measure – which required considerable explanation for those who encountered it and which was subsequently amended almost every year – set up the machinery by which group areas might be declared. Apart from the dedication to the idea of separate group areas for the different groups, the one vision of clarity that its initiators had was that the implementation was to be a slow process so as to avoid serious disruption.[12] Indeed, it was to be seven years after the Act was passed before the first group areas were declared in Cape Town. In the interim, individuals lived lives of uncertainty and were governed by the permit system.

The permit system

The GAA provided that there were three main racial groups, "native", "coloured" and "white". Further, the former two groups could be divided into sub-groups. In September 1950, a proclamation established Indians and Chinese as two such separate sub-groups. Malays were declared a separate group for districts of Cape Town, Simonstown, Wynberg, Bellville, Somerset West, Stellenbosch, Paarl, Worcester, Port Elizabeth and Kimberley.[13] On 30 March 1951, in terms of a proclamation issued under the GAA, the Cape Province became subject to control over the acquisition of property. The idea was to freeze the *status quo* until group areas were declared. All properties henceforth transferred from one race group to another could only be sanctioned by permit. Control over changes in occupancy came as of 26 October 1951 which meant that a new tenant had to be the same group as the previous tenant unless a permit was acquired.[14]

One of the most mixed cities in South Africa in terms of residential neighbourhoods, the inhabitants of Cape Town had been relatively free to buy land anywhere. White residents in many parts of Cape Town (such as Pinelands, Milnerton, parts of Rondebosch and upper Woodstock, did incorporate restrictions in their title deeds to prevent sale to blacks. Separate locations existed for Africans and the City Council did provide sub-economic housing on segregated lines. Apart from these limits – which were slight compared to other cities – an individual was free to live where he wished.

While there were mainly whites living in wealthy areas such as Sea Point and Clifton, many middle- to lower-class people lived in mixed neighbourhoods throughout Cape Town. The older parts of the city stretching from the city centre to Observatory were multi-racial. The residential areas from Mowbray to Claremont contained many pockets of coloureds and Malays, in some instances these were too large to be regarded as pockets. In the outlying areas of Cape Town extending towards the Cape Flats, coloureds, Malays, Indians and Africans as well as pockets of whites lived together. It is estimated that only one-third of Africans in Cape Town lived in the officially sanctioned locations.[15]

The intent of the GAA was to "unscramble a residential omlette"[16] and the permit system intruded now to determine who could buy where, who could sell to whom, and who could rent where.

Unlike residents of Cape Town who were freshly introduced to control by permit, Indians in the Transvaal had been accustomed to this since 1939. Aimed at pegging what was termed Indian penetration into white areas, the system was extended to Durban in 1943. In 1946 this was made permanent in the Transvaal and the whole of Natal and a Land Tenure Advisory Board (LTAB) was established at Pietermaritzburg to administer the legislation. Although it is not possible to examine the nature of the system as it operated, in this chapter, its significance is that the permit control under the GAA was modelled on it.

The GAA also provided for the appointment of an LTAB. This board was according to Donges, the "King-pin in the machinery" for the establishment of group areas.[17] To it also fell the responsibility of administering the permit system. All the members of the LTAB under the 1946 system were appointed to this board.[18] Its chairman was D. S. van der Merwe whom Alan Mabin has referred to as "the Eiselen of group areas", because of his role in drawing up the GAA.[19] Illness and his subsequent death in 1952, prevented him from playing too large a role in implementing the GAA. This passed to Advocate G. F. de Vos Hugo, who took over the post of chairman in 1951.

As the GAA was a comprehensive measure applicable throughout the country, it was decided that the head office of the LTAB would be established at Pretoria, and there would be two regional committees – one in Cape Town and the other in Pietermaritzburg.[20] In September 1953 the Cape Town committee of the Land Tenure Board (CT.LTAB) was relieved of responsibility for the Eastern Cape when a third committee was established at Port Elizabeth.[21]

The CT.LTAB opened in March 1951.[22] Its chairman was J. D. J. Roux. The other member of the board was E. A. Wollaston. He was a pensioner and former secretary in the Justice Department who had on retirement served on the old Pietermaritzburg board since 1949. To these two fell the responsibility of explaining the procedure for establishing group areas to local authorities, organisations and individuals. This involved of travelling as they were responsible for the whole of the Cape though in 1953 this was limited to the Western Cape only. They held monthly meetings (open to the public) where they considered permit applications. These were first held at Marks Building in Parliament Street until they received permanent quarters at the

Magistrate's building in Caledon Street.[23]

Individuals who required a permit to buy or sell or occupy a property would first have to fill in an application form providing full information about the property in question and all parties involved. In addition, they would have to provide a locality sketch indicating the racial character of the immediate surroundings as well as the property's wider surrounding. The board suggested a colour scheme to be used on such maps to indicate racial ownership or occupation: blue – whites, brown – coloureds, mauve – Malays, red – Indians, yellow – Chinese, and black – African. Coloured circles would indicate ownership with dots for occupation. Thus a property owned by a white but occupied by a coloured would be indicated by a blue circle with a brown dot.[24]

After an individual had been through this laborious task and forwarded the necessary information to the LTAB, the board then advertised the application in two local newspapers for two consecutive weeks. The state bore the costs for these advertisements. Thirty days (later reduced to 14 days) were allowed for objections or representations to be made. Individuals were then given the opportunity to be present with legal counsel, if they wished, when the board heard the application. From this time it took about two months or more before the applicant was informed about the outcome. The CT.LTAB forwarded its recommendation to the LTAB for confirmation, which in turn sent this on to the minister of the interior.

The operation of the permit system

For the purposes of this chapter only lists of permit applications considered by the CT.LTAB from September 1951 to the first half of 1954 have been analysed. The intention has been to determine the rate of approvals or refusals, the areas where groups were allowed to buy and occupy, and the rationale behind the board's decisions. This has not been an easy task as the board did not always indicate what its motivations were. The full details of seller and purchaser were not always given in some lists. A list of applications for 1952 which gives fairly comprehensive information has, however, been invaluable in providing clues to the board's thinking and from this inferences can be drawn for other applications.[25]

The board was not exactly flooded with applications in the beginning. In August 1951 the CT.LTAB received 48 applications and 55 the next month. For the period February to May 1952, the average per month was 68. In 1953, for the first 11 months the average per month was somewhat higher at 90. These applications came from all parts of the Cape Province though the city of Cape Town made up its largest component, followed by Port Elizabeth. Most applications were for purchase. Of the 579 applications received in the first seven months of 1954, 381 were for acquiring property and 198 for occupation.[26]

More permits were granted than refused. At the second meeting of the CT.LTAB for instance, of the 36 applications on which decisions were taken, only 5 (14 per cent) were refused. In the next month out of 35, 8 (23 per cent) were refused.[27] This pattern did not change in any significant way for 1952. For 1953, although accurate statistics have not yet been located, from the preliminary data it seems that the rate of refusals soared. In the first seven months of that year, the rate of refusals per month varied from 64 per cent to 81 per cent.[28] In 1954 refusals dropped so that for the period from April to December only 14 per cent of the 819 applications were refused.[29]

The following general pattern emerged in terms of where the different groups (defined under the GAA) were allowed or refused to buy property in Cape Town specifically. These obviously do not reflect all areas in Cape Town but simply those where permits were requested to sanction an inter-racial transfer.

- *Refusals to coloureds*: parts of Salt River, parts of Woodstock, Observatory, Rondebosch, Newlands, Claremont, Wynberg, Plumstead (Meyerhof), Diep River, Southfield, Lansdowne (at Yorkshire Estate and Heatherley Estate, for instance), Bellville (north of the railway line) and Goodwood (north of the railway line).
- *Approvals to coloureds*: District Six, parts of Woodstock (including Walmer Estate and Zonnebloem Estate), north-western part of Salt River, Wynberg (Battswood Estate), Grassy Park, Athlone, Crawford, Kensington, Bellville South.
- *Refusals to Malays*: parts of Salt River, parts of Woodstock, Wynberg (Lotus River Estate), Rondebosch, Newlands, Claremont, Grassy Park (New Retreat Estate), Kensington (in 1953), Athlone (in 1953).
- *Approvals to Malays*: Schotsche Kloof, District Six, parts of Woodstock (including Walmer Estate), parts of Salt River, Wynberg (Battswood Estate), Grassy Park, Duinefontein Park

Estate, Athlone (up to 1952), Kensington (up to 1953).
- *Refusals to Indians*: Schotsche Kloof, Claremont, Wynberg, Constantia, Crawford, Kensington, Grassy Park, Elsies River.
- *Approvals to Indians*: Rylands Estate (as of 1954).
- *Refusals to Chinese*: Lansdowne and Grassy Park.
- *Approvals to whites*: Woodstock, Observatory, Newlands, Claremont, Wynberg, Diep River, Lansdowne (Yorkshire Estate for instance), Brooklyn, Milnerton (Rugby), Bellville (Oakdale Estate).
- *Refusals to whites*: Schotsche Kloof, Grassy Park.

On what basis did the board make these decisions? The board considered whether there were objections to the application and thus devised the lengthy procedure of advertising applications. There were a few cases involving objectors. An application by a Malay to occupy a house at Observatory was opposed by 33 white residents in the same road as well as the Dutch Reformed Church. Although two petitions also with 33 signatories were presented in support of the applicant, the application was refused.[30] An application by a white firm to occupy a stall at the Grand Parade was objected to by Indian fruit stall-owners. The latter claimed that it had been the policy of the Cape Town City Council since the 1920s to lease these stalls to Indians. The applicant was refused a permit.[31] Another case involving coloureds who wished to occupy a house at Cravenby in Goodwood was opposed by 25 whites. The objectors claimed that the area was overwhelmingly white but the board granted the petition as it found the claims of the objectors to be unfounded.[32]

The representations by groups of people on specific applications played a very small role in the end in the board's decisions. Permit hearings, attended by anything between 13 to 42 people, were marked by little or no drama. The board, in late 1952, eventually revised its policy of advertising all applications. This was to save time and money[33] but by this time the board had already had a policy for many areas in Cape Town. It decided to advertise only in those cases where it was uncertain of the area and the policy to adopt.[34]

The permit system was linked inextricably to the ultimate goal of the board to establish group areas and it was this that influenced permit decisions more than anything else. The Durban City Council assisted the LTAB in making permit decisions by indicating its plans in terms of future racial zoning for particular areas. Indeed, the board was heavily dependent on the co-operation of local authorities to devise group areas. The Cape Town City Council, however, refused to co-operate,[35] though the Parow, Bellville and Goodwood Town Councils indicated that areas within their jurisdiction, north of the railway line, should be white group areas.[36]

Faced with some difficulty, because of the Cape Town City Council's attitude, the CT.LTAB used permit hearings to urge groups to indicate where they wanted a group area. Roux, for instance, on considering an application from a Chinese who wished to buy in Grassy Park, enquired: "Have the Chinese decided where they will ask for a separate area?"[37] To an Indian applicant, he commented: "The diffficulty with cases like this is that Indians have made no attempt to tell us where they want their area."[38]

The board thus encouraged ratepayers' associations, other local organisations and individuals to submit applications for group areas. Already by September 1951, the Southfield-Naruna Ratepayers Association, the Ottery-Wetton Ratepayers Association and the Lansdowne-Crawford Ratepayers Association had indicated their preference for white group areas to be established within these areas.[39]

The Dutch Reformed Church, the Upper Ward Seven Ratepayers Association and the Charlie Malan branch of the National Party asked for parts of Woodstock to be declared white.[40] The Dutch Reformed Church was reported to be busy preparing applications to have the whole of Observatory, parts of Salt River, Mowbray and Rondebosch declared as white group areas.[41] Malays, according to Roux, had asked for Schotsche Kloof to be a group area for them.[42] In May 1952, the Coloured Christian National Council met the CT.LTAB and indicated that they wanted Grassy Park for coloureds and that "white spots" there should be removed.[43]

In addition to these requests, the board had its own ideas. It regarded, from the very beginning, areas like Sea Point, Camps Bay, and large parts of Rondebosch as obvious white areas.[44] Kensington was considered an obvious area for coloureds.[45] In 1952 De Vos Hugo expressed the opinion that "non-European pockets" between the railway line and the mountain should be eliminated, while he envisaged a large area for coloureds stretching from Athlone to Bellville.[46]

In 1952, to facilitate the process of declaring group areas, the minister of the interior appointed a Planning and Reference Committee. This committee would consider all proposals for group areas and then refer recommendations to the LTAB.[47] The committee was reported to have had about 32 group areas proposals for Cape Town.[48] The first official proposals of the LTAB were then advertised and a small hearing for objections was held in March 1953.[49] The first proposals for Cape Town were: Gardens, Tamboerskloof, Oranjezicht, Green Point, Sea Point, Clifton, Camps Bay, Bakoven, Pinelands, Thornton and Epping for whites; Athlone, Kew Town, parts of Elsies River for coloureds; Schotsche Kloof and Duinefontein for Malays; and Rylands Estate for Indians.[50]

The significance of these developments for the permit system is that from a very early stage the board began refusing permits to individuals where a group area had been asked for members of another group. Although the board accepted that Lansdowne was a considerably mixed area, it constantly turned down the large number of applications by coloureds to buy in this area and allowed purchases instead in Athlone, Kensington and District Six, for example.

As the board began to define areas for groups in an informal way, the rate of refusals to all blacks, as evident in 1953, soared. One particularly new pattern emerged. Malays, who had been initially allowed to buy in predominantly coloured areas, found that once the board advertised two areas for Malays, such applications were turned down. There were thus numerous refusals to Malays wishing to buy in Athlone or Kensington. Although the board conceded that there were already a number of Malays in these areas, it decided against allowing any "verdere Maleier indringing".[51] In addition, as proposals were advertised in 1953 with more to come, the board seemed anxious not to change the *status quo* in all areas.

Indians, who constituted a small percentage of the total Cape Town population, featured in disproportionally large numbers as both buyers and sellers of property. Practically every application by them as well as the Chinese for purchase, was turned down as the board had no idea where areas would be set aside for them.[52] The Indian buyer eventually had a place where a permit could be granted, after Rylands Estate was advertised but there was no rush of applications.[53]

The permit system was used by the board to stop what it called the penetration of groups into areas predominantly occupied by other groups. In doing so, it made the distinction between the immediate surroundings of an area and its wider surroundings. Applications by blacks to buy in Claremont, Newlands, Diep River and Lansdowne were turned down even though the immediate surroundings of the properties in question might have been predominantly black.[54] In Grassy Park, the board noted on one application by an Indian, that although there were many Indians in the immediate area and there was a mosque, the wider surrounding made it unlikely that it would be an Indian area.[55]

All such applications in mixed areas were marked by comments from the board that "verdere indringing deur nie-blankes moet gekeer word"[56] or as in the case of the constant refusals to Indians "verdere indringing deur Indiërs behoort belet te word".[57] It couched its refusals in the most altruistic, self-justifying manner: "Dit is nie in belang van die betrokke applikante ..." as the latter would eventually have to leave these areas.[58]

In terms of what it regarded as the black spot in Claremont, the board commented that it fell within "'n baie waardevolle blanke omgewing" and that there was little doubt that "hierdie kolle verwyder moet word".[59] Thus the board began to think in terms of cleaning up such areas. Not only were permits refused to blacks to buy in these areas, but the seller was urged to sell to the right group – to whites. This eventually became an important determinant of permit applications.

In 1952 the board was interested not only in who was entering an area as owner or occupant but equally in who the seller or occupant about to be displaced was. Thus it granted permits because a white or coloured or Malay occupant was replacing an African or an Indian: "dit is wenslik that die naturel hier padgee" or "dit is wenslik dat die Indiër hier padgee".[60]

Thus while Kensington was regarded as being for coloureds, a white was granted a permit for occupation because he displaced an African.[61] A white was granted a permit to buy in District Six because the seller was an Indian and the white did not seek occupation rights.[62] A permit to a coloured was granted in Welcome Estate (Athlone) as the seller was an African and the buyer was of the right group.[63]

A Malay was granted a permit to buy from a coloured at Claremont because the board did not regard this as a significant change in the *status quo*.[64] The board was also sometimes more flexible about granting permits for occupation to Malays, Indians and coloureds in Claremont and Newlands provided a white was not being displaced.[65]

De Vos Hugo was satisfied that on a national level the permit system not only stopped new penetration but that individuals who regarded themselves as penetrators or realised that an area was unlikely to be declared for their group were themselves leaving such areas. They were thus doing voluntarily what the GAA would eventually force them to do.[66]

The national statistics do indicate that more property was being transferred to whites than to blacks (see Appendix 1 page 206). According to De Vos Hugo, Indians in Natal who had penetrated white areas were now leaving such areas and in the Cape, coloureds were selling to whites. The situation in the Cape was however more complex given the extent of mixed neighbourhoods.

Appendix 2 indicates that the Cape conforms to the national picture in terms of there being very few transfers to Indians. However, while the largest number of transfers were to whites, property was also being transferred to coloureds in large numbers. In particular, in Cape Town, whites who owned property in Athlone, Kensington, Grassy Park, District Six, Walmer Estate and Battswood Estate (Wynberg) were selling to coloureds. This served the purpose of the board of sorting out areas.

Although the CT.LTAB generally adhered to whatever policy it developed for an area it did make the odd exception. This could have been determined, as already indicated above, by the group of the seller or occupant being displaced. The board did grant permits for purchase if they considered it to be to the advantage of the residents of an area. A white was granted a permit to buy in Grassy Park because he intended using it as a recreational ground for coloureds.[67] Two Indian doctors were granted conditional permits for occupation at Kensington.[68]

The board, on the very rare occasion did grant a permit on compassionate grounds. A coloured wishing to buy the house he currently occupied, which fell within the area the Ottery-Wetton Ratepayers Association had asked to be declared for whites, was first refused a permit. The Malay owner had, however, since then been unable to find a white purchaser. He was a poor man and there was a bond on the house. To rescue him from financial distress the board granted the second application to sell to the coloured occupant.

The board reasoned, the house was already occupied by a coloured as was the neighbouring house. It would thus not seriously affect the area. The buyer was also prepared to take the risk of having to move if the area was declared white.[69] There were many other buyers who were similarly prepared to take a risk, but the board was not generally moved by such arguments. It argued instead that there was no point in granting a permit if the individual might eventually have to move.[70]

Responses to the permit system

The above account which concentrates on how the board viewed the permit system, what general patterns (or exceptions) it developed, and why, only begins to hint at how it might have affected individuals. In this section, the responses of individuals and how they were affected by the system will be examined. The case studies of several individuals – to be recounted here – serve to raise issues such as identity, the meanings attached to space, and the options open to people faced with state intrusion into their lives.

In the first instance, the GAA must have posed the problem of what group one belonged to. The Population Identification Act had only been passed in 1950 and population registers and the identity card system were in slow progress. The GAA defined groups with anything but clarity. A white was any person:

> who in appearance, obviously is, or is generally accepted as a white person, other than a person who although in appearance obviously a white person is generally accepted as a coloured person.

And who was a coloured person? Any person who was not a white or "native" and any female married to a coloured.

Several lawyers, representing would-be buyers of property in Natal, wrote to the government for clarity on the group status of their clients to determine the necessity of applying for a permit. Was a white man with a "coloured looking" wife and child required to apply for a permit? How was a Mauritian who mixed only with other Mauritians and not whites, Indians or coloureds to be classified? Replies from the government deliberately avoided any conclusive answer and lawyers were simply directed to the legal definitions.[71] In the Cape there must have been considerably greater doubts.

The following accounts indicate to what extent the identities claimed by individuals could be situational and determined by the material advantages such an identity offered. Lawyers in Cape Town enquired on behalf of their client who was known as an "Indian waiter". In terms of a government proclamation an Indian was "a person who in fact is, or is generally accepted as a member of a race or tribe whose National Home is in India or Pakistan". Their client's parents had been born in Natal and he had been in the Cape since 1919. He associated with coloured people and not Muslim or Hindu Indians and he did not consider Pakistan or India to be his home. To come to the crunch of the case, the client wished to buy property from a coloured. If he was considered a coloured then a permit would not be necessary.[72]

The permit hearings in Cape Town also brought out similar quests for a useful identity. Omar Osman wanted to occupy a shop in Ida's Valley in Stellenbosch from a coloured. His birth certificate said he was "coloured (Indian)". If he could be considered coloured then a permit would not be necessary. A Malay woman married to an Indian, by law assumed the identity of her husband. One such woman claimed a Malay status for her children so that a business could be bought for them. The CT.LTAB treated these two cases somewhat cavalierly. Roux told Osman's representative "... you will still have to explain how he obtained his name of Osman". To the Malay woman he retorted: "If I claim to be a Chinaman, does that make me one?"[73]

Malays were to find that being defined as a separate sub-group of coloureds had its advantages. Permits were being issued exclusively to them in Schotsche Kloof. However, this identity became disadvantageous as it appeared that they would be confined to only Schotsche Kloof and later Duinefontein Park, thus leaving those living interspersed amongst coloureds all over Cape Town in jeopardy. S. Dollie, writing on behalf of the Cape Malay Board of Deputies, thus urged the government to accept their solution:

> There are certain Coloured and certain Malays who wish to live on their own, then why not declare two areas for each group exclusively and the balance of the areas for common and combined use of these two groups?[74]

Ordinary transactions between landlords and tenants became contests between groups. Initially, as has already been mentioned, the permit system applied to the Cape only for property purchases and not for changes in occupancy. The LTAB however, observed that Indians who owned much property in the Cape Peninsula and who rented out to whites were giving their tenants notice so that they could occupy the homes themselves. This the board believed was a tactical move as the Indians would then have stronger claims to have areas declared for them on the basis of both ownership and occupation.[75] This process was reported in the press to be in progress in Oxford, Regent, York and Essex Streets in Woodstock.[76]

The case of E. G. Durler, a white pensioner who had lived for over 16 years in Oxford Street, came to the attention of the board and also received publicity in the media. His landlord, B. R. Lalla, had now given him notice to leave by the end of October 1951 as he wished to occupy the house himself.[77] The board intervened on behalf of such tenants facing ejectment by quickly extending control over occupation to the Cape. Durler was saved by just a few days and his landlord would now require a permit if the new tenant was not a white.

The response of M. N. to his landlord's decision to give him notice reveals how such a relationship of tenant and landlord could assume an ugly form in the face of the permit system. M. N., a Malay, had been living in a flat in Queens Road, Woodstock for nine years. His landlady was a Cape Malay married to an Indian, who largely spent most of the time in Durban. M. N., who had "spent £50 last year on cleaning the place, with the most expensive paint, and putting in a new sink", was told that the landlady wanted to occupy the flat herself.

Absolutely livid, M. N. wrote directly to the minister of interior on the matter which was "nothing but an injustice". He quoted the government's own law which provided that a Malay woman married to an Indian would be classified as Indian. Thus he reasoned she would need a permit to replace him. He continued:

> I do not think she has a permit, for the government are very strict in issuing permits to Indians to penetrate in Coloured, or Malay areas as in this case ... I hope your department will investigate this case ... These people have been aptly described as parasites, for they trade on nothing but misery in Durban and now they are trying to shift to Cape Town. I appeal to you, Sir, to stop a permit being issued.[78]

The permit system acted to prevent individuals from occupying their own property. In the case of the landlord who owned several properties and already had a home, the hardship was slight but it nonetheless violated his individual rights. The hardship could be severe if one had "no place in the world to go to", and was prevented from occupying the only home one owned. Such was the plight of I. Ebrahim of Hugo Street, Elsies River.

Ebrahim had moved into his own home as the previous white tenant had left and the house stood empty while the newly married Ebrahim needed a place to live in. The LTAB had now informed him that his occupation could not be sanctioned. Ebrahim first unsuccessfully sought an interview with Dr Donges. He then wrote to the minister begging him to grant him a permit even if it was only for five years:

My reasons Sir, is I have already been in the place a year and four months. When I got the letter to vacate I seeked high and low for suitable living quarters but could not find a single place. It is also the first place I have ever occupied and being an inheritance from my father greatly treasured. Newly married my wife has got to get sick in the next few months and I have no place in the world to go to.[79]

James Mathews, a 57 year-old Indian who was married to a coloured woman, found himself "in severe circumstances over which I have no controll". He had lived in Firmount Road in Sea Point for 20 years and had been working in the area for over 35 years. He had now been given notice to vacate the home he rented. Although he owned two houses in the area he had let these out to whites and would now require a permit to occupy either one. He thus wrote to the minister of interior for help as if his application were turned down "all hope will be gone".[80]

These letters reveal the desperation to which individuals were driven. Mathews wrote to Donges because "you have the power to help". He begged Donges, "my last source of help", to *"please"* read the application carefully. Ebrahim tried a different line of approach. He assured Donges, "I have been and are always a law abiding citizen and a supporter of you Sir."

For their efforts, Mathews received a letter from a government secretary informing him of the correct procedure to adopt to acquire a permit. Ebrahim's case was referred to the inspectorate established under the GAA to investigate violations of its provisions. A likely outcome of both cases is that Mathews and Ebrahim had to leave their areas in search of accommodation the law did sanction.

While the permit system traumatised individuals in search of a home, it also served to stifle business enterprise. Indians in Cape Town, who were mainly traders, found it difficult to get new premises. G. Alfred, a Chinese, wished to occupy a premise for business purposes at Elsies River. He lived in Bellville and had a shop there. He now wished to let that shop to his son and to establish himself at Elsies River. This application was turned down.[81]

While Africans appeared only in the rare instance as sellers of property or as purchasers (see Appendix 1), here are at least two cases of applications for occupation. Michael Kalembe wished to occupy a shop for dairying purposes at Retreat. A permit was necessary as a Chinese currently occupied the premise. He appeared in person before the board and explained that there were about 700 African squatters in the area. He supplied them with milk in his horse-drawn cart. He was performing a useful task as none of the established dairies serviced the area because of the sandy roads. Each evening he had a surplus of milk and the health inspectors had objected to him storing it in his house. He thus needed a place where he could store the milk in refrigerators.[82]

The Manyano Trading Co. requested a permit to occupy a butchery in Lansdowne Road. The representative appearing before the board explained that there was no provision for a business premise in the Nyanga location. Until they could start a business there the company wanted a temporary place.[83] Both Kalembe's and the Manyano Trading Co.'s enterprising efforts were snuffed out by the board as permits were denied.

The owners of property found that it was not always possible for them to get a member of the right group to take over the property. William Lewis Roberts, a coloured man who owned a block of shops in Claremont, found himself in difficulties. One of the shops had been vacated by a white tenant and the law now required him to let only to another white. He could not find such a client:

> Meanwhile, I have to pay rates on the premises, which, after 18 months, are still unoccupied. I am losing £15 rent a month, and there are no prospects of my finding a tenant.[84]

Whites appeared unwilling to move into the areas that the board labelled as black-spots and owners there had to absorb the costs of having unsaleable property.

For those who did apply for permits there could be inordinately long delays. Although the average application did take just about two months to be processed, the board did often postpone a decision. In one instance, several coloureds wanting to buy property from a white company were held up for almost one-and-a-half years. The applications were eventually turned down.[85] Individuals who needed to make a quick, urgent sale found themselves strapped as the board's wheels turned slowly.[86]

People who wished to dispose of their property to other groups or who wished to rent property that had been previously occupied by another group found themselves caught in a tight web woven by the state and had to succumb to the permit system. Some found it useful to use the language of the state to attain their own goals. The legal representative of the Indian fruit-stall owners at the Grand Parade who opposed the application of the white firm, in fact asked the question:

"Is it the policy of the Act ... for 15 Indians and a single European to trade cheek-by-jowl under virtually the same roof?"[87] M. N. similarly, used language that the state understood when he complained about his landlord.

Other individuals tried to manouevre out of the web and to have nothing to do with the permit system. Giovani D'Angelo, a white, was living in Harfield in a place which his friend described "as not fit for a coloured what to say for a man like him". He was offered accommodation in Johns Street in Mowbray just behind the Main Road. As the home had been previously occupied by a Malay a permit was necessary. However, D'Angelo's friend wrote to the minister asking that the necessity for a permit be waived. He explained:

> The provisions of the Group Areas Bill is a bit troublesome and the landlord do not like to go to the trouble of applying for a permit. But will be willing to give him the chance to occupy if the permit will be waived ...[88]

It is possible that it was simply the hassle of the procedure that the landlord wished to avoid. It is equally possible that he did not want to use it on principle – a reason D'Angelo was not likely to indicate to the minister. That D'Angelo took as much time trying to get a permit waived as it would have been to get a permit suggests that this is not a far-fetched deduction.

There were other individuals who simply occupied property in violation of the law until discovered by the "G-men".[89] In 1952 the group areas inspectors investigated 52 complaints from the public about alleged illegal occupation.[90] Those who were caught claimed that they did not know. Sherifa Mohedien and her husband had moved into their home in Kensington Estate and lived there for 15 months. One month after her husband died she was visited by an inspector who informed her that the occupation was illegal as the previous occupant had been a white.[91] Similarly, K. P. Cranna, lived illegally in a home in Wynberg for about two years before being detected.[92] After being discovered, both Mohedien and Cranna applied for permits to have their positions legalised.

The permit system largely affected individuals with some capital to buy property and those with property to dispose of. To some extent it also affected those seeking rental accommodation. If Ebrahim felt that he had "no place in the world to go to", there were, however, thousands of residents of Cape Town who continued to live happily where they had always been. If the permit system did produce its fair share of upset, this was going to be nothing compared to the process of removal and resettlement. That remains another chapter in the dark history of group areas in Cape Town when the world of thousands was shattered.

Endnotes

1. The project was motivated for by Wilmot James who now heads it and it is funded by the Ford Foundation, New York. Clive Moses and myself are its two other members. I would like to thank Wilmot for enthusiastically supporting my pursuit of history and Biebie van der Merwe for teaching me enough Afrikaans to read my documents.
2. A. Lemon (ed.), *Homes Apart: South Africa's Segregated Cities* (Bloomington, Indiana and Claremont, 1991); M. Swilling, R. Humphries, K. Shubane (eds), *Apartheid City in Transition* (Cape Town, 1991).
3. *Outcast Cape Town* (Cape Town, 1981).
4. *Group Areas. With Particular Reference to the Western Cape. Legislation, Implementation and Impact* (Centre for Intergroup Studies, UCT, 1983).
5. R. A. Hill, "The Impact of Race Legislation on Kinship and Identity Amongst Indian Muslims in Cape Town" (M.A., UCT, 1980); D. Pinnock, "Breaking the Web: Economic Consequences of the Destruction of Extended Families by Group Areas Relocations in Cape Town", Paper presented to the Second Carnegie Inquiry into Poverty and Development in Southern Africa, Cape Town, 1984.
6. *Open Areas in Cape Town – the Struggle for their Identity* (Mowbray, 1987).
7. J. Knight, "The Economics of Group Areas with Particular Reference to Metropolitan Cape Town" (B.Comm. (Hons), UCT, 1987).
8. S. Jeppie and C. Soudien (eds), *The Struggle for District Six: Past and Present* (Cape Town, 1990).
9. M. Horrell, *The Group Areas Act – Its Effect on Human Beings* (Johannesburg, 1956); *Group Areas in Cape Town* (Johannesburg, 1958).
10. Donges Papers (Cape Archives, Cape Town), A 1646, Vol. 138, L. Pienaar to Donges, 26 May 1950.
11. A white family perhaps lives in an area declared as a coloured area. Such a family moves to an area which is declared white and a coloured family fills the house that the whites have left. In this manner much can be done without any cost for the state.
12. *Debates of the House of Assembly*, 1950, vol. 72, cols 7434, 7452, Donges on the second reading of the bill.
13. See Group Areas Board Series (GGR) (Central Archives Depot, Pretoria), Vol. 28, 9/3 Part 1, Memorandum insake die Wet op Groepsgebiede, 1950, 23 April 1952. It was only in 1957 that Malays were redefined as being part of the coloured group except for the Schotsche Kloof area where their separate Malay identity was retained.
14. *Ibid.*

15. This is largely based on Western, *Outcast Cape Town*, 35ff.
16. *Cape Argus*, 19 October 1951 (editorial).
17. *Debates of the House of Assembly*, 1950, Vol. 72, col. 7439.
18. These were D. S. van der Merwe, Advocate G. F. de Vos Hugo, E. A. Wollaston and W.M. Power (*Cape Argus*, 29 September 1950).
19. A. Mabin, "'Doom at One Stroke of the Pen': Urban Planning and Group Areas c.1935 – 1955", Paper presented at the History Workshop, University of the Witwatersrand, February 1990, 23.
20. GGR Vol. 28, 9/3 Part 1, Memorandum insake die Wet op Groepsgebiede, 23 April 1952.
21. Land Tenure Advisory Board Series (ARG) (Central Archives Depot, Pretoria) Vol. 174, v1/1 Part 2, 18th meeting of the LTAB, 15–16 September 1953.
22. ARG Vol. 173, v1/1 Part 1, sixth meeting of the LTAB, 20 March 1951.
23. For reports on the work of the CT.LTAB between 1951 and 1953 see ARG Vol. 178, v/5 Part 1.
24. *Cape Argus*, 4 April 1951.
25. See GGR Vols 21 and 22, 4/1/1/1 Parts I,II,III; ARG Vol. 179 v/5/1 Parts I and II.
26. These statistics have been drawn from ARG Vol.178, v/5 Part 1, Verslag van werksaamhede van die Kaapstadse Kantoor, August 1951 to July 1954.
27. ARG Vol.179, v/5/1 Part 1, Minutes of the second and third meetings of the CT.LTAB, September and October 1951.
28. This is the impression gained from ARG Vol. 179, v/5/1 Part 1, minutes of the CT.LTAB for 1952 to July 1953.
29. This was calculated from GGR Vol. 31, 9/10, Extracts from the 23rd and 24th general meeting of the LTAB, October 1954 and February 1955.
30. GGR Vol. 21, 4/1/1/1 Part I, Report of the LTAB re P.G. 319/1/219, 29 May 1952. The permit was refused because it meant the Malay would be displacing a white and moving in next to another white.
31. See *Cape Times*, 29 November 1952 and ARG Vol. 179, v/5/1 Part 1, 16th meeting of the CT.LTAB, November 1952, P.G. 319/1/397.
32. GGR Vol. 21, 4/1/1/1 Part I, Report of the LTAB re P.G. 312/3/25–27, 13 March 1952. The board regarded the handful of white homes in the vicinity as constituting a white spot in a black area.
33. In 1951/52 advertising costs totalled £15 416 but with the revised policy costs dropped in 1952/53 to £4 325 (see GGR Vol. 31, 9/10, Memorandum insake die Wet op Groepsgebiede, 1953).
34. See GGR Vol. 21, 4/1/1/1 Part II, Report of the LTAB re P.G. 319/1/387 and others, 28 October 1952 ; re P.G. 319/1/311 and others, 31 October 1952; re P.G. 312/3/61 and others, 31 October 1952.
35. It is not possible in this paper to tackle the contest between the central government and the Cape Town City Council though this looms large as an issue. For a somewhat dry account see A. C. Lakey, "An Analysis of the Response and Background thereto of the Cape Town City Council to Group Areas Legislation of the 1950s" (B.A. (Hons), History, UCT, 1990).
36. *Cape Argus*, 5 September, 10 November 1952; also GGR Vol. 22, 4/1/1/1 Part III, Report of the LTAB re P.G. 312/1/24, 5 March 1953 and re P.G. 312/3/76, 22 April 1953.

37. *Cape Argus*, 27 September 1951.
38. *Cape Argus*, 27 August 1953.
39. ARG Vol. 178, v/5 Part 1, Verslag van werksaamhede van die Kaapstadse kantoor vir September 1951.
40. *Cape Argus*, 9 August 1951; GGR Vol. 21, 4/1/1/1 Part II, Report of LTAB re permit application P.G. 319/1/429, 12 November 1952.
41. *Cape Argus*, 20 October 1951.
42. *Cape Argus*, 25 October 1951.
43. ARG Vol. 178, v/5 Part 1, Verslag van werksaamhede van die Kaapstadse kantoor vir Mei 1952, Dicussion with the Coloured Christian National Council, 3 May 1952.
44. *Cape Argus*, 21 July 1951.
45. GGR Vol. 21, 4/1/1/1 Part I, Report of the LTAB re permit application P.G. 319/1/158 and others, 13 March 1952.
46. Cape Town City Council Papers, Minutes of the General Purposes Committee (Cape Archives, Cape Town), 3/CT 1/4/6/6/1/1/8, Notes of discussion with the LTAB, 14 November 1952, with minutes of the joint meeting of the GPC and the Plans Committee, 23 February 1953.
47. For the motivation to establish the committee see GGR Vol. 42, 14/4 Part I, Memorandum insake verwysings by De Vos Hugo, 30 October 1951.
48. *Cape Argus*, 12 January 1953.
49. *Cape Argus*, 2 March 1953.
50. Horrell, *Group Areas Act*, 74–75.
51. Further Malay penetration (See ARG Vol. 179, v/5/1 Part 1, Minutes of the CT.LTAB for January to July 1953 also GGR Vol. 22, 4/1/1/1 Part III, Report of the LTAB re P.G. 319/1/512 and others, 5 February 1953.
52. See Donges Papers A1646, Vol 135, Wollaston to Donges, 28 December 1954.
53. See ARG Vol. 179, v/5/1 Part II, 29th meeting of the CT.LTAB, April 1954, re P.G. 319/1/1102.
54. See GGR Vol. 21, 4/1/1/1 Part I, Report of the LTAB re P.G. 319/1/126 and others at Lansdowne, 14 May 1952; Report re P.G. 319/1/230 at Diep River and P.G. 319/1/240 at Newlands, 19 May 1952.
55. GGR Vol. 21, 4/1/1/1 Part II, Report of the LTAB re P.G. 423/3/46, 11 November 1952.
56. Further penetration by non-whites must be stopped (see GGR Vol. 21, 4/1/1/1 Part I, Report of the LTAB re P.G. 319/1/230 and 240, 19 May 1952).
57. Further penetration by Indians ought to be prevented (see GGR Vol. 21, 4/1/1/1 Part II, Report of the LTAB re P.G. 319/1/355, 11 November 1952).
58. It was not in the interests of the concerned applicants (see GGR Vol. 21, 4/1/1/1 Part II, Report of the LTAB re P.G. 319/1/126 and others, 14 May 1952.
59. A very valuable white surrounding and this spot must be removed (see GGR Vol. 21, 4/1/1/1 Part I, Report of the LTAB re P.G. 319/1/197 and others, 22 April 1952.
60. It is desirable that the African or Indian leaves from here.
61. ARG Vol. 179, v/5/1 Part II, 28th meeting of the CT.LTAB, March 1954, P.G. 319/1/1040.
62. GGR Vol. 22, 4/1/1/1 Part III, Report of the LTAB re P.G. 319/1/366, 23 December 1952.

63. GGR Vol. 21, 4/1/1/1 Part II, Report of the LTAB re P.G. 423/6/7, 28 October 1952.
64. GGR Vol. 22, 4/1/1/1 Part III, Report of the LTAB re P.G. 319/1/484, 26 February 1953.
65. See, for instance, ARG Vol. 179, v/5/1 Part II, 30th meeting of the CT.LTAB, June 1954, P.G. 319/1/1080, and 32nd meeting of the CT.LTAB, August 1954, P.G. 319/1/1252.
66. GGR Vol. 28, 9/3 Part I, Memo. insake die Wet op Groepsgebiede, 23 April 1952.
67. GGR Vol. 22, 4/1/1/1 Part III, Report of the LTAB re P.G. 423/3/48, 14 January 1953.
68. ARG Vol. 179, v/5/1 Part II, 27th meeting of the CT.LTAB, February 1954, P.G. 319/1/1018.
69. GGR Vol. 21, 4/1/1/1 Part II and Vol. 22, 4/1/1/1 Part III, Report of the LTAB re P.G. 423/R/2 and 423/R/10, 4 September 1952, 31 December 1952.
70. *Cape Argus*, 21 July 1951.
71. ARG Vol. 14, Act 1/1/61, Cowley and Cowley to Secretary LTAB, 16 May 1951, Reply, 6 July 1951; ARG Vol. 14, ACT1/1/6/5 (Part 1), Livingston, Doull and Winterton to LTAB, 15 October 1951, 21 January 1952 and reply 23 May 1952.
72. ARG Vol. 14, Act/1/1/6/1 Part I, D. Chandler to Secretary of the Interior, 30 April 1951.
73. *Cape Argus*, 5 February 1954; 19 March 1954.
74. Donges Papers A1646, Vol. 138, S. Dollie to I. D. du Plessis, 17 January 1956.
75. ARG Vol. 173, v/1/1 Part I, 8th meeting of LTAB, August 1951; ARG Vol. 179, v/5/1 Part I, First meeting of the CT.LTAB, September 1951.
76. *Cape Argus*, 18 October 1951.
77. *Cape Argus*, 18 October 1951, also Cape Argus, 20 October 1951.
78. GGR Vol. 36, 11/2, M. N. to Minister of the Interior, 19 April 1956. The CT.LTAB subsequently explained to M. N. that while the owners could not occupy the flat without a permit, there was nothing to prevent them from giving him notice.
79. GGR Vol. 36, 11/2, I. Ebrahim to Donges, 22 May 1955; note of the Secretary for the Interior, 13 June 1955.
80. GGR Vol. 36, 11/2, James Mathews to Donges, 30 November 1954; reply from Secretary, LTAB, 22 December 1954.
81. ARG Vol. 179, v/5/1 Part II, 31st meeting of the CT.LTAB, July 1954, P.G. 312/3/141.
82. *Ibid.*, 24th meeting of the CT.LTAB, September 1953, P.G. 319/1/799.
83. *Ibid.*, 25th meeting of the CT.LTAB, October 1953, P.G. 423/R/15.
84. *Cape Times*, 25 September 1956.
85. GGR Vol. 22, 4/1/1/1 Part III, Report of the LTAB re P.G. 312/3/5 and others. The properties were north of the main railway line in Goodwood and the board waited for the town council to indicate its proposals for the area.
86. See GGR Vol. 36, 11/2, G. M. Guthrie and Luttig to Secretary, LTAB, 1 November 1954.
87. *Cape Times*, 29 November 1952.
88. GGR Vol. 11, 3/1/3 Part II, F. Carr to the Minister of the Interior, 24 February 1953, also 3 May 1953.
89. A term used by the *Cape Argus*, 20 August 1952.
90. ARG Vol. 227, GA 9, Verslag van die Hoofinspekteur, December 1952.

91. ARG Vol. 179, v/5/1, Part I, 18th meeting of the CT.LTAB, February 1953, P.G. 319/1/528. She was subsequently refused a permit.
92. ARG Vol. 179, v/5/1, Part II, 32nd meeting of the CT.LTAB, August 1954, P.G.319/1/1053. The board eventually granted him a conditional permit.

Appendix 1

Permits for acquisition issued in Natal, Transvaal and the Cape Province

(a) 30 March 1951 to 31 March 1952

To –	European	Indian	Coloured	African	Malay	Chinese	Total
From –							
European		16	39	2	4	–	61
Indian	224		7	–	4	1	236
Coloured	48	3		–	5	–	56
African	16	1	1		1	–	19
Malay	6	–	7	–		–	13
Chinese	5	–	1	–	–		6
Total	299	20	55	2	14	1	391

(b) 1 April 1952 to 31 March 1953

To –	European	Indian	Coloured	African	Malay	Chinese	Total
From –							
European		65	237	3	35	3	343
Indian	409		29	1	22	3	464
Coloured	169	8		–	11	–	188
African	36	4	10		–	–	50
Malay	30	1	25	–		–	56
Chinese	19	–	–	–	2		21
Total	663	78	301	4	70	6	1 122

Source: GGR Vol. 31, 9/10, *Memorandum insake werk onder die Wet op Groepsgebiede, 1950*

Appendix 2

Property purchases sanctioned by permit in the Cape Province in 1952

from white to Indian	2
from white to coloured	206
from white to African	2
from white to Malay	22
from white to Chinese	2234
from Indian to white	87
from Indian to coloured	22
from Indian to Malay	17
from Indian to Chinese	2
total	**128**
from coloured to white	135
from coloured to Indian	1
from coloured to Malay	9
total	**145**
from African to white	9
from African to coloured	8
from African to Malay	1
total	**18**
from Malay to white	18
from Malay to coloured	20
total	**38**

All groups total

to white	267
to Indian	3
to coloured	257
to African	2
to Malay	51
to Chinese	4
total	**584**

Source: GGR Vol. 28, 9/3

Notes on Editor and Contributors

Dr Elizabeth van Heyningen is a Research Associate in the History Department, University of Cape Town. **Associate-Professor Nigel Worden** and **Dr Vivian Bickford-Smith** teach in the same department. **Mohammed Adhikari** is attached to the Academic Support Programme, also at the University of Cape Town. **Naomi Barnett** did her MA in the History Department where **Muchaparara Musemwa** is currently a PhD student. **Dr Uma Mesthrie** teaches in the History Department at the University of the Western Cape. **Wayne Dooling** is a doctoral student at the University of Cambridge, where **Harriet Deacon** has just completed a PhD and now has a research fellowship at the University of Oxford.